Business and the Hardcore Unemployed

A Management Guide to
Hiring, Training,
and Motivating
Minority Workers

Business and the Hardcore Unemployed

A Management Guide to Hiring, Training, and Motivating Minority Workers

by

Lloyd Zimpel

and

Daniel Panger

With a Foreword by ROBERT C. WEAVER, *Former Secretary, U.S. Department of Housing and Urban Development*

A World of Books That Fill a Need

New York
Frederick Fell, Inc.

Contents

Foreword

Business and the Hardcore Unemployed is designed, in the words of its subtitle, as a management guide to hiring, training, and motivating minority workers. It is just that, succeeding admirably in achieving its objective.

The authors display throughout a thorough and sophisticated understanding of the hardcore unemployed. This is a reflection of their complete familiarity with the social and psychological background of those who constitute this group. For the average management, insights into this environment are of crucial importance. Nowhere have I seen them supplied, in terms that management can understand, as well as in this book by Lloyd Zimpel and Daniel Panger.

In addition, *Business and the Hardcore Unemployed* sets forth a series of suggestions and recommendations as to how to recruit, select, train and upgrade minority group workers. In this discussion, recognition is fully given to the key role which foremen and supervisory personnel play in the development of any such program of employment. There are a series of case histories and actual experiences which provide the basis for specific recommendations. While different experts may suggest alternative approaches, I found the principles and procedures suggested sound and comprehensive.

The authors have been able throughout the text to maintain an effective balance between their concern for fuller utilization of the hardcore and the recognition of problems inherent in the employment of this group. They stress and delineate sympathetic understanding of the needs and attitudes of this universe of workers at the same time that the authors recognize the necessity for treating them as an integral part of the labor force once they are oriented to the plant.

The volume is a well-balanced, informative and useful guide to those who want to tap a new source of workers. And it is more. It is a sophisticated, sympathetic, knowledgeable guide to minority group employment. The style is clear, the analyses penetrating, and the philosophy sound.

Introduction

A supermarket manager, wanting to do "what's right," hires the store's first Negro, a young high-school dropout, as a stockroom helper. The new worker shows up an hour late his first three mornings. On the fourth he doesn't come in at all. Eventually, without explanation, he calls for his check. The manager still wants to do the right thing, but now he is having second thoughts. . . .

A white foreman in a bottling plant has long boasted that he will "never have any colored boys" in his section. The company management adopts a policy of opening all jobs to Negroes and Mexican-Americans, and an experienced black machine operator is hired and sent to the foreman's section. The foreman heads at once for the personnel office to complain. . . .

A personnel assistant in a large factory is doing his best to hold to management's new policy of aggressively recruiting and hiring hardcore unemployed blacks. But his business-school training is jarred by the quality of the applications he receives— long, unexplained gaps in work histories, poor education, lengthy arrest records, few references, low test scores. Everything on the sloppy misspelled applications seems to him a danger signal, but he is required to abide by the company's policy. . . .

The president of an office supply house commits his company to a vigorous policy of hiring hardcore minority workers. Over several months Negroes are hired in all departments, with few

9

problems. In the shipping department, however, new black employees usually remain only a few weeks; those who do stay are continually in trouble. Eventually, the problem is traced back to two white employees who make a practice of subtly harassing the black workers until they quit. The president orders the personnel director to immediately put an end to such nonsense. . . .

A supervisor in an electronic assembly plant with a government contract requiring that minority workers be hired finds he suddenly has two young Mexican-Americans on his shift. They are uncommunicative and keep to themselves. When they do talk, it is in Spanish, which the supervisor doesn't understand. They just barely do their jobs and appear indifferent to correcting mistakes that the supervisor points out. He complains about them to the personnel director who tells him the new men must stay and should be given whatever training is necessary. . . .

It is for these harried individuals—company president, personnel officer, manager, supervisor, foreman and others facing similar problems—that this book is meant.

The nation's labor market is shrinking. Economists point out that the pool of ready, willing and able manpower upon which business has so long depended is nearly drained. Increasingly, the employer must turn to the only sizeable untapped labor force remaining and, as best he can, make his selection from the untrained, unskilled, undereducated hardcore unemployed. For a number of melancholy reasons most of the individuals in that group are of minority backgrounds—Negro, Mexican-American, Puerto Rican, Indian—and frequently they are so poorly motivated or have such an oppressive record of failure that they will no longer look for a job on their own but must be sought out on ghetto streetcorners, in barber shops and pool halls. And once they are hired, the employer finds they can't be expected to pull their own weight until they have been trained—perhaps in such simple matters as getting to work on time—for three months, six months, a year. All through that unproductive training period and probably beyond, the new hardcore worker brings a host of perplexing problems that most employers have never before faced.

It is an unprepossessing prospect for even the most sanguine employer. Understandably, he will shy at the start unless he is already wholeheartedly committed to the idea of equal opportunity. It makes little difference how he has arrived at his commitment: by reason of a government contract that spells out requirements for the number of minority workers he must employ; through a pledge to hire the hardcore unemployed exacted from him by the National Alliance of Businessmen; by the persuasiveness of a local civil rights group demanding more jobs for black workers; or by nothing more dramatic than a personal conviction that the social good is advanced through the individual efforts of businessmen such as himself. Whatever the reason, he has involved himself, and now he must seek practical ways to tackle the problems that are sure to beset him.

He is by no means alone. Tens of thousands of employers have involved themselves, or are looking for ways to become involved, with the same problems. The nation is witnessing, say the editors of *Fortune,* "an extraordinary phenomenon in U. S. business—public service operation." It is extraordinary because business is departing from its traditional goal of "profit maximization" in order to confront the problems of hiring and training the hardcore unemployed. It is a phenomenon that was first manifest less than a decade ago, at a time when it became clear that our educational institutions were not assisting minority youngsters to get into the mainstream of business and industry. The failure of those institutions was underscored by the blood and fire of Watts, and it was only after that upheaval that special compensatory training programs, pursued desultorily until then, began to blossom with urgency.

At first these programs represented an uneasy marriage between government, who recruited the men and smoothed off their roughest edges in basic educational courses, and business, who took the trainee off federal hands and put him on a job, frequently with governmental aid to meet his salary until he had matured into a productive worker.

If not overwhelmingly successful, still the arrangement was not unworkable. The government subsidy—unpleasant in theory to everybody but the worker, who needed the money—proved to be no great bugaboo. Indeed, as programs continued to develop, it was established as a fundamental factor enabling employers to take on the hardcore unemployed in the first place. For however much the businessman may wish to make a virtue of necessity and find unrevealed depths of self-interest satisfied by such programs, generally they are unprofitable, at least in their early stages. To carry out effective training programs the employer needs subsidization, he needs tax-incentive legislation, just as he needs the specialized assistance of such groups as the National Alliance of Businessmen.

He also needs more sound advice from the "horse's mouth," such as that offered by H. C. McClellan, the Los Angeles industrialist who took his Management Council into southwest Los Angeles after the 1965 riots and found thousands of jobs for untrained, poorly educated Negroes. McClellan points out that the concept of extensive worker training is not really new; management has always engaged in training its employees in order to keep pace with technological change. "Now," he tells businessmen, "you are merely dealing with a new type of person in a new dimension."

But there's the rub. It is the *new* dimension, the *new* person, the *new* problems that frustrate and stymie management. Employers may hire the black hardcore unemployed by the score. Technically they will then be at work, true enough, off the ghetto streetcorner, earning a good wage and contributing to the economy. But before these new workers ever become assets to the company, management is likely to confront a jungle of practical, nagging, day-to-day problems that require immediate answers to forestall scuttling an entire program.

It is the purpose of this book to look at those problems and suggest answers. From the companies that have pioneered in the hiring and training of hardcore unemployed people of minority backgrounds have come not only concrete procedures —included here—but, more importantly, hints and signals of paths yet to be blazed. We have tried to map these paths as well. This is neither a book of management theory nor a pleading for the cause of equal opportunity. It is meant as a working manual to assist those firms breaking into the hardcore unemployed job pool, a guide to a practical approach for putting the minority unemployed on the job effectively, economically, and to the ultimate benefit of both the employee and his employer.

Business and the
Hardcore Unemployed

**A Management Guide to
Hiring, Training,
and Motivating
Minority Workers**

First Considerations in Hiring the Hardcore Unemployed

"Hire men who aren't trained, who have never held a job, and who aren't even interested enough to come in looking for work?" asked the president of a metal-fabricating plant. "Why in hell would I do something as foolish as that?"

The president was talking about hiring the Negro hardcore unemployed, and his tough attitude is not easily dismissed as outdated business conservatism, for it is not based on overt racism or insensitivity to social issues. His firm has long hired minorities—skilled, well-educated Negroes, to be sure, not the bottom-of-the-barrel hardcore unemployed. But even so, he had given black workers decent jobs during the days when other firms were turning them away and Negro engineers and chemists had to work as postal clerks. His firm had even carried on a recruitment campaign of sorts for minority personnel, hiring all who met high standards and possessed the skills and qualifications to step in and handle the job on the same basis as the qualified white applicant.

But now the president was being asked to consider hiring men off the ghetto streetcorner, the chronically unemployed and often socially alienated individuals who, on the face of it, could contribute nothing to his operation. He was being asked not simply to put those men into jobs, but to take on as well the responsibilities and headaches of training them from scratch for the job, instructing them in all the small, seemingly self-evident details of the working world.

Like any other high company official, the president is answerable to a board of directors and stockholders. His first job is to run his business so that it generates profits, and he sees few opportunities for that goal in the proposal that he hire men who appear to be hopelessly unemployable.

This company president is not alone. Like many other executives he runs his firm fairly, without prejudice, and permits no bigotry in his administrators. Negroes, Mexican-Americans, Puerto Ricans, Indians, and other minorities are hired without hesitation—if they have the full qualifications to do the job. But he balks when he is asked to commit his firm to hiring the hardcore unemployed, a course that strikes him as being well apart from the proper aims of his business. Furthermore, if he saddles himself with a costly hardcore training program and his competitors do not, he feels he will be unfairly handicapped in pursuing business goals. He sees the request as equivalent to being pressured for an outrageously high donation to a charity or social welfare program. It's a handout, not good business.

While this is still a familiar attitude, it is one encountered far less frequently than it was a few years ago. As *Fortune* points out, "a sizable number of companies have plainly staked out positions in job training that are in the nature of public service." This is a manifestation of the growing sense of social responsibility that the corporate citizen, like the private citizen, has developed largely in the past decade, with greatest acceleration since the Watts riots of 1965.

To the president's question, "Why should I hire the hardcore?"

some businessmen are answering, "Because it has to be done, and business can do it best."

"Management's sense of obligation to do something about the Negro problem is far more deeply felt than it was in the past," George Strauss has written. "There is considerable feeling that business should not botch up the Negro question the way it did the union question in the 1930's. It is thought that if business does not take the lead, then the government and civil rights groups will be able to place restrictions on business policy that business will never be able to remove. 'If we don't take the responsibility here and handle it our way,' a top executive comments, 'we will create a monster that we won't be able to handle in the future.'"

BUSINESS SELF-INTEREST

The businessman's stake in the improvement of the social and economic health of the over-all community has never been clearer. "It is in the self-interest of business," says Henry Ford II, "to help reduce dependency, frustration, crime and conflict in the community by treating all people on their merits as individuals. The . . . continuing costs of welfare, crime, disease and waste of human potential [are] costs which are borne by business as well as by the rest of the community . . . Like the rest of American society, American business is now waking up to its own self-interest in doing what is right. The stirrings of conscience have led us to see our own interest in a clearer light and we are now acting more decisively."

There is indeed a self-interested element of "social insurance" for the businessman in hiring the hardcore unemployed. In the nation's ten largest cities are located corporate headquarters representing a capital investment of almost 100 billion dollars. If only to protect that investment from the ravages of urban blight and the disastrous consequences of social disorders, the businessman must take action. The survival of that investment depends increasingly upon business's recognition of the "insurance" it provides itself in hiring the ghetto black and giving him a stake in the urban future that he is willing to protect. A job represents just such a stake.

Theodore L. Cross, chairman of the Banking Law Institute, says that "white businessmen will move heaven and earth to eliminate the will or need to riot." This has become especially true, he reports, since the effects of the most recent riots were felt in "the greater urban economies" and not only in the ghetto, where 90 percent of riot damage had occurred in early disorders. Business in good downtown locations no longer appears immune from ghetto riot damage, and many businessmen have moved with alacrity to take "corrective action to break the isolation of the ghetto—action which formerly might have been considered only in the public interest."

A NEW SOURCE OF LABOR

"Economics makes it evident that more and more companies are going to be recruiting the hardcore," says an industrial journal. "As industry expands, its need for workers expands. The available labor pool simply hasn't been expanding to meet needs . . ."

The pinch of a shrinking labor market has been felt more keenly in some areas than in others. It started some years back in the textile country of Greensboro, North Carolina, for example, where employers suffered from the exodus of the area's best workers to the North and to the new chemical and electronic industries locating in the South. These new job opportunities drained away first the skilled white worker, then the unskilled white, then the skilled Negro, and finally reached the unskilled Negro—leaving only the hardcore unemployed.

Faced with recruiting employees from this group, Burlington Industries took its program into the streets. The company hired a black professional educator who could talk the language. He roamed the ghetto, approached streetcorner loungers, and without beating around the bush, asked, "You want a job? We got one." Taking school dropouts and the unskilled hardcore, the Burlington Education Skills Training (BEST) gave them a combination of classroom work and on-the-job training and put them to work.

There is nothing soft-hearted or philanthropic about Burlington's program. Men who seldom held jobs or worked only as part-time sharecroppers were trained in weaving and spinning and other operative jobs which, a few years ago, were thought to require skills the hardcore unemployed could not master. This belief was shown to be untrue only when the mills were literally forced to find a labor supply and had only the black hardcore to which they could turn. Here the labor market squeeze made itself felt earlier than in other parts of the country, but today many companies are feeling the pinch, and they too are looking to the virtually untapped hardcore pool.

GOVERNMENT CONTRACTS

Other companies, perhaps a majority of those now engaged in hardcore hiring, were led into it by way of government contracts. Under provisions of those contracts, they agreed to hire and train Negroes and other minority workers. This gentle art of the "federal hotfoot," as one writer has called it, prodded business into minority hiring with considerable alacrity. Their fear was that if they did not move, the federal government would, and at a cost which would eventually fall on business in the form of higher taxes or an eroding dollar. Some firms outdid the government's action by setting up their own form of "private sector contract compliance": Neiman-Marcus of Dallas, The Dayton Company in Minneapolis, and Levi Strauss of San Francisco, for example, require that their purchasing departments verify a prospective supplier's minority employment pattern before buying from him. Before losing accounts of that magnitude, most all-white supply firms would go to some lengths to bring minority workers into their work force, just as employers sought to recruit minority workers to avoid losing government contracts.

In fulfilling contract obligations, any one firm has to compete with hundreds of others for the qualified black man ready to step into a job. For such a worker, it is indeed a seller's market. Increasingly, to find the men it needs to satisfy contract compliance officers, business finds itself looking toward the bottom of the unemployment pile. And even here the competition for workers is growing. Under the newly seized-on provisions of a 1965 Presidential Executive Order, contractors in some urban areas must pledge to hire a specific range of nonwhite employees in graduated numbers over a four-year period if they wish to bid on certain federal construction projects. As the 1970's progress, business will necessarily be dealing with the hardest of the hardcore.

While government contracts bring employers the problems of hardcore recruitment and training, they also bring compensating new opportunities. More than one business has found renewed life in the promise of federal contracts that enable expansion into new products or new services: without the contract such expansion would never take place. To many firms, the cost and trouble of adopting the new recruiting, hiring, and training methods is more than compensated for by their new prosperity, which in turn creates more jobs. "The expansion of employment in our type of society is a function of the private sector's finding profitable areas in which to invest—new products, new processes, new industries," says Eli Ginzburg, Columbia University economist.

He goes on to say, "Another way to achieve job expansion in our society is to put the private and public sectors together in more imaginative ways so that there will be new financing, so that certain services, such as medicine and education, which previously were not adequately underpinned, are nourished."

The outlook is for more activity, greater new development, rather than less. A host of new problems confronts the nation, besides the areas of medicine and education mentioned by Ginzburg: pollution control, recreation development, housing, water-resource development, communication, transportation, and an increasing demand for services of all kinds. As these and other areas are tackled by American business, the drain on manpower at all levels of skill will be enormous. A major part of that manpower will necessarily come from today's single largest remaining labor resource: the hardcore unemployed.

WHAT WILL IT COST THE EMPLOYER?

Nailing a cost figure to the training of the hardcore unemployed is an elusive matter, particularly since the results of such a program cannot always easily be measured. Improved public image for the company, the opening of new markets, forestalled labor difficulties, prevention of boycotts, demonstrations and social disorders—these and other results have financially measurable value, but are extremely variable. Yet all these factors must somehow be figured in as cost-reducing items in order to arrive at an honest final figure for a hardcore training program.

Additionally, there must be considered the boost such hiring practices provide to the economy as a whole. If 500,000 people are newly employed, their contribution in federal income taxes alone would reach $158 million. The earnings on which those taxes are paid would not only flow back in part to business, but would also enable the new worker to abandon the welfare rolls, thereby lessening a public expense that becomes increasingly burdensome. Unemployment in general costs business money. Speaking of unemployed school dropouts, sociologist Lucius F. Cervantes says, "Businessmen are coming to realize that it is cheaper to help the dropout through work experience than through taxation. The public, and financially this means business, is taxed roughly $1,000 per year per unemployed youth and no productive work accrues to society."

Estimates are that the outright immediate cost for training one hardcore unemployed ghetto dweller ranges from one to three times the cost for training an employee who comes to the job with some work experience and a high school education. In the experience of American Telephone and Telegraph Company, with a vast hardcore hiring program, this has been said to translate to an actual training cost of $3,000 per employee. Although this is a lot of money, AT&T does not consider the cost excessive. Eighty percent of its customers and 70 percent of its plant investment is located in "deteriorating central cities," and the hardcore hiring program is a practical move toward slowing the process of deterioration and thus protecting its investment.

The higher the skills needed, the higher the training costs. In Boston, the Avco Corporation's printing plant established an elaborate and sophisticated twenty-one-week "vestibule" or pre-on-the-job training period, combined with a system of job-coached apprenticeships in the printing trades, for which they received federal funds of $5,000 per trainee to cover their extra costs. In Minneapolis, Control Data Corporation employed hundreds of hardcore Negroes at a training cost of $2,500, a figure below the estimated $3,000 average for federal job-training programs.

But many employers have found the cost not nearly that high. In Chicago, the Rauland Corporation, a Zenith subsidiary, worked out a one-month vestibule training period followed by on-the-job training for 2,400 hardcore unemployed at a cost of about $1,000 per man. A Philadelphia electronics firm spends only $300 to $400 per man, and a St. Louis aircraft company estimates its cost at $450 per person. Private training firms claim they can put an adequately trained hardcore worker on the job for less than what most companies spend to advertise, interview, screen, test, and place an average worker.

One of the most effective ways to hold training costs to a minimum is through a consortium. In this arrangement a number of small or medium-sized companies band together for the purpose of consolidating training efforts in order to eliminate the costly duplication of similar training activity. In the San Francisco area, such a consortium was formed with Lockheed Missiles and Space Company as the coordinator (see Chapter 12). An early boon to smaller companies was the fact that the coordinator reimbursed them monthly for training costs, which the government only started to do in 1970; thus they did not have to carry burdensome "front-end costs" for a nine-month to one-year period before government subsidies were paid.

The availability of federal funds to subsidize hardcore training has provided a sharp incentive for business to adopt new programs. Largely under U. S. Department of Labor auspices, these programs reimburse the employer for all extra costs above normal training costs that he incurs in taking on a hardcore employee. The bureaucratic red tape that has always been a deterrent to business to enter into agreements with the government has been reduced to a minimum. By lifting the weight of extra cost from the businessman's shoulders, training subsidies have helped clear the way for a wide-scale business effort to bring the hardcore unemployed into the employment mainstream.

GIVE AND TAKE

A company which proposes to hire and train the hardcore unemployed can expect to undergo considerable internal upheaval. Appropriate new methods and procedures must be established, and management and administrative personnel must become comfortable working with such new procedures. The process probably will never be wholly without problems, but it is not a matter of all "give" and no "take" for the employer. In the very process of adapting, changing, revising, rewriting, or totally scrapping procedures in order to bring the new man onto the job with the least trouble, you stand to gain some critical insights helpful in your business overall. At the very least, the procedure forces management, willy-nilly, to look over hiring and training policies with a sharp eye. It is a rare firm that doesn't profit somewhere along the line by such review and evaluation of its practices. And when such a review is undertaken not on a piecemeal, makeshift basis to meet emergencies, but is approached on a planned basis as a consequence of management's firm commitment to a hardcore hiring program, then the value of such review is measurably increased.

For example, one personnel director explained how his company's new hardcore training program backed him into a new managerial technique that provided positive gains for the entire work force. "We found that a smaller percentage of hardcore trainees were leaving their jobs than were newly hired nondisadvantaged workers. So we came to the conclusion that the extra attention provided by our staff, along with special support serv-

ices, would be good for *all* employees, not just the hardcore. . .
Our staff has become increasingly attuned to approaching each
employee on an individual basis, in terms of his particular
strengths and limitations. We believe that because we are now
responsive to the needs of our workers, we have cut down on
job dropouts, across the board."

Another example of unforeseen benefits stemming from a hardcore hiring program is the way it can enhance the recruiting of
new executive talent from among the ranks of bright, socially
conscious young men. The unpleasant fact is that in the past
twenty years there has occurred a general disenchantment of
the young with American business. Questioning business priorities
and values, the talented young turn instead to public service, the
Peace Corps, and other nonbusiness pursuits in which they see a
chance to attack pressing social problems. But the company that
demonstrates its concern with race relations, urban blight, and
the plight of the urban poor attracts the able graduate, as such
companies as Xerox and IBM, with extensive public-service programs, have amply demonstrated.

RESOURCES IN THE PRIVATE SECTOR

Over the past several years, as employers have moved into
the field of job development for the hardcore unemployed, business has acquired a substantial body of knowledge about the do's
and don'ts of such endeavors. In some cases the knowledge has
been systematized by business organizations and industry associations specifically for the assistance of employers hoping to embark
on such a program.

Such assistance was the goal of a group of over 600 businessmen who met in 1968 under the leadership of Henry Ford II.
Charged by the President's manpower message to Congress,

they joined together as the National Alliance of Businessmen and established a Job Opportunities in the Business Sector program (JOBS) for hiring 100,000 hardcore unemployed in an eighteen-month period—a goal reportedly exceeded within the first year. Many of the companies which pledged jobs to the NAB program set up training programs without federal subsidization, or with minimal help from government services such as the Concentrated Employment Program, to aid in recruiting. Others sought the guidance of such authorities as the National Association of Manufacturers, whose Solutions to Employment Problems program was established in 1964 as forerunner to its present Urban Affairs Division. The Urban Affairs Division has studied companies which developed innovative solutions to minority manpower problems, and makes these case histories available as guides to other companies.

Among other resources is the Urban Coalition, comprised of business and public leaders from diverse fields. Located in major cities around the country, the group's purpose is to stimulate and coordinate activity toward solving urban problems, hardcore unemployment chief among them.

Also available are a number of industry developed organizations which specialize in setting up training programs for employers. Among these are the Board for Fundamental Education (BFE), based in Indianapolis, which provides concentrated on-the-job instruction in such basic skills as reading and writing. Another is MIND (Methods of Intellectual Development), supported by the giant food-processing firm, Corn Products Company, to step up remedial education of trainees. In Cleveland, Action for Manpower—Jobs (AIM), was formed by a group of executives from major employers in order to find jobs for the unemployed. Nearly all large communities across the country have one or more similar groups available to aid the employer.

Management consultant firms and human relations consultants also offer a wide variety of services. For a fee they will advise on particular training problems, or set up an entire hard-core training program, including recruiting, classroom and on-the-job training of both new employees and supervisors, and provide regular follow-up (see Chapter 12).

OTHER RESOURCES

Most communities have developed a variety of resources that are of help to an employer starting a hardcore training program. They vary from such agencies as the long-established state employment systems, which aid in referral, recruiting, and screening, to high schools or junior colleges which are willing to participate in 4-4 programs—four hours on the job, four hours in school. Service clubs such as Elks, Kiwanis, and Rotary are also a potential resource; they may be persuaded to underwrite the training of a small group of ghetto residents in much the way that they provide school or college scholarships to needy students. Chambers of commerce are also good sources of aid; many have full-time staff people working in urban job development.

Such resources can be of material assistance—helping to bear extra costs, as in the case of government programs, or alleviating the burden of setting up a separate training machine, as with consortiums. Lessening of program costs may also come through large-scale group training of both hardcore unemployed workers and the supervisors who will oversee them. Community resources such as the Urban League or the National Association for the Advancement of Colored People can be used to feed job candidates to the employer, again lessening recruitment costs. And when the program is underway in your shop, existing personnel can be used as trainers (see Chapter 5) to extend the training process for as long a period as it is fruitful, without the cost of specialized instruction.

Still, many employers prefer to go it alone, not affiliating with other groups and avoiding the federal subsidy so as to eliminate record-keeping and outside control. These self-administered programs promise to get a boost from the probably inevitable passage of tax-incentive legislation, support for which has been increasing in state legislatures and in Washington. In the 91st Congress, Senator Charles H. Percy introduced such a bill, "to provide an incentive for private employers to employ and train unskilled individuals . . . by allowing an income tax credit for wages paid to such individuals." Senator Percy's proposal asked that participating employers "receive a tax credit of 75% of the wages paid to the employee for the first four months of employment, 50% for the next four months and 25% for the balance of the individual's first year of employment."

In view of the growing involvement of business in training programs, some such incentive legislation, uncomplicated and with little red tape so as to appeal to the smaller employer, seems likely to be enacted.

WHAT JOBS FOR THE HARDCORE?

Some businessmen have shied away from hardcore hiring in the belief that such a program is nothing more than a ruinous form of make-work and featherbedding. But the tens of thousands of unemployed persons who have gone to work in thousands of companies have shown the fallacy of that notion. Hardcore trainees *do* become valued and productive employees, performing needed tasks.

But the company launching a hardcore hiring program must

of necessity make a thorough evaluation of the jobs to which it will assign the new men. In a firm manufacturing sophisticated electronics equipment, for example, skilled job functions may be broken up into a number of unskilled component functions suitable for the entry-level newcomer to perform. In some cases such a procedure can work to a company's over-all advantage. The National Association of Manufacturers points out that "for years companies have been taking a hard look at what makes up professional jobs in fields such as engineering in order to determine those functions that can be handled by sub-professionals. The professional is then freed to devote himself to tasks that make use of his specialized training." The elements of a job that require special skills are assigned to the trained worker, with unskilled personnel carrying out routine tasks. "In this way," says Whitney Young, Jr., "skilled workers are more productive and new jobs at entry levels are created. Business did this during World War II, when there was a labor shortage; it can do it again. The new jobs would also serve as apprenticeship positions for future upgrading to skilled levels."

Where jobs are of such a nature as to defy easy restructuring, other possibilities emerge. One West Coast manufacturer of small plastic containers created a new department staffed largely by hardcore "unemployables." The firm sought and received contracts with trucking firms and other fleet operators to supply them with first-aid kits for vehicle glove compartments. The plastic kit itself came from their original product line, and the first-aid components were purchased. The kit was then assembled and packed by the new men. The move proved itself profitable for the firm and provided jobs for a half-dozen previously unemployed young men as well.

Other firms seeking ways to provide opportunity to the hardcore have found it possible to shift parts of their operation from outlying areas to the central city, easily reached by the ghetto dweller. Still others have taken pains to work out advanced vacation schedules to permit hiring of long-term replacements, or have shuffled their production or repair schedules to produce more jobs. Painting and maintenance of equipment, updating of company records, such as filing backlogs, are typical tasks that can be found in most plants and offices.

New production methods can be profitably investigated by almost any firm. The possibility of modification of present production methods for greater operational efficiency should be reviewed, and new equipment considered. In all cases manpower changes would very likely take place, possibly opening the way for the employment of the hardcore unemployed.

ABSORBING THE COST OF "INEFFICIENCY"

With profit maximization as its traditional central purpose, American business has always been uncommonly vigorous in routing out costly inefficiency. A hardcore hiring program, which appears on the face of it to put two workers on a job that one man has satisfactorily performed before, goes against the grain of every manager. Over the long run such an arrangement would be intolerable, of course, but for the purposes of training it has been done matter-of-factly for a hundred years: the trainee or apprentice learns needed skills at the side of an experienced man until normal turnover or expansion of the work force creates a position for him as a full-fledged employee.

A hardcore hiring program is no more than an extension of such a practice, with the guarantee of federal training subsidies furnishing a cushion against the loss suffered because of a trainee's expectedly limited productivity. Such a guarantee makes defensible to company officers and stockholders the establishment of extended training positions or creation of jobs calling for limited production which would otherwise be prohibitively costly.

EARLY QUALMS

Hiring and training the hardcore unemployed is no longer uncharted territory for American business. The qualms that an employer might have expressed twenty years ago about putting Negroes on the job alongside whites were long since revealed as groundless. Today, such fears should not give pause to any employer. Yet, in making your move, you should be aware of the kind of misinformation that still crops up, since the chances are that it will reach your ear before the hardcore program has advanced very far.

The simple fact is that over the past decade, for all the continued race tension and occasional violence, racial prejudice and bigotry have tended to become "unfashionable." The white population has grown in knowledge about the Negro, superficially in most instances, but sufficiently to eliminate open expression of raw and disruptive bias. Stereotyped views of all Negroes as "lazy and shiftless," for example, surely are still privately held by many, but they are voiced far less frequently by today's relatively sophisticated white worker.

With this change in the racial climate, problems that once were serious barriers to Negro hiring today often never materialize. The R. J. Reynolds Tobacco Company in Winston-Salem supplies an example. According to the manager of personnel development, the company had serious fears of "white employee backlash" when it launched its large-scale program of hiring Negroes. But as the program developed, it proved beneficial for white workers as well as the hardcore. What "negated the backlash," says the personnel manager, "was that most of the rednecks tend to be older employees and we found that some of them had been passed over by promotions for one reason or another and many of them have benefited from the training program, too."

Even where a certain backlash is felt, serious problems are often avoided by a "self-adjusting" mechanism, as happened in one Southern manufacturing company when it began hiring Negroes. One of the older white workers, on his way home from work each day, noticed one of the new Negro employees waiting for a bus at the same corner every time he passed. He began to stop and pick up the new man and drive him part way home each day. Another white worker who observed this told the driver that he should not be associating with Negroes, and that he ought to stop giving the new man a ride. When the driver paid little attention to this and continued to stop for the new man, the second worker became abusive and hostile. The driver talked over this problem with his Negro rider, and they decided it would be best for them to stop riding together, at least until the matter cooled off.

The resolution here may not appear to be ideal, but it does show how workers themselves can arrive at adaptive measures to avoid serious backlash problems. It is important to know, also, that the incident occurred in a Southern plant, where white workers were tradition-bound and reluctant at first to accept many of the changes brought on by equal opportunity policies.

The fears and resentment that white supervisors and workers may feel at a sudden influx of hardcore trainees can best be handled beforehand by an unequivocally clear statement from management on the necessity for an extended equal opportunity program (see Chapter 5), and by permitting workers to feel that they too have a role in the success of the program.

"Rather than an ultimatum being handed down the line," suggests the NAM, "managers should bring their work groups together to discuss how the company can best implement its policies concerning hiring and training the disadvantaged. In this kind of setting, employees are often able to express any anxieties they may have about the security of their own jobs. Once this fear is dealt with, useful suggestions are often made regarding the program, which tends to deepen the commitment of those participating."

Doubts about the workability of hardcore hiring plans can be eliminated, says the plant manager for a midwestern manufacturing firm with over 25,000 employees, if you observe the following points:

- Plan carefully—lack of planning invites trouble.
- Develop a good dialogue with all parties concerned; discuss moves with all involved; make sure every worker knows what is to happen and why.
- Use management's equal opportunity statement as a guide, not a club.
- Feel your way—don't plunge.
- Always keep your hardcore hiring plan in the front of your responsibilities, at the top of your priority list; never let it lag.
- Involve union leaders and insurance representatives.
- Ask Negro leaders for suggestions.
- Keep your finger on the pulse of the program; never overlook an incident, no matter how small.
- Don't hesitate to employ discipline, but be sure you have the facts.
- Don't unwittingly discriminate against white workers.

HOW MANY?

"Okay," says the employer, "if I agree to hire the hardcore, how many do I have to take on?"

It is a frequent question and one that has no adequate answer. But such imprecision satisfies no one, and the employer is done no service if the question is avoided.

The fact of the matter is that some black rights groups have begun to ask for "ranges" and "percentages" of Negro employment. Many companies do indeed have unofficial quotas which work to the advantage of Negro workers—at least until the quota is filled. Even the U. S. Department of Labor, with its 1969 "Philadelphia Plan" requiring increasing annual percentages of nonwhite workers in construction jobs, approaches implicit endorsement of a "benign quota." Much the same implication can be drawn from an order of the Washington State Board Against Discrimination, which prevented an ironworkers local union from using union membership or length of service in the trade as a basis for job referrals until Negro membership was within 10 percent of the proportion of Negroes in the population of the union's area.

In San Francisco, a coalition of civil rights groups signed an agreement with that city's hotel employers' association calling for the hiring of a sufficient number of minority group workers to reach "a level of 15 to 20 percent of the total employees." They specifically denied that this was a "quota for hiring," but instead called it an "expected range of non-white employment," or an "anticipated goal."

But whatever name the idea of quotas goes by, an employer engaged in hardcore hiring might avoid the entire quota concept by aiming instead at "maximum feasible participation" for minority employees, at the same time steering clear of anything that could be construed as "discrimination in reverse."

It is admittedly a fine line to tread, and an employer might be excused if he sets his sights on the percentage of Negro or minority population in his community overall and uses that as a rough guide to the ratio of minorities he hopes to achieve in his work force. For example, the Pacific Telephone and Telegraph Company set as its first year's objective under the NAB hardcore hiring program the hiring of one hardcore person for approximately every 100 employees on the payroll in NAB-area cities.

In practice, it frequently happens that a hardcore program sets its own limits on the number of people it can include. An employer takes on no more than he can adequately screen, train, supervise, counsel, upgrade, and effectively absorb into his work force. The idea of quotas or preferential treatment need not enter in. When a company which has not recruited Negroes in the past now makes special efforts to add black workers to its rolls, such effort may well comprise special treatment to include Negroes in the recruitment pattern—but it is not preferential treatment. It only extends to Negroes some of the benefits whites already have.

The point is simply to set all your hiring practices to embrace the complete range of prospective job candidates, including minorities. Look for ways to *include* all, rather than *exclude* some. When you have done that, you have cleared the decks for setting up a successful hardcore hiring program.

CHAPTER TWO

Who Are the Hardcore and How Are They Reached?

The Negro hardcore unemployed are a minority within a minority. Simply to be black (or Mexican-American, Puerto Rican, or American Indian) and unemployed doesn't relegate one to hardcore ranks. What must also be considered are matters of education, training, job experience, motivation, and attitudes; geographic, economic, political and social differences figure in as well. Distinctions between these varied elements of the Negro labor market—from highly skilled professional to "unemployable" teen-aged dropout—are essential to the employer.

What is this market? To answer that question some categories must be drawn—not to satisfy the sociological purist, but only to assist the employer to identify, in a practical way and in terms of his personal needs, the various components of the black labor force, including those other than hardcore.

1. *"The Instant Negro."* At the top of the employment ladder is the fully qualified worker, the man or woman ready to go to work without training and with a minimum of orientation. This group comprises what has been called the "instant Negro," or "super-black," for which there is keen competition since they represent the quickest and least painful way for a company to make a show of integration, however symbolically.

Most college graduates belong in this group, as do workers

who, because of specialist backgrounds, are likely to be pirated off one job for another. But the group also includes those with substantial past work experience who are temporarily unemployed for good reason: older craftsmen, skilled mechanics, clerical workers, production workers suffering from a general layoff. But all have specific skills easily transferable to another job in another company.

Among the younger members of this group, aside from the college graduates, are those who have completed specialized training and, by at least several months on a job, have shown some measure of their ability and the relevance of their training.

This group, then, consists of fully qualified workers. If there were enough of them to go around, a personnel man's lot would be at least 50 percent easier.

2. *The Willing-to-Work.* The members of this group have one thing in their favor: motivation. They are willing to work, and if left to their own devices will eventually find a job without special help. The top-of-the-class high school graduate earnestly looking for work, the young man squeezed out of college before graduation by financial or family problems are prominent in this group. Among the older prospects are the non-high school graduate who has some work experience in a skill still useful on today's labor market, and the recent migrants to a community who have a job background but may have temporary difficulty in finding work because of their unfamiliarity with the area or its labor demands.

3. *The Underemployed.* This includes the large number of workers who have training in a skill but, because of racial discrimination or other factors, have never practiced it. The taxi driver who graduated from a nonaccredited small Negro college as a teacher is an example. While his training is below acceptable levels for some states' teaching requirements, he nonetheless has training which might be helpful as an administrator, office

worker, salesman, or the like, and which he is not using in his present job.

Here, too, are the technological "pushouts," low-skilled workers automated out of jobs, as well as those whose immediate need for "eating money" lead them into an endless cycle of such jobs as dishwasher, brickchipper, car-washer, leaflet-distributor, for which they collect a day's pay at a time.

A large part of this group is made up of the "working poor." These are the men and women who hold only part-time jobs, or perhaps such traditional low-paying "colored jobs" as janitor or other custodial helper, service and domestic worker, laborer, low-level production worker, farmer, and sharecropper.

Groups Two and Three make up a considerable slice of the over-all Negro labor pool. Generally they are the most readily available to the employer. Indeed, many firms desiring to bring black workers into their main labor force could look to their own custodial staff for recruits. You may find a man whose working ability and company loyalty have been proved, and it is frequently only a matter of informal training before he can move up—provided, of course, that he wants to.

These three groups, imperfectly as they may be classified, represent in the main individuals who will probably find work of one sort or another with or without special efforts by business to seek them out. In greatly varying degrees they have all shown either readiness or willingness to work, even if only at jobs that may pay below a poverty level income. They have either a theoretical or practical knowledge of the working world, ranging from familiarity with time clocks and bus schedules to use of safety equipment and how to accept supervision. Such knowledge may seem of slight benefit, but it is an advantage that members of the remaining two groups generally do not have.

4. *The Young Hardcore Unemployed.* These are the individuals under, say, age twenty-five who have dropped out of

high school or, in some cases, have managed to graduate without ever acquiring such basic educational skills as reading. (The Negro youth without specific skills has almost as little chance to obtain a good job with a high school diploma as without one.) Functionally illiterate or undereducated, a member of this group may have some marginal work experience as dishwasher, bus boy, or parking attendant spread over a number of years. He may have skirted the fringe of criminal activity through hustling on the street, and he probably has a minor arrest record. He may well be associated with a militant black nationalist group, and for that reason, or because he is a voluntary social dropout for inarticulated reasons, may hold working for the "Establishment" in deep contempt; or he may be willing to accept work, but only when and where it suits him.

Some of these young people may undergo attitudinal changes once on the job, at the risk, to be sure, of being labeled "Uncle Toms" by their streetcorner colleagues. Others may find that a job brings a wholly new perspective, as in the case of one man who was employed by a company despite his long criminal record. "He was placed in a low-level job and things seemed to be going moderately well for the first few months," reported the rehabilitation specialist. "Then there was a tremendous change and he began progressing very rapidly. He received two or three very quick promotions. His supervisors said that he was outstanding and he was, in fact, one of their best men. At the same time I noticed a startling change in his personality and attitude. When I talked to him I told him that I had noticed this change, and asked him about it. He said, 'All at once I realized that *now* I was one of *them.*'"

Many of the individuals in this group are unemployed because they literally don't know how to work. They have no knowledge of the work market; don't know what jobs are available; what reasonable wages are; where or how to look for leads;

how to fill out an application blank; how to offer one's self as a possible job candidate. They have none of the attributes that nearly every personnel man takes for granted in a job candidate who presents himself at the employment office door.

When the president of the metal fabricating plant quoted at the beginning of this book complained that the hardcore "weren't interested enough to come in looking for work," he failed to realize that most don't even know his plant exists, to say nothing of having the faintest idea of what it does, or why.

It is this group and a part of the next that forms the bulk of the hardcore unemployed.

5. *The Older Hardcore Unemployed.* These are in great part men moving into middle-age and beyond, their life patterns sometimes too well established for easy alteration. Among them, those who show some job history, however dim and distant, and to whom adequate motivation might lend stability, are possible job candidates. These are men who at least have maturity; routinized jobs requiring patience to perform might suit their abilities. Eli Lilly and Company reports that in hiring the hardcore, they have had the most success with "the older applicant from 30 to 45 years of age. Apparently these employees have attitudes which enable them to fit in more easily with their associates at the company." A Lilly vice-president reports that "our retention rate of these persons is 78 percent. When you consider that regular employment is a new experience for most of them, this result is surprising and pleasantly so."

Others in this group are those with recent and relevant training in prison shops, through poverty program training courses, or in vocational rehabilitation. It also includes housewives who, with their children grown, attempt to bring minimum skills to the labor market for the first time or after an absence of many years.

Into this group of older hardcore unemployed falls those in-

dividuals whose chances are slimmest of all—men on the fur-
therest reaches of hope: older, unskilled persons with unrelieved histories of joblessness; those with physical or mental problems unresponsive to rehabilitation or therapy; and those with a
long welfare background and no desire or—as they see it—no
apparent reason to change.

A PROFILE OF THE HARDCORE UNEMPLOYED

The typical urban hardcore unemployed job applicant who
will present himself at your office may be any age, but most
likely he'll be under twenty-five. According to Leo C. Beebe,
Ford executive and an early leader of the National Alliance of
Businessmen, "he'll have a sixth grade education and probably
read at third or fourth grade levels. He'll have no steady employment record, some kind of police record, and he may have
a history of drug addiction or drinking. He has little understanding of the working world. And he probably needs dental work,
glasses, and some other medical treatment to bring him up to
company health standards."

He may desperately be looking for a steady job, or he may
be beyond caring if he works at all. He may be contemptuous
of steady work, or a seasonal employee, one who is underemployed, or who lives by his wits on the streets. Many need only
"an invitation to a job and training to attain productive lives. A
few have problems that far outreach the rehabilitative powers of
. . . any job program. . . . Most need an extra measure of understanding, a sympathetic hand, to turn idleness into output."

This is the surface picture of the typical applicant. Behind
these more apparent traits lie characteristics that have deep
roots. Such manifestations of the hardcore person's different life-
style are less often discussed, but they add a vital dimension to

the over-all picture of the man you are planning to hire and they should be understood.

The low-income slum-dweller—not Negroes alone—lives a way of life that provides him with only the narrowest range of situations and demands. His knowledge of social roles is limited; he seldom participates in any activity which takes him out of the daily routine; he rarely plays roles of leadership or fills any position calling for specialized functioning. Socially, he seldom goes beyond the borders of kinship and neighborhood groups—people very like himself. He reads fewer newspapers, hears fewer news programs, joins fewer organizations, and knows less of the current life of either the community or the larger world than more prosperous, better educated people do. He feels alone and detached, and views the world as indifferent and distant. He believes no one much cares what happens to him.

According to U. S. Welfare Administration social scientists who have studied his life-style, the low-income hardcore person feels helpless in the face of society and its institutions. He has practically no power in the working world. If he finds a job, he can exercise little autonomy and has small opportunity to influence conditions of work. He has seen a sharp decrease in the kinds of jobs he is able to do. Once displaced from a job, he has a harder time finding another. He is close to helpless even to acquire information and training which would change his situation. He has neither the knowledge nor the means to get it. He is widely convinced that individuals cannot influence the workings of society, and he doubts that he can even influence his own life. Correspondingly, he is likely to voice such pessimistic views as, "A body just can't take nothing for granted. You just have to live from day to day and hope the sun will shine tomorrow."

The alien conditions in which he may be caught tend to be unintelligible to him. He does not grasp the structure of the world in which he lives, and never knows what to expect from it. He is discriminated against in many ways, leaving him suspicious and on guard.

He experiences anomie, a term describing situations in which social standards have broken down or no longer influence behavior: there is no norm by which one lives, and socially prescribed behavior fails to lead to expected goals. He becomes cynical, fatalistic. Taught in many ways that economic success is the most desirable thing in life, but barred from legitimate means of achieving it, he may come to believe that illegal behavior is necessary to reach approved goals. He is induced to believe in luck. He blames his difficulties on fortune and chance.

He is deprived—if that condition is defined as lack of resources relative to felt wants and needs. The commercial advertising he sees attempts to stimulate and increase desire for status achievement. The richness of life in the rest of society is displayed on television, which he watches regularly, in newspapers, on billboards, in store windows, and on the very streets. His constant awareness of his own abject status and the "failure" which it rightly or wrongly implies understandably leads to his withdrawal and isolation.

He is insecure. With a low and uncertain income he is more at the mercy of life's unpredictability than are the more affluent. Sickness, injury, loss of work, legal problems—a range of hazardous possibilities—are especially fearful to him. He is unable to secure for himself and his family the regular, preventive health measures which would fend off medical emergencies, and often he finds that he cannot successfully navigate the channels involved in using public sources for emergency help, such as clinics and legal aid agencies.

Of course, not all of these characteristics are found in every member of the hardcore unemployed group. But it by no means requires all, or even very many, to produce a man quite "different" from the job applicant you are accustomed to hire. Yet, for all the difference this list of characteristics implies, none of them necessarily destroys his ability to become a productive worker once he has been adequately trained for the job.

REACHING THE UNEMPLOYED

Since any employer with an appropriate vacancy is usually delighted at finding the fully qualified "instant Negro" to fill it, the workers in Group One above are seldom on the open market for long unless they voluntarily choose to be there. Employer competition for this group is extraordinary. Lockheed Missiles and Space Company reports that its college recruiters have become "somewhat discouraged" in their search for qualified Negro engineering students. They report that "Negro graduates of the high-standard colleges and universities are receiving so many job offers that in some cases the school officials have been forced to limit the number of companies permitted to interview them."

Normally, the recruitment sources you have always used— the state employment service, private employment services—will also reach such members of this group as are available. Additionally, civil rights agencies with professionally staffed employment services, such as some branches of the Urban League (not all civil rights agencies are equipped to furnish competent employment service) should be consulted. Advertisements in Negro or Spanish-language newspapers are frequently effective. If you already employ Negro workers, encourage them to pass along word of vacancies to friends or relatives. At the Oakland plant of Owens-Illinois, Inc., nearly 50 percent of applicants are referred by plant employees, and a Singer plant in South Carolina found white employees recommending Negroes when word-of-mouth advertising was used. Military noncommissioned officers up for discharge are good possibilities, usually they are reachable through military discharge centers.

To reach Group Two, those "willing to work," the same sources should be tapped, along with some important additions: junior college, high school, and trade and business school placement bureaus are obvious sources. You would also do well to make at least perfunctory contact with high school athletic coaches, who often aid their athletes to line up work, and with pastors of churches located in the ghetto to determine the extent of their possible helpfulness. In some communities, inner-city churches serve as virtual clearing houses and dispatching halls for minority job seekers.

To find the "underemployed" worker of Group Three, you may need look no further than your own shop. Can you upgrade custodial workers, for instance, to training positions of greater responsibility where promotional possibilities are clearly visible to them? Another move beneficial to all workers, not just those who are underemployed, is to ferret out the forgotten, deadened jobs in your shop and review them for clues. They may be staffed by potentially able men who have been sidetracked through no fault of their own.

Again, advertise in minority media and inform ghetto churchmen; encourage word-of-mouth advertising, particularly if it will receive wide enough currency so that workers in other plants hear it. Local human rights organizations or fair employment commissions, although primarily administrative agencies, sometimes can be of help in referring you to underemployed workers. Frequently, a man underemployed by another company whose policies have blinded it to his potential will be eager to change work if his new job promises a chance to try his unused skills.

Even in recruiting workers from these first three non-hardcore categories, some measure of extra effort is called for. Negroes will not often apply for jobs where they have been led to believe —perhaps by an acquaintance's experience many years before— that they will not be seriously considered for good jobs. Adding to the problem is the fact that some school placement bureaus and employment agencies simply assume that black applicants will not be considered and, unless specifically directed otherwise, will not refer them. Thus, as one personnel officer writes, experience shows that "worthy members of a deprived group often have to be sought out. Perhaps because of discouraging experiences in the past, they are much less enterprising about applying for jobs than are people from more favored groups. . . ."

LOOKING FOR THE HARDCORE UNEMPLOYED

In some ways, the hardcore unemployed described in Groups Four and Five are easiest of all to find. An abundance of official agencies, with the help of community groups, have been at work since the mid-1960's identifying them and steering them into training programs accessible to the employer. Among such programs are the Job Corps, the out-of-school program of the Neighborhood Youth Corps, Youth Opportunity Centers, Work Incentive programs, and such Department of Labor and Office of Economic Opportunity projects as the Concentrated Employment Program (see Chapter 12).

In most cases, your standard, tried-and-true recruiting methods are worthless in trying to reach the hardcore unemployed individual. He would simply be unaware of them. Word-of-mouth referrals from black employees rarely work because he knows few people who hold a regular job. Advertisements in minority newspapers would be largely ineffective since he never reads them.

What methods, then, do you use?

Recruiting centers set up in the ghetto, away from the imposing corporate offices which many hardcore applicants would hesitate to approach, have proved useful, especially for large employers looking for sizable numbers of men. Such a center can be a mobile unit or a one-man personnel operation which sets up shop in a storefront. In Detroit, the auto industry used this means to recruit large numbers of the hardcore. The Ford Special Training Employment Placement Service (STEPS), for example, successfully attracted many applicants with its inner-city office that advised prospects: "We have factory job openings paying over $3 an hour. No test will be given. Persons with police records will be considered . . ." Ford asked applicants only to fill out a brief form and to pass a physical examination. "If they could do both and were not dope addicts or habitual criminals, they [STEPS] hired them on the spot."

"Job Fairs" are often useful in bringing news to the ghetto about a wide variety of jobs. Set up in a centrally located auditorium, hall, or church, one-day or week-end fairs might invite participation from scores of local businesses. Each company sets up its own informational booth and mans it with a team of personnel specialists to carry out preliminary screening with the authority, hopefully, to hire on the spot. Local grass-roots civil rights organizations are frequently the coordinating forces behind these fairs; groups of companies participating in a National Alliance of Businessmen's hardcore hiring program have also sponsored such events.

Besides ghetto-based civil rights groups, there are a variety of sources within the black community which should be explored. These include directors of athletic teams, social workers, parole and probation officers, and youth groups, not excluding gangs. Ghetto barber shops—the clearing house for much neighborhood news—bars, pool halls, and carry-out food stands, all of which serve as gathering places for the young and not-so-young, should be made regular stops on a recruiter's rounds whenever feasible. For such duties, Honeywell, Inc. of Minneapolis recommends a recruiter who is "an accepted representative of the minority community" and who operates out of a "roving recruiter bus" in the hardcore area.

Some companies have found able workers through the "work pass" or "work furlough" programs operated by many county jails or state prisons to enable persons due to be released from prison into gradually taking on the responsibilities of a job (see Chapter 4). Here an employer receives the assistance of a prison field agent in selecting prospective inmates and matching them to available jobs. At San Quentin Prison in California, an association of black convicts interested in advancement has started a job-finding agency for released convicts throughout the San Francisco Bay Area.

Announcements on ghetto-beamed rock'n'roll radio stations are also worth a try. Many times you will get handsome cooperation from such stations, whose operators are often public-service minded where the welfare of their listeners is concerned.

DIFFICULTIES IN RECRUITING

"We have learned from experience," says a vice president of Eli Lilly and Company, "that it is quite vain to increase Negro hiring—and I believe this lesson applies equally to many other companies—unless there is an upward movement of black and white employees within the company's ranks, leaving suitable openings for the newcomers. Unless this happens, our original objectives will be defeated."

A company that cannot show this "upward movement" (see

Chapter 11), will find it hard to answer the questions one New York management consultant says he hears from black college graduates demanding to know about promotional patterns of the firms he represents. "Blacks want to know . . . how long minorities have been employed, at what levels of employment, the salary levels, and their records of promotion. Quantitative analysis alone bears little weight in the minds of blacks and thus management faces a substantially different challenge today than that of the early sixties."

Such questions may not be put into so many words by the hardcore unemployed applicant, but they exist in one form or another in his mind. If less articulate, he is even more suspicious of the white employment world than the black college graduate. When such questions can be raised and answered by the interviewer during the course of the recruitment interview, the basis on which the new man enters the company is much sounder and his success is more likely. One way this question can be answered indirectly but effectively is if the recruiter himself or a ranking member of the recruiting team is black. The new man sees concrete evidence of the worth your company attaches to its minority employees. He sees that you are not hiring Negroes only for menial work, and he draws his own affirmative conclusions about your policies.

LEARNING ABOUT WORK

Adding to the difficulties of a recruiter is the fact that time and again he will find close to fantasy the ghetto dweller's concept of what work is and the kinds of jobs he feels he is suited for. A teen-age dropout, for instance, barely able to read, will voice vague—or sometimes defiant—aspirations about becoming a jet test pilot. Most job aspirations will be more within reason, but may often be difficult if not impossible to realize under the modest training programs most employers can afford to offer.

One employment authority points out that ghetto young people have an ignorance of realistic job-market opportunities and job requirements in the complex world of the 1970's that is "just as powerful a deterrent to employment as is outright racial discrimination."

Partly at fault for this ignorance is the failure of educational institutions to prepare black young people in skills American business needs today. Also responsible is the pervasive feeling in the Negro community that many of the jobs considered for generations as "colored jobs" by white employers and black employees alike—such service tasks as janitor, maid, delivery boy, and the like—are all that is open to them anyway, no matter what skills they acquire.

Economist Eli Ginzburg says, "From the point of view of the Negroes there are too many poor service jobs in our economy. If this were the period of American industrial history when there was a great expansion in manufacturing jobs, the Negro would be in a better position. In 1900, when immigrants who could not speak a word of English came to the United States, they got jobs within twenty-four hours. The recruiters took the immigrants right off the boats and gave them jobs. At that time American industry needed brawn and little else. . . . Today we do not have a large number of blue-collar entry jobs for poorly educated people. And when we offer a poor job to a Negro, he says, 'Is this what freedom means, that I can carry the parcels or wash dishes or shine shoes?' It is unfortunate that Negroes were hired almost exclusively for so long in these kinds of jobs."

Although totally untrained for a job requiring any skill whatsoever, a hardcore unemployed person may still choose to remain jobless rather than take the only work he is able to perform if he feels that the job will subject him to humiliation and further underscore his sense of personal failure. The white employer may believe that an applicant without skills or talent should be grateful for any job he can get. But, of course, the black applicant brings only the same regard for the job, or contempt for it, that prevails in the greater community. If a job is considered dirty and undesirable by society, the hardcore person is not so isolated from that society that he, too, will not find the job undesirable, no matter how unsuited he may be for more elevated work.

Business Week magazine writes, "To ghetto dwellers, unskilled service jobs mean demeaning work, small paychecks and no future—and they won't take them. 'Hundreds of jobs pushing racks in New York's garment district will go begging,' says a placement officer, 'because nobody will take them.' This attitude puzzles—and angers—many whites. But, cautions an interviewer, 'these people don't have middle-class values. To many of them no job is better than a bad job.' "

However, many of the jobs that business is now in fact capable of offering look better to Negroes than the prospect of pushing racks in the garment district. An assembly line, for example, the magazine concludes, "has some promise for tomorrow—good work can mean hefty incentive payments and a future on a bonus line."

In his book *Tally's Corner* (Little, Brown, 1967), about the Washington, D. C. ghetto, the anthropologist Elliot Liebow comments incisively on the "why Negroes won't work" question:

> Men who have been running an elevator, washing dishes, or "pulling trash" cannot easily move into laboring jobs. They lack the basic skills for "unskilled" construction labor, familiarity with tools and materials, and tricks of the trades without which hard jobs are made harder. Previously unused or untrained muscles rebel in pain against the new and insistent demands made upon them, seriously compromising the man's

performance and testing his willingness to see the job through.

A healthy, sturdy, active man of good intelligence requires from two to four weeks to break in on a construction job. Even if he is willing somehow to bull his way through the first few weeks, it frequently happens that his foreman or the craftsman he services with materials and general assistance is not willing to wait that long for him to get into condition or learn at a glance the difference in size between a rough 2″ x 8″ and a finished 2″ x 10″. The foreman and the craftsman are themselves "under the gun" and cannot "carry" the man when other men, who are already used to the work and who know the tools and materials, are lined up to take the job. . .

When we look at what the men bring to the job rather than at what the job offers the man, it is essential to keep in mind that we are not looking at men who come to the job fresh, just out of school perhaps, and newly prepared to undertake the task of making a living, or from another job where they earned a living and are prepared to do the same on this job. Each man comes to the job with a long job history characterized by his not being able to support himself and his family. Each man carries this knowledge, born of his experience, with him. He comes to the job flat and stale, wearied by the sameness of it all, convinced of his own incompetence, terrified of responsibility—of being tested still again and found wanting. Possible exceptions are the younger men not yet, or just, married. They suspect all this but have yet to have it confirmed by repeated personal experience. . .

These are considerations that many businessmen, however firmly embarked on a hardcore hiring program, cannot easily confront and competently deal with. But they should be firmly in mind as you structure your hardcore hiring program.

Right from the beginning, the initial contact with the prospective worker must be more than simply a bare-bones way of measuring the man's raw potential, although that must be done also. Ideally, the first recruiting contact should be a well-thought-out first step in the training itself, a kind of pre-orientation session in the educational process which the new job represents to the new worker.

In this first session, however informally it is carried out, the applicant should come away realizing that your company offers him a good job at good pay, and that he is not being asked to take a dead-end spot. If the job is necessarily low on the totem pole, it should be pointed out that this is the normal entry position for everyone and that in six months—or nine, or twelve—he will be moved up as others before him have moved. He must be convinced, too, that company management provides full back-up support through the training period and beyond, so that he does not shy away from taking the job for fear he will be led into one more failure. He must believe that so long as he faithfully attempts to master his job, he will be given every opportunity to prove himself. One Philadelphia company puts these principles into practice by telling recruits, "Once you have completed your initial qualifying period, you are eligible to bid for any open job posted on the bulletin board—and all openings are posted."

These are not unusual measures for business. In fact they only describe a course that is usually followed in practice by most companies, even though it may not be routinized or set forth as policy. With the hardcore unemployed, however, it should be spelled out at first contact in order to counteract the bitter "what's the use" attitude that the unhappy experience of the ghetto has instilled in many of its residents.

Reporting on the difficulty of recruiting the hardcore, Lockheed's personnel director told the editors of *Fortune* magazine that they "simply don't believe what you tell them; they think what you're offering is just another chance to fail. You have to persuade them that notwithstanding any disappointments they've had, there's really something for them now if they prepare themselves, apply themselves, and work. That isn't easy."

WHITE MAN'S WORK

In the few brief pre-hire minutes you have with an applicant, it may be difficult to convince him that his chances are totally unimpeded, for his experience tells him such is not the case. Writing about attitudes in a town in the deep South in which a textile plant furnished much of the employment, an observer points out how deep-seated this belief is throughout the entire community, black and white. "Domestic work is regarded as suitable for Negro women and unskilled or semi-skilled factory work for Negro men. Few Negroes hold jobs regarded as 'white man's work.' Everybody seems to know what jobs have always belonged to white men."

What the competent recruiter must do is find ways of revealing by statement and examples that your company has no exclusively "white man's jobs," that all jobs are open to whoever qualifies. He must shore up that contention with evidence that the job is regarded as important within the company. In this regard it is helpful to have a simple brochure with photographs that show Negroes, among others, working at decent jobs. The prospective employee must find reasons to believe his new job will provide him with a certain status—at least within the plant itself and, hopefully, without as well—and the recruiter must supply the basis for that belief by an honest appraisal of available jobs and what they can lead to.

OTHER PROBLEMS IN RECRUITING

A Santa Monica machine shop found it was having no luck at all in attempting to recruit hardcore unemployed blacks at the state service center established in Watts after the 1965 riots. Seeking the reason why, a company personnel man began inquiring among the Negroes who reported to the center and who would, presumably, be interested in at least checking on what the recruiter had to offer. He got one standard reply: "Too far to go. You need wheels for that job." Few of the unemployed men had cars, and public transportation would have meant three hours on buses every day.

With a prospective employee, most personnel men would see little need for discussing something as simple as how the new man will get to work, or what route he will follow. Yet such questions in the mind of the hardcore unemployed individual might loom as an unbreachable barrier to taking a job. If he does not have a car, he is dependent upon public transportation for getting to and from work. Unfortunately, business and industry has become more and more suburbanized at the same time that public transportation facilities have grown fewer. A trip by bus from the central city ghetto to the suburbs may represent an enormous expenditure of time and considerable money to the prospective trainee. But rather than spell this out, he may simply shrug his shoulders and walk away, leaving a bewildered interviewer.

The recruiter from a company located in the central city has an obvious advantage, particularly if the company's plant is large and well known. It is likely to be accessible to the hardcore applicant, and he probably has at least a general idea of how to reach it. Even so, the personnel manager of one Los Angeles wholesaler has drawn up a simple large-scale map showing the fastest and cheapest ways to reach his plant from the ghetto neighborhoods. Because it relieves a new man's anxiety about travelling blindly through strange territory, the manager claims it is a helpful recruiting tool.

The company located in outlying areas has different problems.

The original move to the suburbs may have represented an attempt to get away from the problems of the central city, but now, having embarked on a hardcore hiring program, it finds itself dealing with those same problems, somewhat compounded. To many a hardcore unemployed person, a trip to the suburbs is unthinkable. Even if he does take a suburban job, his energy and enthusiasm is sorely taxed each day by the commuting trip, and he may soon drop out.

The suburban company has to face up to the problem of transportation from the very first, solve it, and present the solution as part of the recruitment package to sell its program to the unemployed. Toward this end, some companies have had their section heads coordinate car pools: rides with older workers are arranged well beforehand for the new men. Such an arrangement has the additional value of assuring that the new man gets to work regularly and on time. In some cases municipal transit authorities will reschedule bus runs to meet a large employer's peak needs. Or bus routes may be altered to accommodate a group of fifty or sixty workers; or additional vehicles may be added for morning and evening runs. Another possible solution is the hiring of private bus lines, or the use of shuttle buses, the cost of which may be figured into Labor Department training contracts. One company gives a two-week supply of free bus tickets to new men.

Whatever steps are taken to assist the new man in getting to the job, they should systematically be incorporated into the recruiting pitch, to help alleviate the prospect's concerns from the very beginning.

The range of assistance your company offers its new hardcore recruits is limited only by what you see as necessary to keep and develop them as valued workers. Some firms have gone as far as helping its new Negro workers find housing in nearby communities. At times this has meant running counter to community traditions, but at least one Kentucky company found that its economic influence in the community forestalled any complaint about its Negro workers buying homes wherever they could afford them. The house-buyers, of course, were workers employed at skilled levels. Most hardcore unemployed individuals won't be immediate candidates for bungalows in all-white suburban developments. But in many cases they *will* need the full range of their employer's help, in more ways than one, to find their way out of the ghetto and onto a productive job.

CHAPTER THREE

The Interview:
Vital First Contact

How many hardcore or other minority applicants have been thwarted in their attempts to secure employment by overzealous security guards, information clerks, receptionists, secretaries and other front office personnel, we will never know. But a few unfortunate experiences have come to light. In Kentucky, a large defense subcontractor embarked on a program of hardcore recruitment. Following considerable effort by the personnel manager, two young black men were referred to the plant by a social worker in the Louisville ghetto. But when they came to the plant to apply, both men were barred at the gate by a security guard—a retired policeman. One of the young men left without trying to explain who he was or what he was there for. The other, who sported a bristling beard, tried to explain and was detained in the guard shack for his trouble. Only the timely appearance of the personnel manager prevented the bearded young man—no expert in tactful communication—from being arrested by the Louisville police who had responded to a call from their retired colleague. Needless to say, neither black man showed further interest in working for that company, and their job-hunting enthusiasm may have been dampened generally.

Another example: A shy nineteen-year-old Negro girl, a high school dropout who had been motivated after the birth of her baby to finish her education at night school, applied for a file clerk's job at the home office of a large Chicago insurance company. After instruction by the pastor of her church—who had been contacted by a company vice president who was concerned because there were few minority individuals in his work force— the young lady carefully groomed herself, left the baby with her mother, and arrived precisely at 9 a.m. At eleven-thirty she was still waiting. She had given her name to the receptionist who brusquely told her to be seated and then forgot all about her. Fortunately, she was noticed by an office manager. Her face was hidden behind a magazine, but the manager noticed that her hands were trembling. Had she not been spotted she might have remained in the corner of the busy reception room, confused and frightened, until closing time.

An unusual case, perhaps. But abundant evidence points to the uninstructed receptionist as an often unwitting but effective barrier to a smooth-running minority recruitment program.

Regardless of how sincere management is in its desire to bring minority group members into its work force, and regardless of the effort expended by personnel managers and recruiters, the most artfully conceived program can be undermined by unsympathetic, insensitive, or careless functionaries with distorted notions of their authority.

Generally, a set of hard and fast rules governs the duties of a plant security force in matters regarding checking identification, treatment of unauthorized personnel, handling attempts at theft, and the like. When a minority hiring program is initiated, management should add a new rule or two covering admission of minority job candidates. Unaccustomed though the guard may be to seeing Negroes or Mexican-Americans on the grounds, he must be instructed to offer assistance, to go out of his way to direct such individuals to the personnel office. It may be asking a lot from some of the grizzled old-timers found glaring suspiciously through guard-shack windows, but it would be immeasurably helpful if they can find it in themselves to greet the uneasy applicant with a smile and a word or two.

Instructing guards in the gentle art of greeting job applicants may be difficult but it is not impossible. A Tennessee ordnance company so thoroughly educated its security personnel that one gate guard, a man who normally spoke in only one tone—bull elephant bellow—mellowed to the extent that over several months he personally recruited five black hardcore workers. His technique was the original one of hailing black women who passed by the plant gate on their way to work in a nearby laundry and urging them to refer jobless sons and husbands directly to him. It had gotten through to this man that management was determined to increase its numbers of minority workers; authority-oriented as he was, he acted accordingly.

PAST THE GUARD AND INTO THE FRONT OFFICE

In their inimitable but charming fashion, receptionists, as most employers know, can virtually make or break a business operation. Salesmen worth their salt quickly learn that getting to know the receptionist can be the difference between an hour or two of heel-cooling next to the magazine rack followed by a hasty and interrupted interview, or the chance to make a full and effective presentation. With rare exceptions, minority job applicants have never had the opportunity to study at close hand the exotic receptionist subspecies, and they may well be ignorant of the treatment her exalted position traditionally demands. Thus, here again, even before the applicant reaches the interviewer, a recruitment program can suffer serious setbacks, unless the lady can be persuaded to modify her behavior, at least in her dealings with the minority job-seeker.

Necessary as it is for the receptionist to master the latest hair styles and eye-makeup skills, she must also have the ability to smile at other than potential boyfriends. She should greet the job applicant pleasantly, tell him he is expected, inform him if there will be a delay in seeing the interviewer, and give him company literature to look over. If it is necessary for the applicant to wait more than a few minutes, she should let him know from time to time that he isn't forgotten.

One technique for getting a receptionist off on the right foot is to have her call the interviewer to inform him an applicant is waiting and, in the hearing of the applicant, remind the interviewer of others who are waiting, asking specifically how long it will be before the applicant can be seen. It assures the applicant that the important gentleman in the back office is thinking of him too, and he is not solely at the mercy of the receptionist.

In many offices it is the practice for the receptionist to hand the job-seeker an application form and tell him to fill it out. Every job candidate completes his own application; it's a long established policy with most companies. But it may not be wise to follow that policy with the hardcore unemployed applicant. Handing him an application to fill out while he waits to see the interviewer is often the first sign to him that he is once again being asked to reveal his inadequacies. A blank form, a pencil, surroundings that threaten by their unfamiliarity, and no one to offer uncritical assistance may prove to be so unpromising a combination that the applicant simply gets up and leaves. Or in defense he may adopt a hostile manner and dare the interviewer to challenge him. To avoid either of these, it is a useful practice to have the interviewer help the applicant with his application.

At this point an employer's voice is heard: "Enough is enough. We won't change our method of operation for anyone, whatever his color. After all, we're going to a lot of trouble to recruit them. Do we have to coddle them when they come in too?"

But consider what a hardcore jobless applicant brings to

your office. In a curious way it is not unlike what you would bring to his environment if circumstances forced you into it. Let us say you find yourself in a typical central city black ghetto. You walk past barbershops that double as pool parlors, markets that feature hog maws and chitterlings, past record shops crowded with teen-aged boys with "konked" hair and girls with bushy natural hairdos; past groups of mustached men idling before a shoeshine parlor. In these littered streets and under the cold stares of the residents, you'll soon grow aware of your white skin, conservative dress, and middle-class demeanor. Let us suppose, absurdly, that you are here to apply for the job of rack-boy in one of the pool halls. Elbowing through a score of dark-skinned pool players, you are soon far away from the door; retreat is blocked. The environment is so alien you're not even sure of what to do first, or who to talk to, if anyone. Yet you are in debt, broke, you need the job, and if you get it you'll have to work surrounded by these apparently unfriendly people. In these unlikely circumstances your own behavior would be markedly altered. You might become nervous, frightened, and perhaps a little angry at the unsympathetic treatment you are sure is coming.

To the ghetto-bred black or Mexican-American or Puerto Rican, your personnel office may be every bit as threatening as his pool hall would be to you.

TAKE THE THREAT OUT OF YOUR OFFICE

An expanding Northern California electronics firm responded to the urging of a federal contract compliance officer and contacted the minority specialist of the local state employment office who referred a twenty-two-year-old black man for a trainee position. The young man had worked only on and off as a car-washer since dropping out of high school, but he was recently married, his wife was pregnant, and he was eager to find steady work. The company's employment interviewer was impressed by the young man's friendliness when he met him in the lobby. They chatted sociably on the way to the interview booth. But once inside the interview booth with the door closed, the young man became ill at ease and reticent. He answered in monosyllables, stared at the floor, and fidgeted. Before the interview was completed he mumbled that he had something important to do, and got up and hastily walked out.

What had happened? The interviewer later tried to puzzle it out. He came to the conclusion that the young man had simply been too threatened by the situation to endure it to its end. Even though he had seemed comfortable earlier, once he was closed off in an austere booth with a stranger, deep inside a stone and steel building far from his familiar surroundings, subjected to questions that revealed his past failures—all this had pushed him against the wall. Unable to deal with the pressure, he had escaped it.

But the conditions that led to the young man's discomfort needn't have existed. In most companies a few fairly obvious changes can be made to prevent such a situation from recurring.

Try to arrange for interviews in rooms that have an outside window. Leave the door open if possible. A minimum of furniture and a maximum of space should be the rule. Don't barricade yourself behind your desk; sit on the edge of it or in a chair, at least at the beginning of the interview. Don't cow the unlettered applicant with a surplus of printed material on display. A picture or two on the wall and even a potted plant can also help soften the severe character of too many interview rooms.

PREPARE YOURSELF

Not only should the surroundings be adjusted to lessen the threat, but the interviewer himself should spend a minute or two in advance preparation to make sure the interview is a success. The personnel man generally has his first contact with the white, work-oriented job candidate when the job-seeker enters the interview booth carrying a freshly completed application. Traditionally, that has been enough. It hasn't been necessary for the personnel man to acquaint himself with the applicant's background beforehand.

But with the hardcore unemployed applicant it is advisable that he does. When possible, before the interview the personnel man should contact the referral source—social worker, pastor, training institution or employment department representative. It may give him insight into the applicant he may not get otherwise.

But with or without advance information, the interviewer should always walk out to greet the applicant and personally accompany him to the interview office. If the man in authority —in shirt sleeves—comes to the applicant instead of the applicant coming hat in hand to him, the level of threat is reduced and the interview starts on a more promising footing.

As one observer has pointed out, the attitudes of the hardcore person being interviewed are very likely different from those of other job-seekers. He may well be thinking:

Why should I work 7 to 4 o'clock for eighty dollars a week? I can make more hustling in the streets—that's where the action is.

They really don't care; they just want to make themselves look good.

They're only going to put me on cleaning toilets anyway.

What's the use? I never finished high school and I've been arrested twice.

If I go to work, will my mother lose her welfare check?

There aren't any black people in this section.

I haven't got money for the bus or for lunch anyway. How could I get to work?

I'll try it for a day or two, but it won't work. They're all against me.

Obviously, a little extra effort on the part of the interviewer is necessary to overcome these negative factors.

HOW TO MEET THE MAN

And now, from the employer's point of view, the hiring process really begins. This is where it happens or doesn't happen. Here is where the interviewer makes his first assessments of the applicant's employability. Frequently he will make those assessments—and they may be the final ones on which he bases his decision—before a single word is spoken.

This was revealed in a recent survey of 150 employers who were asked their most common reasons for rejecting applicants during the initial interview. A list of forty-two such "negative factors" were compiled from this survey. Four of the reasons that played a large part—if not the *only* part—in deciding not to hire were assessments made by the interviewer *at first sight* of the applicant.

"Poor personal appearance" was the reason that led in frequency. Second was "nervous—ill at ease," followed by "fails to look interviewer in the eye," and finally, "limp, fishy handshake."

Applied routinely, with nothing else taken into consideration, these four factors alone would eliminate 99 percent of all the hardcore unemployed who ever apply at your shop.

Consider the applicant who is rejected out of hand because of "poor personal appearance." Processed or natural hair, beards, colorful closely cut clothing is the style among many young ghetto inhabitants. The black man in his teens or twenties who aspires to the admiration of the opposite sex and the envy of his friends wears his hair either in a bushy natural or carefully processed in a shiny, high wave. He sports a beard or at least a tuft of whiskers on his chin. He wears tight-fitting, cuffless pants that may be rich purple or dark green in color, possibly a satin shirt, and glossily shined shoes. Among black women, natural hairdos are more and more the style, along with large earrings, bright-colored dresses, textured stockings, and a noticeable absence of restraining underwear.

These young men and women who are looked upon by their peers as well dressed and attractive may be judged by the white personnel man to have "poor personal appearance." Rejected on sight on that basis alone, whatever case they can make for their value as workers is never heard.

An applicant's nervousness or his failure to look the interviewer in the eye is seen among experienced white applicants too, and should hardly be unexpected in the hardcore jobless. But it should not weigh disproportionately in the decision on whether to hire. Anxious and ill at ease, an applicant will avoid his questioner's eyes almost as a matter of course. What's more, among an element of black and brown ghetto-dwellers, a direct stare into the eyes implies a hostile challenge. With a black woman it can have even more complex implications: prostitutes frequently signal their tricks by direct eye contact, often without exchanging a word.

The firm, manly handshake has long been a trademark of the American businessman, but not all segments of the population value the gesture so highly. Many Mexican-Americans have a different concept, and a Chicano's handshake with one of his fellows may be limp, without pressure. This serves as a badge of identification among some *barrio* dwellers, and the Mexican-American who delivers a vigorous shake to a compatriot might find himself treated roughly for his display of manliness.

Further, a handshake involves touching another person. Many black ghetto inhabitants have lived lives wholly lacking in social contact with Caucasians. In the presence of whites, they are often distrustful and their handshake reflects this distrust.

Aside from the handshake, you should have no reason to touch the applicant. No matter how sincerely sympathetic or fatherly you feel, a friendly arm around the shoulder or a pat on the back is likely to be misinterpreted and resented.

Nor will you establish rapport by references to "what a hell of a ballplayer Willie Mays is," or how much you enjoy the comedy of Bill Cosby. Racial or ethnic references dragged in by the heels at this stage of your acquaintance with the applicant will also be resented. If you seek to put the hardcore applicant at ease, your purpose may be better served by some slight reference to yourself—"I'm feeling lousy this morning. Guess I'm catching a cold," or "Great day to be at a ball game, isn't it?" Many personnel men make a practice of greeting all applicants in such a manner.

CALL HIM MISTER

No matter how young the applicant is and no matter how much distinguished gray has descended on your own locks, always address the applicant as Mr., Mrs., or Miss. Until you become much better acquainted, and only after you have asked the applicant to call you by your first name, should you lapse into the familiar. This may seem a small matter, but the reason for it is grounded in the hundreds of years Negroes were denied the dignity of being addressed as Mr. or Mrs. Even today, in some sections of the country, black septuagenarians are referred to as "boy" or "girl," addressed by their first name only, or affectionately called "Auntie" or "Uncle." Even to the sixteen-year-old black, "boy" may be unpleasant; to anyone past twenty it is certain to be offensive.

Unless faced with a rare direct question, don't mention your "tolerance" toward Negroes; and even if you genuinely admire the well-kept lawn of the Negro family who recently bought a house three blocks from you, this is not the time to mention it.

You are not required to prove to the applicant that you "like" Negroes anymore than he need prove to you that he admires whites. Time may soften the attitudes of both, but in the meantime you and the applicant are engaged in a business relationship. Whether the minority applicant is the first of his race to be considered by your company or whether 25 percent of your work force is already black, references to race, racial problems, and the good job your company is doing in minority hiring can prove damaging to the success of the interview. The personnel assistant who tells black applicants how eager he is to hire more of "you people" will receive his share of cold stares, probably because few people wish to be crudely tagged according to the color of their skin and without regard to their individuality. And none of the applicants you are likely to see will be willing to stand as spokesman for his race anymore than a white personnel man would assume responsibility for the attitudes of all the whites in the world.

The same applicant who will bridle at being called "boy," may well elect to further display his individuality and manhood by refusing your invitation to sit down. If he doesn't take a chair in response to your bid, don't press him. Be flexible; if necessary start the interview standing. Later, as the applicant grows more at ease, try again.

OTHER COMMON REASONS FOR REJECTION

Sloppy application blank.

Inability to express himself clearly—poor voice, diction, grammar.

Answers only "yes" and "no" to open-end questions.

Indefinite response to specific questions.

These reasons for deciding to reject an applicant were also listed as leading "negative factors" by the 150-company survey. Again, none touch directly on the applicant's ability to perform on the job.

The problem of a sloppy application blank should never arise. The form should be filled out with the assistance of the interviewer. Completing an application blank on his own would be, to many a hardcore applicant, an enormously difficult task. Yet, under the tactful guidance of a sympathetic interviewer, all the necessary information can be obtained fairly painlessly.

In a secretarial job or public contact position, "inability to express himself clearly—poor voice, diction, grammar" would probably serve to disqualify the candidate, but it should have little bearing if the applicant seeks a job such as truck driver or machine operator.

Undeniably, differences in the language and speech patterns of hardcore ghetto dwellers do exist. Based on Southern rural influences and often further complicated by colloquialisms common only to the black community, the language of black men often sounds exotic to the white middle-class ear. With Mexican-Americans, a strong Spanish accent can have the same effect.

If it is any consolation, it is probably no harder for you to communicate with the applicant than it is for him to make himself understood to you. As you toil through the application blank together, don't yield to the temptation to give the applicant a lesson in English. But do make a point of explaining complex or detailed questions. Find ways to rephrase questions until an appropriate answer is given. Make sure that a confident nod of the head by the applicant does not simply cover up a misunderstanding he is afraid to reveal. Ask more questions if you don't clearly understand his answers.

Even highly trained old-timers in personnel work bewail their experiences with hardcore applicants who answer only "yes" or "no" to open-end questions designed to elicit a flood of volunteered information. Yet the one-word answer makes sense to the hardcore individual who comes out of the literal tradition that is part of the ghetto experience. Black and brown ghetto life has deep agrarian roots. More than half of the ghetto-dwellers you are apt to see were born on farms or in small country hamlets. Most of the others are a single generation removed from direct contact with the soil. American folklore is replete with tales of the monosyllabic farmer who responds to the city slicker's complex question with a terse "nope" or "yup." Such responses from the Yankee farmer are part of hallowed tradition; yet the black or Mexican-American country-bred individual who responds similarly is considered deliberately uncooperative. Usually that is not the case, and if you invest a little time and patience, you'll get the information you need.

When the applicant's response to questions is "indefinite"— another negative factor—there is a strong possibility that he does not fully understand what is being asked of him. Many employment interviewers are conditioned to consider indefinite answers as deliberate evasiveness or attempts to gloss over damaging information. If this is the case a few other questions can soon establish it. But if it is a matter of simple misunderstanding, take care to restate the question, approach it from another angle. Problems will arise if you fail to do so. Consider the experience of a motherly, middle-aged personnel technician who screened applicants for a precision-instrument manufacturer in upstate New York. During an interview with her first hardcore black lady recruited from the Rochester ghetto, she asked the applicant to give her a "resume of outstanding financial obligations" and to estimate her "anticipated financial needs for the next annual period." At these examples of bureaucracy at its best, the applicant could only stare blankly at the ceiling.

DIG BENEATH THE SURFACE

The hardcore applicant is not likely to put forward his own interests even when you provide the opening. He may minimize, misstate, or fail to mention skills and past experience. Unlike the experienced white job-seeker, he will tend to put his worst foot forward. Asked what job he wants, he may respond, "Anything." This is not because he lacks ambition or direction. He simply does not know the make-up of the job market. A white applicant is acquainted with a wide range of jobs by virtue of family associations. He knows what his father, brothers, cousins, uncles all do for a living. The black applicant may spring from a welfare family; possibly no one in his immediate circle has a steady job. He may be badly misinformed about the job market, as evidenced by one job-seeker who claimed it was futile to look for work in the auto industry since it was his understanding that the electric auto would soon make all the existing Detroit plants obsolete. Added to this fact is his feeling of defeat: the pressures of his life have convinced him he has no choice anyway so there is little use in pretending to voice a preference.

Here, too, take the time to dig beneath surface answers. A few probing questions may uncover helpful information, as in the case of an applicant who described his last regular job as "laborer." Questioning as to the exact tasks he performed revealed that he had, in fact, operated a fork-lift, although he had been classified as a laborer and paid accordingly. A forty-year-old Negro woman who described her entire employment history as "day work" was discovered to have worked on and off for years in a cannery where she had developed skills of which she was unaware. In another instance a black school dropout who said he had never worked was found to have held several temporary jobs greasing cars and doing minor auto repairs for service stations.

Probing beyond the catch-all answer can yield results in other ways, too. One twenty-five-year-old black man told an interviewer that he lost his last job because he was arrested. The tough appearance of the applicant made it easy for the interviewer to believe that here was a hardened criminal; and obviously other interviewers had thought so too, since the man had been unable to find a job since his arrest. But a few questions revealed that the arrest—his first—resulted from an unpaid traffic ticket. The man spent five days in jail because he lacked the twenty-five-dollar fine, and he was fired although he had been a satisfactory employee for over two years.

Where gaps exist in an applicant's job history, you may find that he is confused about dates, has forgotten the name of an employer, or needlessly fears a poor reference. Since any previous employment experience must be counted as an advantage when you consider hiring the hardcore unemployed, use all your interviewing skills to make sure that a full history is uncovered.

IF YOU'RE GOING TO HIRE . . .

With the interview drawing to a close, the application completed, and all necessary questions answered, don't undo all your hard work by reverting back to normal procedures and telling the applicant, "It will take a day or two to check your references. If everything works out all right, we'll call you."

Personnel experts have long lamented the drawbacks of such a procedure when applied to the experienced, relatively sophisticated job-seeker. To the hardcore unemployed it is almost certain to be taken as a roundabout way of telling him he's rejected.

If you see any possibility of hiring the man, don't let him leave your office with the thought that he is not being considered. Arrange on the spot for his medical check if one is required. Take him out to the job site where he will work, introduce him to his future supervisor, show him what he will be doing and the product or service which will result from his work. But don't turn this visit to the job into a second interview. Keep it brief so the worker doesn't feel he is being exhibited to the other workers. If he is the first black to be employed, it can be helpful if a representative of top management accompanies the applicant to the job. In this way other workers are informed of the high level of interest in the new man, and potential troublemakers in the ranks may be squelched in advance.

If you can't hire the applicant on the spot, before he leaves make sure he understands the employment procedure—who finally hires, what information you have to verify, when and how he will be notified, and any further interviews or tests that will be required.

Accompany the applicant back to the reception office. Ask if he has any questions. Thank him for coming in, and offer your hand. If you've done your job well and sympathetically, he'll accept it without hesitation.

CHAPTER FOUR

Picking Your Man:
Selection and Testing

There's an old story about an executive who needed a new secretary and interviewed three girls for the job. One typed a hundred words a minute and had rare recommendations from previous employers. Another had a college degree and all the qualifications for a first-rate "Girl Friday." The third was a mediocre typist and barely able to take dictation—but she had a terrific figure. She got the job—thanks to the precise science of employee selection.

No doubt American business would pay a pretty penny for a foolproof method of selecting personnel, male or female, white or black. Despite the highly trained, hard-working personnel technicians, despite dozens of sophisticated screening tests, despite decades of trial and error that have led to greater refinement of techniques—despite all this, selecting new personnel is still a chancy business.

The polished look-you-straight-in-the-eye young college graduate fails at a job that seems tailor-made for him. The hesitant, half-educated, scruffy individual fits right into a complex operation and within weeks brilliantly proves his worth despite the selection techniques that almost screened him out of the job. Why? With hindsight it's easy to find the answer, but hindsight is no help until months after the man is hired.

If traditional selection techniques don't always work in the regular employment process, they work even less well where the hardcore unemployed are concerned. The experience accumulated by progressive employers over the past few years shows that here traditional selection procedures simply won't work. The old tried-and-true criteria of what makes a good loyal employee, despite its apparent usefulness to old-line personnel men, has to be modified if the hardcore hiring program is to be successful.

BRING IN THE SUPERVISOR

Successful employment of the hardcore depends upon the response of your entire organization. It may be traditional in your plant for the personnel officer to actually hire the new employee, with the supervisor seeing the new man for the first time on the morning he reports to work. In other firms the personnel department only screens applicants, with the right of final selection resting in the hands of the supervisor. In either case, some shifts must be made to accommodate the procedure to a well-planned hardcore hiring program.

Generally, the best course is for hardcore selection to be made by personnel officer and supervisor acting together. The personnel man carries out the usual preliminary screening, with the supervisor having an opportunity to meet and talk with the prospect before hire. The actual decision to hire should be shared equally by personnel and supervision, after a full discussion of all information available and a review of anticipated problems.

Besides hewing to the "two heads are better than one" notion, this method allows the supervisor to get a line on the new man beforehand. He has a chance to consider job options for him, and to work out such arrangements as choice of working partners, decide as to the best shift, whether or not to start the new man on full days, and the like.

At the same time, the supervisor should not have full responsibility. He has his own job to do overseeing production schedules and managing his work force. The personnel officer, who does not have the pressure of production and whose duties keep him in touch with management's current concerns, should be an equal partner in the hiring decision.

INDUSTRIAL UNTOUCHABLES?

A study by the Kaiser Steel Corporation plant at Fontana, California, has shown that most "disadvantaged minorities"—that is, the hardcore unemployed—were unable even to get past the employment door because of selection requirements. But once those requirements were modified, all but a small percentage adequately performed the entry job. A report on the study showed that among the things keeping the door closed to the applicants was their "fondness for goatees, beards, wild hairdos and outlandish clothes." Additionally, they brought with them "police records ranging from petty thievery, drunk driving and brawling on up to armed robbery, narcotics peddling, burglary and other serious offenses." They revealed "lack of education, lack of skill, susceptibility to bad influences, lack of basic work attitudes and habits, lack of hope. . . ."

With masterful understatement, the reports concludes, "These are not characteristics we are used to looking for in employees. In fact they are the very traits and background that have made these people industrial untouchables in the past. . . ."

What about these undesirable traits? As American business enters the 1970's, enough has been learned by such employers as Kaiser and others that these characteristics can no longer be used as excuses to bar employment. The bugaboo of "poor personal appearance," cited in the preceding chapter as the leading reason 150 employers gave for turning down applicants, is an example of a barrier that the Kaiser study showed to be unrealistic.

The fact of the matter is that in a large number of jobs, personal appearance makes no difference at all. Only in public-contact positions can a case be made for considering appearance as a selection factor. True, acceptance of such an idea requires some adjustment in our own thinking. Clean-shaven, middle-class white Americans tend to look upon Afro hair styles, beards, moustaches, and the like not only as bizarre manifestations of a vaguely unpatriotic conspiracy but as devices employed deliberately to antagonize. This is not the case. As the monocle and dueling scar were the badges of the Prussian, and long hair and moccasins were marks of the pioneer, so too exotic hair styles, colorful clothing and the like are badges of cultural identity and racial pride among large numbers of ghetto dwellers. To the personnel officer these signs should not be evidence of mysterious difference but rather of the applicant's sense of his own worth as an individual—a quality not without value in an employee.

Also tied into the question of personal apperance are such matters as the wearing of dark glasses—frequently seized on as an indication of something sinister, perhaps drug addiction. But the ever-present "shades," too, are most often either badges of identity or shields the uncertain individual uses against the unfamiliarity of the threatening white employment world. As one young man explained, "When I'm wearing 'em, I can look out, but nobody else can look in."

The combination of shades and the smell of liquor would doubtless be fatal to any applicant's chances, no matter how well he stacked up otherwise. No employer can be expected to assume the headaches a problem drinker brings with him. Yet there are considerations here too which should be taken into account. Is the man indeed a problem drinker? Or has he only resorted to a drink or two to bolster his courage before facing you? To a black man who has never worked, or who has not looked for work in years, a job interview is loaded with tension and uncertainty which he may not be able to handle without some artificial help. If he is a chronic drinker, careful questioning and a phone call or two to references should provide sufficient information to so determine.

OTHER COMMON REASONS FOR REJECTION

Among other reasons the group of 150 employers gave for not hiring were many which, like "poor personal appearance," had nothing to do with ability to perform a job. Primarily they stem from the interviewer's subjective reaction to the applicant. As reasons for rejecting a man, they are only as good as the interviewer's judgment. One interviewer might find a man's attitude "hostile"; while another would judge the same man to be "solemn, grimly determined." Or an applicant may seem to "lack vitality" to one interviewer, where as to another he appears "calm, easygoing."

Keeping in mind the wide differences of opinion possible, let's look at more of the reasons most often given by the 150 employers as to why applicants fail to survive the selection process, and consider these reasons in relation to the hardcore applicant.

Hostile; overbearing; overaggressive; conceited; know-it-all. Hostility or aggression in the hardcore unemployed applicant may well be a mask for insecurity—as it may be in anyone. Both undesirable traits are amenable to modification as the new man learns to trust you, and to find comfortable reference points in his new environment.

One executive of a Boston mail order house tells about an unsmiling, tight-lipped young black woman who was interviewed by the office manager for a clerical trainee position. The office manager's first impulse was to reject the young woman. "The way she talked and handled herself practically said to me 'Go to hell,'" he commented. But he felt he was on the spot, since the young lady was related to a woman who had worked for years for the company president. Rather than risk turning her down, he hired her, determined to keep a close watch over her. After a week or two on the job the young lady's attitude dramatically softened. "I was wrong," the office manager confessed. "She wasn't arrogant, she was just scared. After she saw we were all human too, she became as civil and polite as anybody else."

Lack of interest and enthusiasm; passive; indifferent; apathetic. In a minority culture, a high premium is placed on the ability to "keep one's cool," to remain unruffled under stress or tension. Passivity and lack of interest may be manifestations of the keeping-cool syndrome. Then too, as a part of the cultural inheritance, many ghetto dwellers develop a facade of passivity, indifference, apathy, as a way to ward off disappointments or thwarted hopes. But as many employers have found, as soon as the worker meets with a minimum of success, in most cases there is a marked change in attitude.

Overemphasis on money; interested only in best dollar offer. A job-wise applicant applying for an entry-level job whose interest is only in the almighty dollar might give any employer pause. Yet what such interest is most likely to indicate in the hardcore applicant is his lack of realistic information about the job world. The personnel man may find himself explaining again and again that he has no thousand-dollar-per-month entry-level jobs open just now.

Unwillingness to start at the bottom; expects too much too soon. If the bottom happens to be a janitorial position, the dirtiest job in the shop, or other traditional "colored work," his point is well taken. On the other hand, as pointed out in Chapter 2, lack of understanding about the requirements for a given job may lead an applicant to express interest in a position far beyond his ability. Answer his questions seriously. While they might indicate job-shopping if asked by a job-wise white applicant, from a hard-core job candidate such questions are generally just what they appear to be on the surface—attempts to elicit information.

Makes excuses; evasive; hedges on unfavorable factors in record; lies badly. A man who has grown up on ghetto streets, who has never been employed or has a spotty employment record, very likely will be close-mouthed about his past. He doesn't know what information will hurt his chances and what will enhance them. Evasiveness during the employment interview shouldn't lead you to automatically bar the man. A great deal depends on what he is evasive about. A little reluctance to tell you about his marital status isn't of much importance; but a song-and-dance about an arrest record is something else.

It appears also that the major objection to a few white lies (notice they're not "black" lies) from an applicant is not because he isn't telling the truth, but because he "lies badly." What it comes down to is that he has not acquired the sophisticated facility of presenting the polished half-truth, of knowing what to omit, of arranging, for example, with a friend of the family for a favorable employment reference, or tailoring gaps in his employment history to hide certain information. He may frankly tell you, for example—which an experienced applicant never would

—that he was fired from his last job for "cussing out the boss. I called him a son-of-a-bitch, so he fired me." The applicant with polish would refer to the incident as a "personality clash." In a word, the hardcore applicant has no mastery of putting his best foot forward. Don't expect it.

Lack of maturity. Just how this can be handily measured in a selection interview is hard to say. Usually it takes considerable knowledge of a man to be able to judge his maturity. Supreme Court justices involved over the years in momentous decisions have been known to behave like teen-agers at supposedly secret times. Some industrial tycoons throw tantrums. Ph.D. research scientists have silly moments that astound their colleagues. Yet all are considered successful, "mature" men in their everyday lives. The ghetto black who may be thought "immature" because of one glimpse of his behavior during a job interview may in fact have had thrust upon him the responsibility for raising half-a-dozen brothers and sisters, shopping, cooking, disciplining, while the mother was away working as a domestic on the other side of town.

Lack of courtesy; ill-mannered; failure to express appreciation for interviewer's time. What pass for good manners in one group may be looked upon by another as affectations, and in a third may be totally unheard of. The polite, meaningless exchanges between people when they meet for the first time—references to the weather and the like—are far less common to the average ghetto dweller, who is more literally inclined. The "what's happening," or "how's it going" greeting is reserved for a fellow black. Behavior that might be considered rude from a middle-class white cannot be so considered when it comes from a man whose environment places no stigma on such activities as chewing on a toothpick, cleaning fingernails in the presence of others, leaving one's hat on, lighting a cigarette without asking permission, or responding with a shrug or a grunt. Codes of manners differ greatly between cultures—and between generations, as many of us learn from our sons and daughters—and the hardcore applicant will not have at his command such fine touches as thanking you for the time you've deigned to spend with him. Gratitude is probably the last thing on his mind. Considered dispassionately, his failure to express appreciation is a good deal more forthright than the rote response of the job-wise white applicant, who knows how to butter up interviewers. After all, the applicant may feel he is doing you as much a favor by going to work as you do him by offering the job.

Condemnation of past employers; no tact. This is an area where the ghetto applicant may prove himself *too* honest. While the experienced applicant has learned the unwritten rule that forbids speaking ill either of the dead or a former employer, the hardcore jobless is apt to "tell it like it is." It's a situation in which he can't win—either he lies badly or tells the truth too well, and in either case he doesn't get the job.

Lack of vitality; shuffles; slow-moving; lazy. What looks at first glance like a symptom of laziness may in fact be something else entirely. For example, some time back a big New York City hospital brought in a new deputy administrator to improve efficiency. He went to work with a vengeance. One of the first departments he surveyed was the medical records section. Here his eye fell on Ella, an overweight black woman who was extremely slow-moving. The deputy administrator watched her shuffle through the files and quickly left. The next day he sent the record room supervisor a memo highly critical of Ella and suggested her replacement or reassignment. The supervisor marched to the deputy's office and indignantly pointed out that

Ella's production rate was the best in the record room. She moved slowly, true, but she was tireless and seldom wasted a motion. Besides doing her job well, she was well liked by her fellow workers.

There is no foolproof way of knowing whether the hardcore applicant—or any other applicant—is or is not lazy. He may have been considered lazy in school because he didn't understand half of what he read and so never completed an assignment. Or he may have spent months or years hanging around streetcorners not because he was lazy but because he gave up looking for work after meeting endless rejections. Properly motivated and given a chance, he may turn into an entirely satisfactory worker. Not knowing how to work does not mean a man is lazy; it only means he does not know how to work.

Wants a job only for a short time. Many a man seeking employment for the first time bolsters his courage by telling himself that, after all, he'll only stay on the job for a short time. The concept of permanent employment, of a total break with the easy old routine, may otherwise seem too overwhelming. One of the goals of a training program for the hardcore is to assist in the development of new concepts, such as an understanding of the prevailing work ethic. Again, this is an area in which attitudes change as a result of exposure to a new environment.

Lack of knowledge of field of work; no interest in company. Both reasons are, again, in the nature of definition of the hardcore jobless person. If he had the knowledge and the interest, he'd be a different man. Don't expect the unskilled, untrained hardcore applicant to have more than a sketchy familiarity with work in general or you'll run into situations such as this: A foreman in a St. Louis job shop told the plant manager he didn't want to work with a new black trainee who had been charged to his crew. In the foreman's words, "He don't know the machines; he don't even know the difference between a drill press and a lathe."

Although an applicant for a sales or executive position who shows no interest in the company quite properly would raise management's eyebrows, it would be unfair and self-defeating to a hardcore hiring program to view the ghetto dweller in the same light. As pointed out in the "Profile of the Hard-Core Unemployed" in Chapter 2, with rare exceptions the experiences of his life have not brought him into contact with the complex world of work. He probably never heard of your company or of any of your competitors, and has only a slight and erroneous idea of how companies are run or what they do. Matters that you might assume to be common knowledge because of their frequent mention in the business pages of the newspaper may be totally unknown to him. But this is a vacuum that a few months in a well-planned, on-the-job training program will help to fill.

Cynical. The contrast between the life in the ghetto for the hardcore unemployed person and that brewed up in television studios, between what he is taught in school and what he sees on the ghetto street every day—these discrepancies are bound to produce a certain degree of cynicism. If he expects to be disappointed in his desires and if he has been conditioned to failure, he has undoubtedly learned to cushion the shock with cynicism and professed disbelief in a fair order of things. This does not, however, make the man any less capable of becoming a productive worker.

Low moral standards. Low morals among the poor or minority groups are more often suspected than proved. For instance, whenever the sexual pursuits of Negroes are mentioned, there arises a smokescreen of exotic myth. In any case, such "standards" scarcely affect a man's employability—unless he is applying for a position as chaplain's assistant. Increasingly, management is recognizing that a man's morals are his own business, and the lecher, the dirty-movie addict, the homosexual, the adulterer, and others are not automatically barred from jobs simply for following their curious inclinations—provided their activities do not interfere with their ability to do their jobs.

Intolerant; strong prejudices. In recent years, a black nationalist movement has given rise to open expression of bitterness toward whites, especially such whites as landlords and merchants, with whom Negroes come into contact most frequently. But however loud and outspoken they are, this group is a minority within the black community. While many black people will listen with delight to the nationalist antiwhite invective, they are by no means prepared to take the violent action often called for.

At least one important reason for the upsurge of business interest in employing the hardcore individual is the attempt to relieve the growing tension in the ghettos. A good job and fair treatment all around is an excellent antidote to the spreading poison of antiwhite feeling.

Narrow interests; no interest in community; lack of social awareness. Here again is another reason for rejection that has little to do with ability on the job. The personnel man who uses such a reason to turn away an applicant may mean only that "his interests are different from mine." And that should be assumed from the start.

The fact is that the ghetto dweller does indeed have a stake in his community. Writing in *Look* magazine, George Leonard says, "The Negro culture has flaws . . . but it also has qualities this country now desperately needs. In the ghettos you find a rare sense of community and brotherhood . . . just what is lacking in white suburbia. Pallid and sterile, the suburbs could use a large portion of what the Negro calls soul . . ."

True, the hardcore unemployed person may have little interest in politics, which he often sees as an alien intrusion, and he is not concerned with middle-class institutions that are superimposed upon his community, such as P.T.A. and related activities. But he is interested to a remarkably high degree in the flow of life he understands and knows best—that of the ghetto.

Poor handling of personal finances. This is a perennial problem, and it is recognized as such in the training programs that include supportive services such as counseling in the handling of money. The hardcore person's inexperience in managing his finances can be costly and troublesome to employers. Garnishments, repossessions, attachments, and the like are matters that you must be prepared to deal with right from the beginning in your training program.

A large number of the unemployed are from a rural background where they had little experience with money. They lived in a perpetual condition of debt through which the institution of sharecropping was maintained. Individuals who for much of their lives have never known luxuries, and perhaps lacked necessities as well, may go off on a spending spree when they begin to receive regular paychecks. Overbuying is common, and serious indebtedness results. Contributing to the dismal picture is the fact that in the ghetto prices for food, furniture, household goods, and services are routinely higher than elsewhere. Rents are often exorbitant. Armies of peddlers, suede-shoe boys, fast-buck merchants, and others who prey upon the ignorant poor can be found day and night skimming away the cream. Because of their lack of financial experience, ghetto dwellers fall frequent victims to glib talkers and fast operators who, once an inflated contract has been signed, are quick to turn to the courts for garnishments when the stiff payment terms cannot be met.

But whatever reasons lie behind the ghetto dweller's inability to manage his finances, they do not lessen the trouble caused to employers. For that reason many employers have taken the bull by the horns and immediately provided the hardcore new worker with expert counseling on handling his finances.

Marital troubles; poor personal life. Until such matters intrude on the job—as well they might—they shouldn't be a bar to employment. To the white middle-class suburbanite, any poor man in the ghetto has a "poor personal life." He is often denied the barest minimum of privacy in unsuitable housing. His major form of recreation may be the streets. His children lack adult supervision and are exposed to violence and degradation. His wife may have to work as a domestic to support the family because he cannot find a job. Or he may have moved out so that his family can receive the welfare money which his presence in the home would deny them; and now he can visit them only by sneaking in at night.

Here, too, business has found that counseling pays off. In some cases the buddy system (see Chapter 5) is used to support a new hardcore worker's efforts to solve his personal problems. It has been found, too, that a good job and a regular paycheck go a long way toward smoothing out an irregular personal or marital life.

Inability to take criticism; won't accept instruction. Here again, it's almost necessary to try a man on the job before you know whether he'll take instruction or criticism. A lot depends upon how that criticism is offered. Today, the efficacy of criticism as a means of managing workers is increasingly questioned. The concept of "positive reinforcement"—the constructive use of praise—is more and more a useful technique, especially in hard-core training programs.

To a ghetto dweller, particularly one who has had little contact with Caucasians, criticism from a white man can be interpreted to mean that the white man holds him in contempt and is challenging not only his ability—which he doubts anyway —but his manhood as well. A popularly held ghetto concept is that only children are criticized, and adults criticize only if they are willing to risk a punch in the nose.

In time, after solid relationships are established—and helped along by a proper training program that avoids the pitfalls of the school classroom where the hardcore dropout doubtless heard all the criticism he ever wants to hear—modification of the worker's behavior will generally take place.

Lack of appreciation of the value of experience or education.
The hardcore unemployed person would be neither hardcore nor unemployed if he did indeed have work experience or edu-cation. In a very real sense, the reason your company has em-barked on a training program is to give the man a chance to gain such appreciation.

Late for interview without good reason. In employing the hardcore person, few problems are likely to crop up more often than those centered around time. But fortunately tardiness or absenteeism are correctable problems, as many examples in this book point out.

So far as failure to keep an interview appointment is con-cerned, it may evidence fear or confusion as to where to go and whom to see. Or the man may be seeking to assert his independ-ence by strolling in late. Such behavior may well signal the beginning of a continuing problem—or it may be a matter that quickly corrects itself once the training program begins to take hold. But in any case, be prepared to deal with it.

There are probably few personnel men who haven't used one of the foregoing reasons for rejection as an excuse to turn away a job applicant, perhaps someone they "had a hunch about." But today, if your company is seriously launching a hiring program for the hardcore unemployed from the ghetto, the men who do the selecting must remember that the old standards, the old ways, the comfortable tried-and-true methods developed over the years don't always apply to the hardcore applicant—or they apply in different ways. It's this difference that provides the challenge.

SHOULD YOU HIRE AN EX-CON?

Selection procedures in many companies are kept nicely loose and flexible until the possibility of hiring a hardcore applicant with a police record presents itself. At that point rigor mortis sets in. "No sir!" says the boss. "We only hire honest men." Or, "After all, they'll be working around valuable mechandise." Or, "All our employees have to be bondable."

None of these explanations are frivolous or unreasonable. Yet there do exist many businesses that are successfully hiring men with police records. Their experience should be examined by other companies for whatever guidance it might provide. A large aerospace employer, for example, seeks out hardcore applicants who not only have unstable work records but police records as well. Over the several years the policy has been in effect, says a personnel spokesman, it has given them "no special problems." And in the Midwest, the colorful president of a large novelty manufacturing firm many years ago established a policy of hiring ex-convicts, some of whom have worked their way to top executive positions.

Such major employers as the federal government and the State of California no longer ask for information about arrest records on application forms, although questions pertaining to convictions are still permitted. A great number of employers in the private sector have done the same.

How do you decide if a calculated risk is justified in hiring a man with a police record? First of all, take into consideration the following points:

Make a distinction between an arrest record and a conviction record. A man living in the ghetto is more liable to be "brought in" by police—for suspicion, for loitering, for gambling, for exuberant horseplay that is called disorderly conduct. In some Southern states, police activity in Negro neighborhoods is so great few black men grow up without a record even though nothing criminal may be involved. Therefore, carefully evaluate the frequency, severity, and location of violations for which the applicant was arrested.

How old was the applicant when he was arrested? An eighteen-year-old may commit impulsive, reckless acts which would be unthinkable to him a few years later.

How long since his last arrest? If he has gone straight for fifteen years since he was last arrested for siphoning gas, chances are he won't backslide.

What is the nature of the work he'll be doing? If he will be closely supervised, you might be more lenient in your selection standards regarding an applicant with a police record.

Most important in this area, as in all aspects of the selection process, consider the *whole* man—his background, his interests, his aptitudes—and don't let one lone negative feature overwhelm you into failing to see his other points. A man with a police record is not always a dyed-in-the-wool liar and cheat. For instance, one ex-convict who had gotten a job without telling the employer that he had served time in prison was troubled by the thought of losing the job when the employer found out the truth. After a few weeks on the job, he went to the personnel manager and confessed that he had misstated the facts in order to find work. While the employer was not happy with the situation, he did keep the man on, and after an extended probationary period, the man proved himself a satisfactory employee.

It's true that many ex-convicts can't be fitted into the normal work force. They may have serious personal problems, or the nature of the work may require a bond which, even under the relaxed standards of some bonding companies who recognize the problem of the hardcore ex-convict, is simply not available. Yet men who have served sentences in state prisons for such serious crimes as armed robbery, aggravated assault, rape, and even murder have time and again proved to be satisfactory employees. Years spent in prison, whatever else they do, can also modify behavior and teach men to accept orders and adapt to a routine. Additionally, most state prisons, unlike county jails or city lockups, make serious rehabilitative efforts, teaching inmates useful skills and adapting them to a disciplined work environment. Auto repair shops, machine shops, and clothing manufacturing facilities are a part of many modern penal institutions. Courses in blueprint reading, electrical theory, metallurgy, and other skills are available to inmates, so that once out of prison they may bring to your plant abilities that other hardcore applicants do not have.

One way to determine whether an ex-convict is potentially a good employee is to ask his parole or probation officer. These officials usually have detailed knowledge about the attitude and behavior their charges revealed in prison, know what skills they have developed and, additionally, have a pretty good idea of whether the man is trustworthy. In many cases they can also guide you to work-furlough programs. In these a prisoner due for release is freed for daytime work in order to provide him with a transitional period to grow accustomed to the new demands he'll experience outside prison walls. There are also many "half-way house" programs which guide the newly-released prisoner in his readjustment to the working world, and the Department of Labor has developed a job-bonding program specifically for released prisoners that is available in certain prisons and can help an employer meet bonding requirements.

Numerous issues are involved in hiring the hardcore unemployed with prison records—plant security, insurance rates, bonding, and others. But business and industry has enough experience under its belt to show that the risk is not inordinate and in the long run the problems encountered are not much different from those of the normal rank-and-file work force.

WHAT GOOD ARE TESTS?

To test or not to test? So far as the question applies to the selection of an over-all work force, the personnel world is not-so-neatly divided. "Testing is necessary. It's the only objective means for selection," say the old-line managers. Others claim, "Tests have a built-in bias against certain job candidates—minorities, the poor, the uneducated, the disadvantaged. If you use aptitude or intelligence tests, it's only because you want to screen out these groups."

When the issue is narrowed to hiring the black hardcore unemployed person, however, personnel men are less divided. Obviously, most standard selection tests would badly undercut the very purpose of such a program, which is to draw into the employment cycle people who lack the background to get in through the usual screening processes—which include tests.

"Many companies are eliminating the use of standard test batteries as a screening device," reported the National Association of Manufacturers in 1968. Hard-headed business reasoning lay behind the move: the tests were not doing what they were supposed to do. The companies found that men from the ghettos who were already performing well on the job failed the standard tests, even though they had already proved their ability.

Some critics suggest that this irony results from the inappropriateness of some tests to the jobs for which they are used as screens. "Should a company seeking manual workers," asks the U. S. Commission on Civil Rights, "test for verbal proficiency?"

Examples of items from such misapplied tests abound: What is the difference between "exoteric" and "esoteric"? Fill in the correct word: "He treated me as though I ——— a stranger." Such questions seek to test an applicant for information in no way required on the job.

Other test questions can be misleading in more subtle ways and thus serve inadvertently to specifically eliminate some minority candidates. Consider the following:

"A man who spends his money lavishly for nonessentials is considered to be: (1) fortunate; (2) thrifty; (3) extravagant; (4) generous; (5) economical."

To the middle-class applicant, brought up to respect traditional virtues, the obvious answer is "extravagant." But to the young man who hustles on ghetto streets, with his goal the ability to conspicuously display his capacity to "make it big," the correct answer might be "fortunate."

The same kind of thinking could be applied to this question:

"In general it is safer to judge a man's character by his: (1) clothes; (2) voice; (3) deeds; (4) wealth; (5) face."

These are isolated examples of a test which contains many

other questions. But they do raise doubts as to whether a test valid for one group of applicants may not inadvertently discriminate against other groups.

A further barrier to fair employment comes when the test cut-off point—that is, the score which must be achieved in order to be hired—is set artificially high or reflects unreasonably lofty standards. One good-sized East Coast company found that it suddenly needed a large number of relatively unskilled workers to staff a new plant. A company executive says, "So we hired lots of people we ordinarily would not have taken because of their test scores. And we found that lower test scores than we had previously set were perfectly okay."

Regardless of test content, the very process of testing in itself has pitfalls for many minority job-seekers. Coming from economically deprived backgrounds, many blacks, Indians, and others are handicapped in successful test performance by social and cultural factors that differ from those generally attributed to the dominant population. Puerto Ricans and Mexican-Americans may be limited by language differences as well. Speed of performance, verbal ability, certain modes of thought—all these may be built-in requirements in certain tests. Yet such qualities may be foreign to some minority life styles. Out of this discrepancy arises a feeling against tests among ghetto dwellers that reaches peaks of sensitivity and apprehension hard for many whites, who have grown up with tests, to understand.

A San Francisco job counselor describes the feelings of one young black man who at age seventeen "left home amid much fanfare to enlist in the Marines. He failed the entrance examination after having been told that a third-grader could pass it and he returned, defeated, to his home. The effect on him was devastating. He has never passed a test since, and has walked away from any situation which required a competitive entry, whether it be job or school. He said, 'Every time I'd pick up a pencil I'd feel as if my brain was split open and the whole world was looking in.'"

One prominent test publisher admits that tests "may place a premium on types of backgrounds, or types of information that are not possessed to the same degree by all examinees." Test results, then, also vary accordingly among different groups, with Negroes generally achieving lower scores which bar them from jobs. However, since it has also been shown that Negro performance once on the job is just as good as white, some personnel men suggest simply setting a lower passing score for Negroes. Practical as this seems, such a procedure would run afoul of federal and state antidiscrimination provisions, just as would giving separate tests to black and white applicants.

To underscore the seeming unfairness to Negroes in many white-oriented tests, a Watts social worker not-so-facetiously devised the "Adrian Dove Counterbalance General Intelligence Test." By employing aspects of ghetto culture unfamiliar to most whites in the same way that aspects of the dominant middle-class culture are used in tests given to ghetto-dwellers, the tongue-in-cheek test emphasizes the perils of holding sacred the results of any test.

A few questions from the Dove test:

A "gas-head" is a person who has (A) fast-moving car; (B) stable of "lace"; (C) "process"; (D) habit of stealing cars; (E) long jail record for arson.

If a man is called a "blood" then he is a (A) fighter; (B) Mexican-American; (C) Negro; (D) hungry hemophile; (E) Redman or Indian.

Cheap chitterlings (not the kind you purchase at a frozen food counter) will taste rubbery unless they are cooked long enough. How soon can you quit cooking them to eat and enjoy them? (A) 45 minutes; (B) 2 hours; (C) 24 hours; (D) 1 week (on a low flame); (E) 1 hour.

If a judge finds you guilty of "holding weed" (in California), what's the most he can give you? (A) indeterminate (life); (B) a nickel; (C) a dime; (D) a year in County; (E) $500.00.

A "handkerchief head" is (A) a cool cat; (B) a porter; (C) an Uncle Tom; (D) a hoddi; (E) a preacher.

Which word is most out of place here? (A) splib; (B) blood; (C) grey; (D) spook; (E) black.

The answer is (C) in each case.

TESTS SHOULD MEASURE ACTUAL ABILITIES

Any test is only as good as its validity—which means that the scores applicants make on tests should have a proven significant relationship to the quality of their job performances. An Ohio company's personnel psychologist suggests one way to validate tests: "Give the proposed test to a group of employees and then compare the scores they make on the test with some measure of the quality of their job performance." Many companies call in certified psychologists or testing specialists to perform this task. If it is not done and unvalidated tests are used, the chances for inadvertent unfairness in the selection process is greatly increased. Even so, there is an "almost universal willingness to use unvalidated tests," says testing authority Professor Robert M. Guion. "Testers seem to be hoping that they will never be called upon for evidence that their tests are nondiscriminatory, rather than doing something to seek evidence one way or the other."

On one point many testing specialists are agreed: tests which in fact measure actual ability to perform a specific job are far more likely to accurately reflect an applicant's suitability for a job than are tests designed primarily to measure aptitude or intelligence. Validity of such tests is established by evaluating the relevance of the content of the test to the content of the job.

On a job-related written test, specified questions, such as the following, leave less room for cultural or educational differences to creep in:

"The best way to clean a casting is with: (A) Dutch cleanser; (B) Ivory soap; (C) solvent; (D) alcohol."

More to the point still are actual on-the-job tests—a method of selection of special value to companies embarked on hardcore programs. The prototypes of such tests have long been around —typing tests and shorthand tests, for example—but the extension of the concept to measure *potential* abilities is a more recent development.

At the bottom of a hardcore program is the employer's acceptance of the candidate's lack of training—he has no skills to test for. Thus it would be pointless to expect the new trainee to pass a test in, say, machine operation. After he has been on the job a few months and has had the chance to learn, such a test for checking his progress would be appropriate. But with the new man it would reveal nothing useful unless to infrequently turn up an applicant with some half-forgotten job experience.

Yet most companies need some way to measure a trainee's capacity for learning and following through on certain kinds of jobs. What is his latent potential for doing certain kinds of work? An employer needs certain basic information about his new man. Will one trainee prove to be good at certain repetitive tasks or will he be bored by them and soon quit? Will another be capable of a job that requires considerable dexterity and coordination? With the hardcore applicant, paper-and-pencil and most job-related tests fail to satisfactorily reveal these potential capacities.

Information about the prospective worker must be dug out in other ways.

INTERVIEWING FOR POTENTIAL

There are other perfectly respectable means of measurement beside tests which give a good picture of the man. Chief among these is the in-depth oral interview. As described in Chapter 3, the skilled and scrupulously fair personnel man can sympathetically probe, asking and re-asking questions, looking all the while for reasons to hire the man, not for reasons to turn him away.

While it may be time-consuming to administer, the in-depth interview provides the best means of assessing an applicant's common sense and his all-important motivation to learn. Motivation may well be the primary quality needed for entry-level jobs. If the new man can develop enthusiasm for his work, the chances are good that he will grow into a productive worker. And it is in the extended interview that the personnel specialist has the opportunity to best gauge the capacity a man has for generating this enthusiasm.

In some situations, depending on the nature and level of the work available, such in-depth interviewing can serve as the bulk of the screening process.

SELECTING BY WORK SAMPLE

One effective way of testing individual potential is through "work sample" techniques, an idea originally developed in the 1930's for use in evaluating vocational abilities of the physically and mentally disabled. More recently, the Department of Labor reports adoption of the technique as a tool for steering the hard-core unemployed into suitable jobs. It is used in federal job-training programs such as the Work Incentive program (WIN —see Chapter 12), which seeks to train people on welfare for productive work.

The work sample procedure substitutes job tasks, tools, and equipment for the standard written test. Typically, a job task might involve putting together nuts, bolts, and washers. How the task is done indicates a person's tolerance for simple repetitive routines, manual and finger dexterity, coordination, form perception, physical stamina, and ability to follow directions. Another task, disassembling and reassembling a lock, might show dexterity, spatial and form perception, eye-hand coordination, adaptability to routine, and skill at working with the hands.

One program that helped develop work sample techniques was conducted with Manpower Administration funds among people from the slums of North Philadelphia. Over a two-week period, the trainees were assigned twenty-eight progressively more demanding tasks, ranging from sorting nuts and bolts to taking apart a telephone or proofreading. Each task involved various abilities, and completed work samples were judged according to their complexity. Throughout the process applicants were observed and evaluated on work attitude, accuracy, promptness, learning speed, acceptance of instruction and authority, and other work-related factors.

In addition, personality factors of the trainees revealed during the work sample process were helpful in determining employability, especially if the individual "exhibited emotional problems which would affect his job performance," says a report on the Philadelphia program. "Assessment of such factors as persistence, dependability, independence, initiative, motivation, reaction to criticism and praise, social judgment, leadership, distractability, ability to handle stress, ability to channel energy, etc., helped the counselor to understand the individual better and to suggest suitable vocation goals."

Do work sample techniques help employers get—and keep—productive employees from the hardcore ranks? In Philadelphia, 56 percent of those placed on jobs from the work sample program were still on the job three months later. This compares to 35 percent of a control group of hardcore persons who were placed on jobs without the work sample program. Counselors in work sample programs claim that the technique greatly increases their knowledge of the trainee and enables them to refer trainees to a much wider variety of jobs than would standard testing, screening, and selection techniques.

It seems clear that business will have best results in hiring the hardcore through work sample procedures or techniques based on this concept. No other mass testing means appears to do as well in assessing a hardcore individual's potential.

In setting up such a program, cost would be a major factor. However, many large companies could establish work sample programs or modifications with costs figuring in as part of the federally reimbursed training schedule. A program could be worked out in alliance with other companies, using the consortium approach (see Chapter 12). Personnel officers can persuade employment services to sponsor broadscale programs of this sort. The graduates from it would provide well-screened recruits for a wide variety of businesses. The guiding principles for setting up such work sample programs have been well established. In Boston, Buffalo, Detroit, Milwaukee, Phoenix, Pittsburgh, St. Louis, San Francisco, Washington D.C., and the Mississippi Delta region, work sample techniques have been applied in the federally funded training and placement programs for the hardcore.

WHEN TESTS "MUST" BE USED . . .

Whatever other screening procedures are available, still many companies have an investment in written testing procedures that can't be flushed down the drain. At best, the testing procedure can be phased out; or perhaps it can be used only in conjunction with several selection techniques. This is the case at General Electric where testing "is only one of three steps in the recommended G.E. hiring procedure, and G.E. recruiters are frequently warned against giving too much weight to any test."

Only college-trained job candidates and not production employees are tested by the Norton Company of Massachusetts. Even in those cases where tests are used, a Norton executive says, they "never carry more than 15 percent to 20 percent weight" in the final decision.

Where tests are "unavoidable," the testing process itself, or the conditions under which tests are administered, should be reviewed with an eye to improvements. Such changes may result in a better score from applicants who don't have "test-savvy." For example, one study found that the presence of a Negro examiner in the test room was helpful to black job candidates, and it has been shown that Negro job applicants scored higher when they believed that the test would be graded leniently, or that the test score was not a determining factor in getting the job.

Additionally, a simple warm-up test given before the actual test provides the applicant with a familiarity of what is expected and tends to work off his nervousness. This, too, has produced better scores. Some companies have also found it feasible to give applicants who fail a second chance, either on the same test or a similar one.

When tests absolutely "must" be used, many firms follow the

lead of one Minnesota-based company, whose vice president for personnel told an interviewer, "I, personally, feel that anyone who did hire or reject on the basis of tests as a major factor in the decision, either believes in magic or has rocks in his head."

WHAT ALTERNATIVES?

The employer involved in a hardcore program is in it for better or worse. And if he hopes to continue using his standard battery of tests as the core of his selection procedure, he will run up against endless frustration and confusion which may eventually scuttle his program.

Fortunately, not many programs end up that way, and not for that reason. New ways to measure human potential continue to be found. Besides in-depth interviews and work samples, another still in experimental stages is the use of leaderless discussion groups. With this technique, a body of trainees, or pre-trainees, is monitored in a series of discussions about jobs, the world of work as they perceive it, and their career aspirations. Such a program requires expert help to set up, but to a company or group of companies so inclined, it could be integrated with a special training program, such as that outlined for supervisors in Chapter 6, or conducted as an adjunct to it, possibly using the same specialist personnel as trainers.

At the very least, such experimental programs add one more alternative to the uncritical use of job tests, and any employer committed to a hardcore hiring program will want to—indeed, *need* to—examine all alternatives to find the one that suits him best.

CHAPTER FIVE

Setting the Stage in Your Plant

Some years back, the no-nonsense manager of the Southern plant of a big national manufacturer called his supervisors together. "Gentlemen," he said, "head office has instructed us to integrate this plant. We will be hiring Negroes, starting immediately."

One supervisor jumped up and avowed that as a dyed-in-the-wool southerner he simply wouldn't be able to work under those conditions.

"Whatever you wish," said the manager. "You'll get two weeks' pay."

The supervisor quickly changed his mind.

Another supervisor spoke up. "You know damn well those colored boys will get to fighting with our men. How do you expect to handle that?"

"I'll fire the men who are fighting," said the manager. "I'll fire their leadman, I'll fire their foreman, and I'll fire the supervisor of that section."

The plant was integrated without incident.

That took place in the early 1960's. Nearly a decade later, there are few employers who haven't had at least limited experience in hiring Negroes. Today, installing a hardcore hiring program doesn't present exactly the same considerations as did attempts to get the first Negro on the company payroll. All the same, employing the hardcore will call for internal adjustments, and to bring them off successfully plans have to be laid in advance. As in any business venture, the more thorough the planning, the smoother the program.

Starting with an explicit and firm policy statement in writing by the president, planning should include briefing sessions for management and supervisory personnel; labor union officials should be brought in on early discussions; insurance representatives should be included. All aspects of the program—recruiting, training, support services, follow-up, and the like—must be explained in detail to supervisors. Personnel inventory charts should be drawn up to show where the new trainees will be placed and to what jobs they will move as the program progresses. Arrangements must be made for an employee education program, and for establishing a reporting system for administrative control and feedback.

THE FIRST STEP

To kick off a hiring program for the hardcore, top management must first issue a firm and unequivocal statement of policy, spelling out the minimum expected of all employees to make the program workable.

One company, which we'll call XYZ Company, issued this statement:

> In order to effect full utilization of all available labor resources, XYZ has entered into an agreement with the National Alliance of Businessmen to bring into our work force, to train and to employ in permanent jobs at all levels, a number of new minority trainees. The company management has volunteered to join the thousands of other companies across the country in participating in this important program in

order to better serve a large segment of its market, as well as to assure continued availability of federal contract work.

XYZ has long been an equal opportunity employer. Management is committed to move forward aggressively and affirmatively in bringing our minority citizens into the economic mainstream by means of employment within our company. We will renew our active recruiting efforts in minority communities so as to increase the representation of Negroes, Mexican-Americans, Indians, and others within our work force. These trainees will augment our present work force, and in no case will they displace workers now on the job.

In this endeavor I earnestly solicit the assistance of every member of the XYZ family. Our new training procedures will reach into most departments of the manufacturing plant. All supervisors have been instructed to receive and pass along constructive suggestions from all employees. I am sure that, as in the past, I can count on your wholehearted cooperation to implement this program and help XYZ maintain its leadership in the industry.

Copies of this letter signed by the president were distributed with paychecks to every employee. It was posted as well on all bulletin boards in proximity to copies of the fair employment regulations administered by the Federal Office of Contract Compliance, the U. S. Equal Employment Opportunity Commission, and the State Anti-Discrimination Commission. The letter was also printed in the "XYZ Zephyr," the company house organ, along with an article signed by the plant manager which explained briefly the NAB program, and the kinds of training the company was making available. The article also pointed out that federal funds would enable the company to set up support services involving job counseling, promotional reviewing practices, and legal and financial counseling—all of which would benefit any employee, new or old, who chose to avail himself of them. It urged employees with questions or suggestions to bring them to their supervisors. Not so coincidentally, the "Zephyr" also began printing more pictures of black workers, in uncontrived on-the-job shots and in "departmental man-of-the-month" profiles.

A company executive later explained why the firm went to such advance pains. "It was our thinking that we'd get the whole-hearted cooperation of the work force if we let them have at least a chance to participate in setting it up, and we wanted to show that it would bring in services from which everybody would benefit. The program is a year old now and it's worked out fine."

How had it helped employees other than hardcore?

"I think that what's happened is our staff is more attuned to looking at every man on an individual basis, looking for his particular strong points and weaknesses. With all the trial-and-error experiences our supervisors have gone through in training these new men, they've learned a lot about the needs of the work force. In my opinion this has been responsible for a cut in our over-all rate of job dropouts."

GETTING SUPERVISORS INVOLVED

Essential to the success of a hardcore hiring program is the total commitment of the top men. Management's statement of policy won't do the job itself. Managers and supervisors right on down the line must understand the policy and be made aware that the company wants it carried out at every level.

"Unless top management lays it on the line," says Kodak chairman William Vaughn, "lower-echelon people won't do it. Even then they may not do it without follow-up." When Ford undertook its hardcore training program, ten thousand supervisory employees received a letter from Henry Ford II, telling them that he expected them to tackle the program "in new ways and with a new sense of urgency" toward making it work. Another company president admitted frankly, "We put a lot of pressure on our managers and supervisors to get to work and implement this policy. As a result we didn't have any serious foot-dragging."

To assist supervisors in understanding the new program and to help them be most effective in carrying out new and demanding duties, many companies establish comprehensive "sensitivity training" programs (see Chapter 6), which are coming to be seen as necessary to successful hardcore training. But even if your company does not enter into a full-blown supervisorial training program, it is still essential to schedule an advance meeting or two with the supervisors who will have any part in the hardcore program.

The way you handle such an introductory meeting is important. The southern plant manager quoted at the beginning of this chapter adopted a tough take-it-or-leave it approach. It worked for him at that time and in that situation. But that was a different situation than most companies are in today, and the kind of muscle the manager showed is better implied than openly displayed. A candid appeal for help is more likely to get the cooperation needed.

As one executive suggests, "When people help in formulating a program they often develop a sense of ownership. It becomes *their* program, not just something the company cooked up. They feel that they have a stake in making it work."

It was that approach that was used by the plant manager of a Kansas City bottling plant. Upon receiving instructions from the president, he called together his thirteen supervisors. "I told them straight out," he says, "that the old man had put all his weight behind this thing and was holding me responsible for it —no ifs, ands, or buts. So they could all be damn sure I meant to see that it worked. 'I need your help on this, boys,' I told them, 'or I'm not going to get it off the ground and we'll all be in trouble.' They were all old-timers and we knew one another pretty well. They knew I wasn't kidding. I laid it on the line that I needed their help and I got it—100 percent. They went out of their way to help these new men. Some of them put in lots of extra time too. Before this program started we only had two or three Negroes on the maintenance crew. Now in the last year we've got to the point where about 8 percent of our production force is black, and most of them came in through the training program."

DISCUSS PROBLEMS

The key to obtaining commitment from supervisors lies in free and open discussion of all aspects of the new program—including the ways supervisors will be compensated or rewarded for their extra efforts. In your first meeting with supervisors, forthrightly state your company's case for entering into the program. This can take the over-all form of an appeal to fair play combined with economic considerations. The president of General Foods, for instance, in demanding greater affirmative minority recruiting efforts from his staff, told them he wanted company practice to square with his "ideas of American Democracy [and] religious teachings." He warned management that the company "could not sidestep a personal involvement in the Negro's economic problem," and even though the company was making progress in equal job opportunity, at the same time he was convinced "not enough was being done."

From a broad statement such as this to set forth the company philosophy, move on to specific points:

The need to obtain federal contracts or retain existing contracts which require the hiring of minority workers.

The desire to expand into new markets among minority communities, or avoid the narrowing of existing markets.

The necessity to avoid inviting boycotts or demonstrations from the community.

The need to act as a good corporate citizen in promoting the benefit of the larger community and the welfare of the nation.

The need to help the minority community "catch up" after generations of underprivileged status, and to help get persons off the welfare rolls and established as tax-paying consumers.

Frankly set forth the problems that might crop up, but also point out that you are not blundering into a new venture without some experience and knowledge of what to expect. Very likely your company, if it was in business during the 1940's, had a concentrated war-effort training program, not unlike the one you are now undertaking. "Our country entered World War II with inadequately trained manpower," says Donald M. Kendall, Pepsico president. "Yet within one year, we had so well mobilized our training structure that we were teaching housewives and farmers how to make complex electronic assemblies and close-tolerance machines." Some of the old-timers among supervisors may well remember these training programs. The point to be made is that hardcore training, although it calls for extra effort, does not represent any sharp break from business tradition, and that it is not somehow vaguely subversive in appearing to give preferential treatment to one group. It's been done before.

Suggest to supervisors the kinds of problems they might expect. Extra time will be required from them; production schedules affecting not only the hardcore but others as well may have to be readjusted. Ask for their ideas on how to deal with such possibilities. Discuss how supervisors will be compensated for their work. The National Association of Manufacturers says it should be made "absolutely clear that supervisors will be tangibly rewarded for their efforts," since they cannot respond adequately to the trainee's need for extra time and attention if production as usual is expected. The form such rewards will take —and they will vary between companies—should be determined by management as an integral part of the over-all program.

Where there is resentment against the hardcore from the supervisors, it frequently centers on the notion that "nobody else gets any special deals, why should they?" It is here that recourse to a full-fledged sensitivity training program as outlined in the following chapter is helpful. But if no such training is available, management must deal with such attitudes through discussion. Get all supervisors to throw in their ideas in answer to the complaint, and by guiding the discussion, allow all points of view to be aired. Many of the old myths that should have died when the first Negro came to work for you will still pop up: "Those kids are all dope addicts; they can't work with machinery; they won't take orders from a white man; they'll steal the tools; they're always late; they're hostile to everybody; they'll make passes at the white women workers."

During these discussions it is useful to have in mind—and perhaps throw out for comment—the findings of various surveys which have sought over the years to probe the difference between what whites think Negroes want, and what Negroes in fact express as their chief goals. At the top of the list of what whites *believed* Negroes wanted was intermarriage with whites; and near the bottom was "economic improvement," that is, better employment opportunities. At the top of the list of *actual* aspirations of black people was free access to a good job, and at the bottom was "unrestricted social relationships with whites." This exact reversal of priorities on the imagined list and the real list is a dramatic subject for discussion, and it serves to allow supervisors the opportunity to ventilate deep-seated anxieties and hostilities which, if they exist, should be identified early.

Infrequently, a supervisor may show an unshakable reluctance to cooperate, and has to be talked to in the summary fashion used by the Southern plant manager quoted earlier. An executive of an Indiana bag factory, for instance, reported that one of his foremen told him that he "didn't like the idea of having to teach his job to a bunch of pool-hall bums." He was taken aside and talked to privately. The executive said, "I told him that we weren't asking for his approval of the program. All he had to do was carry out his orders, and if he felt he couldn't do that and hold to company standards, we'd have to find someone who could. He didn't like it, but he stayed."

If the supervisor's objection to a new man is based solely on the basis of his race, the company has few alternatives if it really wants to pursue a successful hardcore program. One company's experience, although not specifically involving a hardcore worker, illustrates one method of handling the problem. A Negro employee was brought into the all-white department of a large food-processing plant. "There was no apparent resentment or resistance by the other employees in the department," the company reported to the National Industrial Conference Board. "However, the foreman of the department . . . said he could not bring himself to supervise an integrated work force. He was informed that if his personal feelings interfered with the efficient direction of the department, there was no longer a job for him with the company. As a result, he left. The entire action convinced employees in the plant that the company was indeed sincere. . . ."

Discussion should be free and open but, all the same, supervisors should not get the impression that they are voting on whether the company should install a hardcore hiring program. Management's decision has been made, and the meetings are a means of education and information regarding that decision.

Don't try to hide the special problems the new trainees will bring with them—a total lack of familiarity with the working world that may show itself in repeated tardiness, absenteeism, turnover, unusual ways of attacking a job. But point out at the same time that corrective and support services will be available. Deal frankly with the rumor that invariably gets into circulation that trainees are being groomed to replace present employees. The sooner that is laid to rest, the better.

INFORMING THE WORKERS

What must come out of your meetings with supervisors, then, is their understanding, support, and suggestions for implementing the hardcore program. The discussion will also provide the supervisors with the information they need to answer the questions and satisfy the doubts of the general work force. If supervisors wholeheartedly buy the program, there will be little likelihood of kickback from the ranks. Give the supervisor the full responsibility of answering the questions from his men. One company approached its hardcore program so full of doubts that it assigned the industrial relations manager the job of informing all workers and answering their questions. The reason was logical enough—such an approach would centralize the information function and lessen the chance of passing along misinformation. But the actual result was to seriously undercut the supervisorial authority and to greatly overburden the industrial relations office with specific individual gripes and observations which had to be referred back to the supervisors anyway.

Once the statement of company policy has been distributed, the supervisor should be prepared for questions. And he should answer them honestly. As an arm of management he cannot afford to get into arguments over the advisability of the policy, nor should he engage in an apologetic defense. Even if he has personal reservations about the policy, his attitude must be "this is our job and this is how we must do it." If he shows vacillation in his support of the decision, his workers will quickly seize on it and, if they are of such a mind, take advantage of it by failing to cooperate with the aims of the program.

The anxious worker, fearing for the security of his job, should be treated with understanding. But where the worker's fears or misunderstandings serve as a roadblock to the program, or threaten the authority of management, disciplinary measures must be taken.

Generally, in today's enlightened civil rights climate, the loss of an employee because of his disagreement with a company's nondiscriminatory policy is rare. Today, if prejudiced sentiment is overtly displayed at all, it generally takes the following form: A company reported to the National Industrial Conference Board that it employed a Negro in its office in a white-collar capacity, "doing minor clerical work, sorting mail and reproducing material. When he started to work, four white girls went to their supervisor and said that if he was going to be allowed to sit down in the office, they would leave. Their supervisor went to the manager of the office, and the manager told the supervisor to tell the girls to get their checks and leave if they were unable to adapt themselves. The girls went back to work immediately and no further incident occurred."

In this case management's strong hand forestalled the endless difficulties that may have resulted if a less determined stand were taken.

UNIONS AND INSURANCE COMPANIES

Whenever possible, bring the union in right at the start for discussion of the hardcore program. Shop stewards, business agents, and union officials should be asked for suggestions. If the union plays a big role in worker recruitment and hiring, its participation is especially vital. Many unions are founded on the idea that their duty is to take care of their members. A hardcore program which is tossed at them on a take-it-or-leave-it basis may well be regarded as seriously undercutting the job security of union members. Union cooperation is more likely if you can show that opportunities for all workers will be enhanced, as would be the result when strong support services are written into the hardcore hiring plan. In a number of cases where the union has been brought in on the initial planning, fears that their position would be weakened were allayed and they supported the new program. Instances are reported where the union consented to an extended probationary period for new hardcore recruits.

In certain instances, it is sometimes advisable to seek help from the international union, which frequently takes a broader view of minority recruitment and will assist the local in working with your company. Help can also be sought from the AFL-CIO's Human Resources Development Institute (see Chapter 12) which was established to expand job opportunities for minority workers.

But most unions, like most employers, are willing to work out reasonable procedures for employing the hardcore, if for no other reason than that they—just as the greater community—are beginning to respond to increased pressure to take a more active role in solving social problems.

For insurance companies, too, a growing number of hardcore workers produces a new set of conditions. How they finally deal with those conditions will affect your efforts and in some part limit what you can attempt. Adequate insurance coverage is essential, especially if there is an added risk factor resulting from extensive hiring of untrained personnel.

Talk over the problem beforehand with the insurance company's representative. It is not unusual for an insurance company, after such a discussion, to decide that it has an obligation to play a role in a cooperative effort that benefits the entire community; as a result, insurance rates may be maintained at previous levels, and the insurance company suffers no loss by its support of the program.

THE BUDDY SYSTEM

The "buddy system" is a means of pairing off a mature and sympathetic old-timer on the job with a newly hired trainee on a one-to-one basis. It provides essential built-in support for the new man. As problems arise on the job, the new man has someone at his elbow to provide the needed help and assurance.

Buddies must be men from the regular work force who are willing to take on the job of helping the hardcore worker succeed. They should be well liked by present workers so that their new assignment is viewed with respect. Just as supervisors should in some way be compensated for the demands made upon them by a hardcore program, the buddies' chore should also be sweetened. One possible way of doing this is to make the buddy assignment a preliminary step to a promotion or a desirable transfer. The value of buddies to the success of the program should be recognized by management, perhaps through letters of commendation, a service award, special mention in the plant newspaper, or the like.

Should the buddies also be Negro? Some uneasy hardcore trainees have obviously made faster adjustments under the tutelage of supervisors of their own color. If the pattern of Negro employment in your plant is good, with black workers at all levels, so that it will not appear that segregation is being practiced when the new black trainee is paired off with an older black worker, then such assignment is possible. But don't match up the new man with the only other Negro in the shop. At best this is a tricky business. The job welfare of the new man must be considered, but this has to be weighed against the problem of apparent segregation and the consequent possibility of establishing new "color-line" traditions in a department or throughout the plant.

The men selected as buddies should get an early pep talk from top management and attend a special orientation session. Wherever possible the buddy should have the chance to meet the new man before he starts work. If it is not practical otherwise, he can meet his charge in the personnel office a few minutes before the trainee's first shift and accompany him to the job site.

The buddy system is one element of the hardcore hiring program that most companies swear by. Some companies report that many buddies have taken hold of their jobs so enthusiastically that they even assist the new man in his off-the-job problems. Instances are reported of buddies seeing to it that the new man comes in on Mondays or the day after payday, or helping a new man shop for a decent used car; and cases have come to light of buddies even attempting to arbitrate a new worker's marital difficulties.

SPECIAL SUPPORT SERVICES

The National Association of Manufacturers points out that a perennial question regarding hardcore workers is, "These guys are here one day and gone the next—how do I keep them from disappearing?"

Companies seeking the answer to that question have found it by building strong support services for the hardcore into their operations. Such services permit them to deal with problems that business and industry generally have not tackled before, such as job counseling, legal and financial counseling, special meetings to improve communication between workers and management, medical service, arranging for child care, and similar problems usually thought of as beyond the scope of employer-employee relations. But the companies who exhibit an understanding of the special needs of the ghetto-dweller have the best success in holding them on the job. From these special support services, the worker gets a sense that the company is seriously interested in him, and he responds by sticking to the job.

The extent of support services that a company can afford to build into its hardcore program varies widely with the size of the company, local availability of similar services, economic considerations, and the breadth of the training program. Some businesses might well furnish only a sympathetic ear in the personnel office to hear problems and offer advice. Others might set up the impressive full range of services, receiving reimbursement for the expenditure from the Department of Labor through the National Alliance of Businessmen or a similar program.

Support services such as legal counseling often can be arranged through local Legal Aid Societies; and assistance in financial and family affairs can be obtained from community agencies set up for those purposes. Such support is, in effect, tacked on to the hardcore program. Other support services can, like the buddy system, be built directly into the program; job coaching and counseling are two such services.

THE JOB COACH

Usually the job coach works through a community agency that seeks jobs for the hardcore. The Concentrated Employment Program (see Chapter 12) has adopted the job coach concept with considerable success. Besides helping the unemployed find jobs, one coach reports he works on such problems as telling people "where to go for food stamps, bailing someone's brother out of jail," or advising how to pay back a one-dollar loan.

While the job coach's background is usually not that of a formally educated social worker, he does need some special abilities. Most important is his capacity to work with people sympathetically, honestly, and realistically, whether they are ghetto dwellers or high-level company management personnel.

"We're one step from being the people we're serving," says the black supervisor of job coaches for the Washington, D. C. CEP program. He points out that most of the coaches are or have been on parole after time in jail on charges ranging from car theft to armed robbery and narcotics. To the hardcore, they make themselves understood in the tough language of the ghetto, and they have a "knowledge of the con"—the ability to recognize when someone is feeding them a line or just plain lying.

In California the job coach concept has been adopted by the state civil service, which has established the position of "job agent." Job agents not only work to find training and jobs for the hardcore, but for an eighteen-month period after a man goes to work, they stick with him to help clear up problems and to steer him into whatever support services he may need.

In his daily rounds, the typical job coach keeps in touch with the new employee, offering him encouragement and assistance with family, legal, or medical problems—anything that would interfere with the man's job.

The coach's duties do not end there, however. He also stays closely in touch with company personnel, especially the hard-core employee's immediate supervisor. To the supervisor the coach offers whatever help and guidance he can toward most effectively developing the positive side of the worker.

The value of a job coach lies in his ability to always be on top of a situation, so that he can deal at once with a problem before it gets out of hand. The NAM says that companies report that "the performance of persons seen regularly by a job coach is superior to that of individuals not receiving personal attention. Some company officials frankly state that without the constructive involvement of this third person they most probably would have terminated some hardcore workers who later turned out to be good employees."

COUNSELING

When individual difficulties require personal attention in greater depth than the supervisor or job coach can provide, the counselor is one means some companies use to provide such help.

Professionally trained, a counselor may work with up to about thirty workers, and may counsel them individually or in group sessions. Workers are helped to face and understand their conflicts and tensions, and hopefully are relieved of some of the inner pressures that may otherwise erupt in a manner troublesome to the employer.

Establishing a regular counseling service for employees may seem like a fringe benefit of extreme luxury to some employers.

But again, according to the National Association of Manufacturers, "by and large, companies offering a counseling service say they have been amply repaid in terms of increased morale and, many feel, increased productivity."

CHILD CARE

Another support service, which may appear almost exotic to some companies, is the provision of child-care facilities. But companies with women employees, whether black or white, find a major cause of absenteeism is laid to the need to be home with children. The course one company followed is described in the following case history.

The KLH Research and Development Corporation of Cambridge, Massachusetts, established a child-care center for its eight hundred employees, about half of whom are women, many of them heads of families. The program enables the company to offer employment to some mothers now on welfare, since all-day care for their children is assured. The center is located near the factory to encourage greater parent participation in the family-oriented program. Tuition is based on ability to pay, the fee generally running about six dollars per week per child. Actual costs per child are about thirty-five dollars per week, part of which is covered by funds from the U.S. Department of Health, Education and Welfare.

The child-care center also functions as a school, with plans that call for four teachers and eight teachers' aides to every sixty children between the ages of two and six years.

"The project was inspired mainly by the need of KLH employees for better child day care," NAM reports. "Because of lack of satisfactory baby-sitting arrangements for their children, many of the mothers are forced to take time off from their jobs. In some of the more critical cases the parent was actually forced to quit the company and seek some form of public assistance. The KLH program is mainly aimed at solving this problem. It has been shown by many government surveys that women on welfare . . . would like to work if given the chance."

WHERE TO PLACE THE NEW MAN

What job the new man will perform and where in the shop it will be located depends entirely upon the needs and nature of your operation. But it is useful to draw up beforehand a job inventory to chart trainee positions and show the promotional channels leading from those positions. This gives management the necessary long view of the program, and can help prevent "plateauing," in which the hardcore program unexplainably gets stalled at one point, requiring extensive and concentrated effort to get it moving again.

Some plants have long-established practices of assigning new workers to the dirtiest or least desirable entry-level job for a probationary period. In working with the hardcore trainee this practice should be abandoned. Traditionally, such work may have been shunned as "no work for a white man," and new black workers won't see much promise in a training program that assigns them to it. "Dirty work" assignments can cause other kinds of difficulty, too. This was the case in an Ohio ceramics factory which had always put new workers in "the hole," as it was known to employees, where bags of clay and chemicals were received and stored. "If my own son came to work here he'd have to start in the hole—everybody has to," the manager told the representative of an equal employment regulatory agency who had found that the only five blacks employed by the firm were all in the hole. The representative was not satisfied, nor was a local civil rights group which had reported the matter in the first place. The company eventually changed its practice.

Choosing the specific jobs to be assigned to new workers is a matter that management, supervisors, and the personnel staff must jointly decide upon, perhaps in consultation with the agency that will participate in recruiting. The decision has to be made according to such considerations as production schedules, availability of supervisory time, past experience with given jobs, possibilities for upgrading and promotion, and similar matters. Individual differences in new employees should be taken into account too, and matched to the job wherever possible.

Often, existing jobs can be restructured to provide new jobs (see Chapter 1). Such is the case in one St. Louis plant where the category of "electrician's helper" has been established a step below the previous entry-level position of "electrical maintenance assistant" in order to provide niches for the hardcore. And in a number of hospitals, nurses are relieved of routine chores by workers filling the newly created position of "clinic assistants." In most supermarkets, the job of check-out clerk has been broken down, with newly employed sackers relieving the checker to devote all his time to more rapid processing of customers—a clear addition to efficiency so far as the customer is concerned, and in promoting rapid customer turnover as well.

In job assignment, just as in the selection of the most appropriate buddy, carefully consider the disadvantages of placing black trainees in departments which already have substantial numbers of black workers. Instead, this may be the point at which to tackle the department or section which has somehow managed to stay all white. If a black supervisor is employed in your plant, there may be a general impulse to assign new black workers to him. When he is that rare "right man," he can greatly facilitate training. But the more militant young blacks are sometimes hostile to older Negroes whom they see as having sold out in order to advance to elevated positions in the Establishment. On the other side of the coin, Negroes who have worked hard to achieve the comforts of middle-class life are sometimes leery of hardcore ghetto dwellers. A Northern California luggage manufacturer who had long employed blacks ran into problems when three hardcore youths were assigned to a sixty-year-old black supervisor. The supervisor, who had for years lived comfortably in a suburban community, took as a personal affront the language, dress, and mannerisms of the three new workers, and he rode them until the plant manager stepped in and reassigned them. But other employers report good results in assigning hardcore workers to black supervisors. Much depends on the individuals involved. Don't make the mistake of thinking that a similarity of color alone will override extreme differences in education, achievement, or personal philosophy.

Such "segregated" assignment can serve a beneficial purpose, however, in cases of Spanish-speaking workers with little understanding of English. The entire training process will be facilitated if they are paired with bilingual, Spanish-speaking buddies or supervisors.

FAILURE—WHOSE FAULT?

Careful advance preparation for the new hardcore man can do much to anticipate and head off problems. But you won't be able to anticipate everything that could possibly happen—and a lot will. Sometimes when the trainee falls by the wayside it may be impossible to determine whether he failed the program or the program failed him. The NAM suggests that "in the end, the payoff is likely to be greater if the assumption is made that somewhere along the line the program is at fault."

If management makes this assumption, the program will be held up for objective review, and if flaws are discovered, strengthening measures can be taken.

CHAPTER SIX

A Two-day Sensitivity Training Program for Supervisors

Industry was among the first of American institutions to accept the idea of sensitivity training when the concept was introduced some twenty years ago. In time the idea caught on in other quarters, and today there are many variations of the original human relations training concepts—encounter groups, marathon confrontation sessions, and nonverbal exercises being among the most popular.

But most useful to business and industry, as it faces the challenge of the hardcore unemployed, is the applied human relations training that deals with re-education and organizational problem-solving. Essentially, such training is based on the "T-group," or training group principle: ten to sixteen people are brought together for an extended period with the objective of creating an emotional atmosphere which draws underlying motivations to the surface for examination and understanding. For business in the 1970's, such training, says the National Association of Manufacturers, "is increasingly viewed as a vital component of any successful effort to employ and retain the hardcore."

There are a variety of ways your business can set up sensitivity training programs. The most common are: (1) through arrangement with a local school or college that offers courses around which such a program can be constructed; (2) by employing the services of a professional training firm, or management consultant firm, who can deliver a complete packaged training program; or (3) by assigning to personnel within your own organization the responsibility for formulating and carrying out an in-house training program for supervisors.

While information on the first and second approaches is readily obtained within your own community, the whys and hows of implementing number three are less easily come by. This chapter is meant to provide a working—if skeletal—guide enabling a personnel man to set up a worthwhile training program for supervisors involved in hardcore employment.

WHAT COMES FIRST?

The program outlined here is for a two-day training session. The following initial preparations should be made for it.

1. Select a training officer. He should be an individual whose personality, intelligence, and interest in the program are such that he can do the job thoroughly and with enthusiasm. He may be the personnel officer, the industrial relations manager, or, in smaller companies, possibly the chief executive or a top-level manager. The individual selected must be willing to undertake considerable advance homework, including a study of selected books listed in Chapter 12. He should be given complete responsibility for preparing the supervisor training program as outlined here. The remainder of this chapter is addressed to him.

2. Lay the groundwork by having top management meet with supervisors as described in Chapter 5. Consider various rewards

as inducements to more willing participation—extra compensation or time off, for example.

3. Set aside two days for the program for each group of no more than sixteen supervisors. If you choose two working days, consider the resulting need to compensate for the supervisors' absence through altered work schedules, doubling up, and temporary use of managers as supervisors. It is possible to conduct the program over a series of two- or three-hour after-work sessions, but the best combination of concentrated training time and least disruption of work comes by using both days of a weekend, or two consecutive Saturdays.

4. Choose a site. It should be comfortable, relatively quiet and private, and with sufficient room to move about. If your company does not have such space available, a local school, church, or fraternal society can usually provide facilities. However, home grounds are best.

5. Make your arrangements beforehand for necessary materials, such as a blackboard, questionnaires, instruction sheets, printed forms, exercises, and reading materials as described in the following pages.

6. When possible, obtain the services of an assistant trainer. Such an individual should ideally be Negro or of other minority background. He may sometimes be reached through the social science departments of local colleges, or community social agencies. Local human relations commissions or governmental fair employment agencies often will provide expert assistance without fee; try them first. If your business employs a Negro supervisor or manager, consider assigning him temporarily to the training program. It may also be possible to borrow a minority group supervisor from another company. In the training program, practical experience on the part of the trainers is more valuable than impressive academic degrees.

Once each of these matters has been cleared, the training officer should prepare a check list to make certain that all points have been covered. When this is completed, the supervisor training program is ready for launching.

TIMETABLE FOR SUPERVISOR TRAINING

As much as possible conduct the training period in one and one-half hour segments, with a fifteen-minute break after each such segment, and a lunch break of one hour. Don't press for longer sessions, since attention spans—even of seasoned workers —are limited, and heightened emotions need time to simmer down. Too much material stuffed into one unrelieved session may choke rather than nourish.

The time periods suggested below for each phase of training are by no means absolute, but should serve as a flexible guide to permit covering all material in two days without crowding.

FIRST DAY

Part I   *Suggested time*

   A. Negative expectations   20 minutes
   B. Historical review   15 minutes
   C. General fears   30 minutes

Part II

   A. Expected problems and solutions   45 minutes
   B. General discussion   30 minutes

Part III

A. Outline of Negro history	30 minutes
B. Details of ghetto life	15 minutes
C. Minority workers in business	15 minutes
D. Language differences	15 minutes
E. Discussion	15 minutes

Part IV

A. One-way communication	20 minutes
B. Two-way communication	30 minutes
C. Illustration of work situation	20 minutes
D. Person-to-person communication	45 minutes
E. Describing observed behavior	30 minutes
F. Making judgments	15 minutes
G. Direct *vs.* indirect description	20 minutes

SECOND DAY

Part V

A. Practicing new techniques	45 minutes
B. Soliciting information	30 minutes
C. Clear writing	20 minutes
D. How to observe performance	45 minutes
E. Developing positive reinforcement	1 hour

Part VI

A. Experiments in role-playing   2 hours
B. Concluding session   1-2 hours
C. Follow-up   2 hours

PART I

A. *Negative expectations.* Start the first session off straightaway by calling for the supervisors' most negative expectations regarding minority workers. This should be far more structured than the similar preliminary discussion described in Chapter 5.

Each man is asked to write down the three most negative things he thinks will happen as a result of the employment of hardcore Negroes. He need not sign his name to the list. The trainer collects the lists and kicks off discussion by reading what appear to be the most common concerns. Don't minimize the importance of any concerns so long as they have any basis in reality. Attempt to explain causes where possible. Suggest ways of coping with problems—if the group agrees they are indeed problems. Strip down stereotypes and discuss the needs of minority group individuals. After the participants have had sufficient opportunity to express their beliefs, turn to authoritative source material (see book list, Chapter 12) to clarify popularly held stereotypes. Don't expect—or ask for—agreement. Simply state the factual argument.

B. *Historical review.* Now provide a sudden shift of emphasis. The trainer says: "Before we move on to the area of personal feelings and concerns—and I have my own share of concerns about members of minority groups—it might be a good idea to lay out some facts about the Negro in the United States that you might not be aware of."

Using historical source material, rapidly recount a series of significant facts, such as the following sample. This phase lends itself to a "did-you-know" format:

"Did you know:

"that the first man to die in the Boston massacre when the British opened fire in Boston Commons and killed five Americans was Crispus Attucks, a Negro sailor?

"that two of the outstanding heroes of the battle of Bunker Hill were black men, Peter Salem and Salem Poore?

"that over five thousand soldiers who served under George Washington during the Revolutionary War were Negroes?

"that although generation after generation of Negroes were said to be content under slavery, they showed their 'contentment' in such ways as runaways by the thousands, local uprisings, burning of crops and houses, and by major insurrections such as those led by Gabriel Prosser in Virginia, Denmark Vesey in South Carolina, and Nat Turner in Virginia?

"that though most blacks were slaves there were a number of 'free colored,' so called, who made major contributions to our society?

"that Benjamin Bannecker, a black man, was appointed by George Washington to the commission that planned the city of Washington, D. C.?

"that Phyllis Wheatley, a black poet, was sent by Washington as a cultural representative of this country to the crowned heads of Europe?

"that the battle of New Orleans was fought by Negro troops under the command of Andrew Jackson?

"that a good majority of the sailors manning our men-of-war during the War of 1812 were black?

"that 300,000 Negroes served in the Civil War?

"that black cowboys comprised a full one-third of all cowboys in the West from 1870 to 1900?"

Many more examples can be cited: Here's where the trainer's homework makes itself felt.

C. *General fears.* After ten or fifteen minutes of showering the group with facts, turn back to the discussion. You or your assistant should straightforwardly present a list of generally held fears concerning Negroes: intermarriage with whites; job competition; neighborhood integration with resultant loss of property values; loss of personal status or prestige through association with minorities; increase in crime and violence.

Discuss each fully, but don't expect problems to be resolved. At best you may soften some rigidly held prejudices. But the exposure of fears and discussion of prejudices is designed to force participants to take a look at beliefs that they have never really examined before.

PART II

A. *Expected problems and solutions.* Focus now on specific day-to-day problems by giving participants sheets of paper ruled into three columns with headings as shown below, and ask them to write in Column one the working problems expected as a result of employing black hardcore workers.

After each participant has listed as many problems as he can, divide the group into subgroups of three each. Instruct these subgroups to discuss and write down in Column two what factors exist in the company that will lead toward a solution or modification of the expected problems listed in Column one. At least twenty minutes should be devoted to this phase. An additional twenty minutes should be given over to discussion by the subgroups of negative factors in the company situation that might interfere with successful solution to the problems. These factors should be set down in Column three. Column headings on the paper will look like this:

Column 1	Column 2	Column 3
Problems expected from minority workers	Conditions in company that will help solve such problems	Conditions in company that will hinder solutions of such problems

Some of the entries will probably be along these lines:

Problems expected:
  Always late; won't show up.
  Lazy; won't care about doing a good job.
  Inappropriate dress.
  Won't respond to discipline; hard to manage.
  Will be hostile, aggressive, sassy; get into fights.
  Will be oversensitive; take offense at any excuse.
  Will be difficult to talk to.
  Won't be able to find housing in the area.
  Will have problems getting to work because they live so far away.
  Won't be loyal to the company.
  Will fight supervision; want to do the job the way they please.
  Will try to get fresh with the women on the staff.
  Won't be good bets for promotion.
  Will come to work drunk or doped up.
Conditions in company that will help:
  Favorable and determined attitude on the part of management.
  Concerned supervisors.

Counseling service through personnel department.
Other minority workers already successful on the job.
Past success with training programs.
Large number of old-timers willing to help.
Sensitivity training programs.

Conditions in company that will hinder:
Older workers' resentment at coddling of new workers.
Union objections.
Normally slow turnover may prevent advancement of new men.
Heavy production pressures.
Existing education or testing requirements for entrance jobs.
Bonding requirements.
Rigid union seniority contract provisions.
Racial prejudice on part of other workers.
Bad past experience with one or two minority workers.

Participants should be encouraged to write down items that specifically reflect conditions unique to your operation.

B. *Discussion.* Bring the entire group together again. Each subgroup presents to the group the anticipated problems they have listed and the factors bearing on it as listed in columns two and three. After each subgroup has made its presentation, the entire subject is opened up for general discussion. Guide the discussion toward a consensus as to which problems are most serious, which least serious. Seek tentative ways to deal with those factors within the company which work against solution.

If the thrust of the discussion is toward constructive problem-solving, much valuable material may be developed. Make every effort to elicit specifics. As suggestions are being made, jot down notes to yourself. This helps stimulate discussion since it is seen as evidence of sincere interest in the proposals.

PART III

This section consists of a general survey of the hardcore unemployed. Although comments and discussions should be permitted, in this part of the training you and your assistant mainly present information to the group.

A. *Outline of Negro history*. In brief, the information on this subject which results from your homework should be introduced somewhat as follows:

> In the main, black men and women who fall within the general classification of the hardcore unemployed are direct descendants of slaves. There are thousands of black men and women still alive whose parents were born into slavery. The impact of slavery is still felt by millions of Negro-Americans who know it as a degradation suffered by their grandparents and great-grandparents. Even after slavery was abolished, the condition of most Negroes in the rural South—and most of the hardcore are their descendants—improved very little. Most lived in abject poverty and struggled for survival as tenant farmers, or sharecroppers. They were little educated, and malnutrition and disease were common. Most of the hardcore individuals with whom you will work are either themselves recent arrivals to an urban area, or are the sons and daughters of those who left the farms and moved into the cities during the thirties, forties, and fifties. They or their parents brought with them few usable skills, serious educational lacks, a total unfamiliarity with the ways of life in the city. They experienced the open and continuous pressure of racial prejudice. You might say they had two-and-a-half strikes against them from the start. . . .

B. *Details of ghetto life.* Detail the impoverished life to be found in most black ghettos—the crowding, high unemployment, isolation from the white community. Mention the inherited anger of many blacks, caused by the abuse they or their parents suffered, and the disappointment when they discovered that conditions in the ghetto were often little better, and sometimes much worse, than what they knew as sharecroppers. Point out that this life style leads to poor or nonexistent work habits, with much absenteeism and tardiness, and to difficulty in concentrating on a task for an extended time.

This picture of ghetto influences which alienate, isolate, and produce rage and frustration is followed by a recounting of positive aspects of ghetto living: "By the very condition of their life, ghetto dwellers manage to develop a high degree of self-reliance as well as a good ability to adjust to trying conditions."

To assist better understanding of the hardcore worker, offer a glimpse of the black subculture. Point out that it develops self-sufficiency, places a premium on comradery and extended family relationships; that it does not tend to isolate individuals as some cultures do; and since ghetto life often permits only a minimum of privacy, a considerable degree of sharing of time, responsibility for child care, problems, and joys is demanded.

C. *Minority workers in business.* Briefly survey the experience of business and industry over the past thirty years in employing minority group workers. Thirty years ago the vast majority of black workers were employed only in "traditional" jobs—janitorial work, unskilled hard labor, domestic work, personal services. Wartime jobs in the 1940's brought many into skilled work. Today, millions have moved into every rank of business and industry. Most have made the move successfully, and this promises good results for the hardcore worker if the initial period of adjustment can be satisfactorily weathered by both worker and employer.

D. *Language differences.* Discuss language differences. This subject is best handled by a black assistant who can explain ghetto slang with possible hidden meanings. Describe some of the aspects of "private" use of language in a way similar to the following.

In struggling for their own identity, most minority groups, such as the Italians, Jews, Irish, and Germans in their day, developed their own special idiomatic language. It helped them to develop a sense of community and specialness. As one or another group becomes integrated into the general population, the need for this special language as a sign of a special identity diminishes and finally disappears. Of course, those who already spoke a foreign language will continue to speak it. Then, too, fragments of the language filter down through generations, and young people whose parents and even grandparents speak English may retain certain special "in" words based on their language heritage. Similarly, black people have developed a rich "sublanguage" which is constantly changing. What is in use today may no longer apply a year from now, although some words and expressions are longer lived than others.

To a black man a Caucasian may be a *gray boy*, a *paddy*, a *honkey*, or a *Mickey Mouse*, none of which are exactly compliments. The black man may need some *dust* so he can see his *mink*—that is, he needs money because he plans to visit his girlfriend. If he says he is going to *hit* on a *fox*, he is planning to try his luck with a girl. On the other hand, a *half* might not be interested in *foxes*, since he is homosexual. If you hear the word *blood*, it refers to a *brother*, a *bootsie*, or a *member*—all references to Negroes. If a black man says he will drop by your house to *rap* and that he will bring some *pluck,* he plans to come by for some conversation and will bring wine or other liquor. In order for him to get to your house he'll have to use his *short* or *rubber*—automobile. If you try to *hype* or *run a game* on him—that is, make fun of him or use him—he may get *up tight* and *split.* . . .

In the discussion also point out the sensitivity among blacks to such words as "boy" or "girl" or to expressions such as "you people."

E. *Discussion.* Wind up this section by asking for comments from anyone who feels he has discovered anything as a result of the presentation. Concentrate the discussion around these areas of new understanding. Don't re-hash other matters.

(Since this training program has been designed in sections that are largely self-contained, appropriate training films—see Chapter 12—can be shown, if desired, following the completion of Parts I, II, or III. Be sure to follow up the showing of any such films with a discussion of the points it raises.)

PART IV

Tell supervisors that from this point on training will consist primarily of activities in which they will personally participate. Ask them to volunteer their own refinements and improvements of techniques as the sessions progress. Encourage them to assume creative roles.

A. *One-way communication.* Set up two-man teams. Ask each team to do the following as demonstrated by the trainer and his assistant: without looking at the other team member who must remain silent, one team member talks for three full minutes about any matter that interests him—a hobby, a recent trip, a book, a movie. After three uninterrupted minutes, the listening member of the team attempts to repeat, or "feed back," the gist of what has been told him. This he must do without looking at his team partner and with no corrections or comments from the partner.

After you have demonstrated this procedure, allow the teams about ten minutes to perform it on their own. Then call the group together for comments and accounts of the experience. Ask them to spell out their difficulties. Some participants will be annoyed or angry at having to play the game. Recognize the irritation as justified, sympathize with the complaint, but don't get bogged down with explanations or apologies.

B. *Two-way communication*. Using the same two-man teams, instruct each to make a second presentation on a different topic. This time the talker looks the other man in the eye. Questions are permitted, and the talker asks the listener if he understands whenever he has doubts. Then the listener feeds back to the talker; he also looks him in the eye, and again questions are permitted. Allow at least fifteen minutes for these exercises. After each team is finished, assemble the group again. What similarities and what differences did they find between one-way and two-way communication? Which way was easier? What were their emotional reactions to each of two approaches? What did they learn about communication?

C. *Before the above discussion fades out, select one team of two men to act as an instructor and a trainee.* Construct a believable work situation in which the instructor is training a worker in an unfamiliar job. Prepare in advance a set of fairly complicated instructions for a task not related to the usual jobs in your plant. Give the instructor member of the team time to familiarize himself with details of the instruction sheet. If possible, have tools or equipment available. If the instruction calls for building a wooden box, for instance, a hammer, nails, and boards add to the effectiveness of the illustration.

Have the team carry out the instructions, first with the instructor team member using one-way communication. With a different set of instructions, run through an example using two-way communication. Designate several two-man teams to go through the exercises in turn while others watch. Encourage detailed discussion of what they observe. Relate this to examples drawn from the actual work experience of individuals in the group. Offer one or two examples of your own, and then solicit response to such questions as "What was the biggest problem you had on your first job? What was the worst mistake you ever made? Who was the best supervisor you ever had and why?"

D. *Person-to-person communication.* Choose two participants who have demonstrated enthusiasm and some dramatic flair. Designate one man to play the role of a recently hired worker; the other man assumes his usual role of supervisor. Select one of the following situations—or a similar one from your experience—and brief the team on it:

1. Worker arrives an hour late and says his car broke down. Since he couldn't afford a tow, he says he had to wait for his brother-in-law to arrive to help him push the car back home. His lateness has interfered with production and has made it necessary for the supervisor to do some of the work himself.

2. Worker has just scrapped an expensive casting because of failure to carry out detailed instructions. Because of the press of other responsibilities, the supervisor had not kept a close eye on the worker.

3. Worker has spent an unusually long time in the toilet several times during the past few hours. His absences have interfered with production. Worker states that he is not feeling very well.

4. Worker informs supervisor that he believes a list of items to be picked for shipment is in error. Supervisor prepared the list himself and is under pressure to make immediate shipment.

5. Supervisor instructs worker in a new procedure to be followed in drawing tools and supplies. Instead of simply requesting what he needs from the tool room clerk, he must now prepare a detailed list which is first to be initialed by the supervisor and then presented to the tool room. Worker's use of tools or supplies has never been questioned before.

6. Worker requests that he be given overtime work at premium pay. He claims other workers with less seniority have been awarded overtime and he has not. Supervisor does not feel that worker should work overtime because he performs poorly when not directly supervised. During overtime work supervision is at a minimum.

After describing the situation to be acted out, explain that there are three "filters" serving as obstacles to communication, and the team must use them in discussing the problem. They are: prejudiced attitudes, distractions, preconceptions about what the other means to say.

1. As the basis for "prejudicial attitudes," select different political party membership, different religion, different race, or different country of origin.

2. "Distractions" can be provided by your own interruptions of the discussion, a radio played at full volume, or a steadily ringing telephone.

3. "Preconceptions" about what the other intends to say can be established by having actors assume that the other is lying, that one does not like the other and is trying to "sandbag" him, or that the other is of low intelligence.

Use your imagination and introduce other filters, or obstacles, that make the situation as difficult as possible to discuss rationally. Then instruct the team to act out the situation. Encourage them to follow it through to the very end, however disastrous the misunderstandings become.

Following is an example of such a dramatic scene, with stage directions, constructed around the first situation suggested above —a worker whose car has broken down and the supervisor has had to do some of his work.

The worker is Negro. He is a member of a strict Fundamentalist church in which he serves as deacon. The supervisor is Caucasian, and has no connection with organized religion.

The scene is set in the glass-enclosed office of the supervisor. It overlooks the noisy production line. During the scene, about once a minute someone barges in to thrust a note at the supervisor, urgently ask him a question, or simply to shout hello.

The supervisor considers the worker to be basically lazy, although he has no evidence of this. He also believes the worker is more likely to lie than tell the truth—a belief he holds about all black people.

The supervisor had to carry several heavy loads of parts to the assembly line, a job the worker normally performs. In the course of this work his hands got dirty and some of the grime has soiled his white supervisor's smock.

The worker senses that the supervisor is racially prejudiced. He expects to be treated rudely and he is upset at the prospect of the interview. Because of his strict religious beliefs, he is scrupulously honest in every way.

The worker knocks on the door of the glass cubicle and waits half a minute before he is asked to enter. After entering, the worker stands inside the door for over a minute while the supervisor continues to do some paperwork without once looking up at his visitor.

The playing out of this situation may be set up to begin something like this:

Supervisor: Adams, do you know that your being late caused problems for the entire section?

Adams: I'm sorry. You see my car broke down and I had to wait for my brother-in-law to come and push it back home.

Supervisor: You know, half the men who come in late claim it's because of trouble with their cars.

Adams: Well, the fuel pump just gave out. It started up all right and then about half a mile from home it just gave out. It was almost new, too. I just put it in myself last month.

Supervisor: Strange how fuel pumps, or transmissions, or some damn thing like that always "just gives out" on the way to work. Funny that it seldom happens on the way home. . . .

Have the actors take it from there, with many interruptions as suggested above.

Now select another situation and have the same team play it *without* filters and with a free flow of two-way communication. Invariably, this second exchange will move toward a satisfactory resolution of the problem. Guide the situation if you observe filtering taking place. It may stem from nervousness of the participants or remarks from the audience.

Select a second team and run through another situation. Then have the entire group offer their observations. Ask participants to relate examples of filtering from their own lives, possibly relating to experiences with their children, neighbors, or spouses.

E. *Describing observed behavior*. Select another two-man team. By now, participants should be familiar enough with this technique so that those who were irritated by it earlier will accept it. Send one member of the team out of earshot. He is to serve as the supervisor, observing a worker. He is not to communicate with the worker, but is to tell the group what he thinks the worker is doing. While the observer is out of hearing, explain to the worker member of the team and to the audience what the worker will in fact be doing. Situations can be similar to the following:

1. Worker suspects there is a structural defect in a piece of metal stock and examines it minutely, turning it over, carefully rubbing it, tapping it. From a distance of twenty feet, the supervisor observes his actions.

2. Worker is in the process of picking and packing a complicated order. He has just read the instructions and is considering in what order the merchandise should be picked so that it can be efficiently packed. For several minutes he stares down into the packing carton with the order in his hand. Supervisor observes from ten feet away.

3. Worker is loading heavy cartons onto a skid. He is working erratically because he has never done heavy work before and he is in poor physical shape even though he looks fit to the casual eye. He has skipped breakfast and hasn't money enough to buy lunch. From across the room, supervisor observes his poor performance.

(Also include in this segment one example of a worker assessing the behavior of a supervisor, as in the following: Supervisor is assigned by manager to observe and record every movement made by workers in a particular job in order to evaluate the efficiency of a certain phase of production. Following instructions, the supervisor observes every third man. Worker becomes aware of supervisor standing several feet behind him, taking detailed notes.)

When everyone but the team member who plays the supervisor has been informed of the situation to be acted out, call the supervisor in and ask him to explain what he thinks the worker is doing. To induce him to get into the spirit of the occasion you may have to coach him. In the first example, for instance, you might start off by saying, "What the devil is he doing with that piece of metal stock?"

Run through three or four such situations with different teams, without permitting team members to communicate verbally. After this, set up two or three situations where the supervisor-observer watches for a short time and then checks his perceptions by: (1) questioning the man directly; (2) double-checking through follow-up observations—he checks back periodically to see whether worker's behavior has changed; (3) comparing notes with the observations of others—any member of the audience will do since all have heard the instructions.

Following this series of team performances, conduct an in-depth discussion on problems of describing observed behavior. Encourage participants to offer examples of times when they misunderstood what they saw, either on or off the job. The discussion should lead to on-the-job problems that result from misinterpreting behavior. If possible, draw forth actual examples from the company's experience. Point out that cultural differences may intensify the problem of correctly interpreting behavior. Don't elaborate at this stage; cultural differences will be taken up later in greater depth.

F. *Making judgments.* Devote ten or fifteen minutes to considering the differences between describing behavior and making judgments. Use examples similar to the following to make clear the difference.

"Tony frowned when I warned him about being late." Description of observed behavior.

"Robert lacks ambition." Judgment.

"Danny works slower than the other men in the warehouse." Observed behavior.

"Mike struck Tom first when they got into an argument." Observed behavior.

"John is belligerent." Judgment.

"Mary has shown herself not to be trustworthy." Judgment.

"Shorty is a neat dresser." Judgment.

"Roger made five mistakes in preparing orders yesterday." Observed behavior.

"Roger is always making mistakes." Judgment.

"The boss really likes his secretary." Judgment.

G. *Direct versus indirect description of feelings.* During this fifteen- to twenty-minute segment, consider the difference between the direct statement and innuendo, veiled threat, or the statement that contains double meanings. Point out that the direct statement is particularly important in talking to the hard-core trainee, who may not be familiar with the evasive, ambiguous language used as a matter of course by many middle-class whites.

Set the stage with this or a similar example:

A worker assigned to unload a truck is observed by his supervisor as he leans against the side of the truck and stares vacantly into the sky.

Here are some possible direct and indirect statements related to this example:

"You're really working hard, aren't you?" Indirect statement.

"I didn't know you were a student of cloud formations." Indirect.

"What do you mean by standing there staring into the sky?"
Indirect.

"I told you to unload that truck. Now get to work." Direct
statement, but a little severe.

"It makes me angry to see a good worker goofing off. You
know I'm under pressure to get this merchandise into the warehouse. I'll be back in ten minutes to see how you're doing."
Direct statement with positive overtone.

Another example:

A black worker accidentally breaks a fairly expensive tool.
Instead of reporting the accident, he hides the tool, but it is later
discovered.

The following are possible statements the supervisor might
make:

"What kind of knucklehead are you anyhow?" Indirect.

"Do you think you'll ever learn how we do things here?"
Indirect.

"Is that how you people think you'll advance yourselves?"
Indirect and insulting.

"I'm angry and disappointed that you didn't trust me enough
to tell me you accidentally broke the tool." Direct statement, but
overly critical.

"I'm angry that you felt you had to hide that broken tool. I
guess you haven't had time enough to get to trust me. Try to be
more careful from now on." Direct and appropriate.

PART V

A. *Practicing new techniques.* Distribute rulers, paper and
pencils to all participants. Have prepared in advance copies of
different drawings showing geometrical designs; one might be
similar to this:

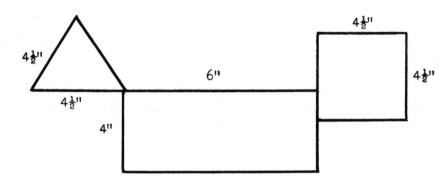

Altered combinations of this same design should be used to make up enough different drawings so that each two-man team has its own.

1. Set up a two-man demonstration situation where one man describes the drawing, which the other has not seen but which he must try to draw on the blackboard from the verbal description alone. Allow about five minutes for this.

2. Then erase the blackboard and have the man start again, this time helping him by verbal hints, or by drawing on another part of the blackboard an example of the way a line should be executed. Do not assist in completing the drawing itself. Have the class compare the results of drawings done by Method 1 and Method 2.

Set up the entire group into two-man teams. One man of each group receives a copy of a different drawing which he does not show the other. He then instructs his teammate in drawing the design, first only by describing what is on the paper, and second, by supplying additional help and details as described in Method 2 above.

After about thirty minutes of practicing this technique, initiate a general discussion. What difficulties were encountered without the extra help? With the extra help? What was the emotional reaction of participants? Did they feel frustrated? Did they get annoyed? Direct the discussion into the desirability of showing *versus* telling as the most effective way of instructing a new worker in a new job.

B. *Soliciting information.* Use the same two-man teams as above. One member decides what kind of information he wishes to solicit from the other and then informs the other as clearly and concisely as he can. For instance, he may wish to solicit all relevant data about his team member's route to work, or the floor plan of his house, including location of all furniture, or something similar. When the second man has given the requested information, the first man feeds it back with frequent questions to check his accuracy. After making suggestions to each other on how to improve techniques, the men exchange roles, and the second man solicits different information from the first.

In a group-wide discussion based on team experience, consider the problems that may arise in soliciting information from hardcore employees. Demonstrate such problems by taking the role of the white supervisor, with your assistant assuming the role of hardcore worker. First present a situation where cultural and language differences provide obstacles and there is no feedback or checking for accuracy of perceptions and responses. Then repeat the situation with feedback and checks. Rehearse this demonstration beforehand, but don't attempt it if the assistant trainer is not himself black, or feels uncomfortable in playing the role of minority worker, since an unskillful demonstration may degenerate into buffoonery.

C. *Clear writing.* Conduct a brief discussion on writing memoranda and instructions clearly and unambiguously to avoid misinterpretation. During this training session, you can only touch on this broad subject, but emphasize the problem that many hardcore workers will have when faced with written instructions.

Direct this discussion toward the realization that written instructions or memos should be read aloud to the man, with allowance for feedback and checking techniques to assure understanding. Point out that written memos and instructions are a necessary part of business and can't be avoided. But if they are used without explanation with workers who have poor reading comprehension and are unwilling to reveal their ignorance, serious misunderstandings may result.

Following is an example of a memo that might create problems of comprehension.

This Memorandum supercedes Memoranda No.'s 451-A and 451-B, as well as the earlier related Memorandum No. 228.

Regulations pertaining to procedures involving safety of personnel will apply in their totality from the point any employee enters upon the premises of this company. For purposes of this memorandum, premises is hereby defined as all those properties owned, leased or under any usage whatsoever by the company, not excluding (but not limited to) parking lots, vehicles or other transporting devices, as well as all bonded warehouses, however physically removed from company headquarters.

In addition to the mandatory use of approved safety equipment and devices in areas posted red or yellow as detailed in Memorandum 506-B and further explained and defined in Memorandum 518-C, all employees are required to exhibit behavior such as will not jeopardize either their own safety or the safety of others. Boisterous or such other behavior as is deemed inappropriate on company premises for purposes of safety will result in the taking of disciplinary measures against the offender(s).

Future amplification of this directive will be forthcoming as the need arises.

Attention is also directed to Memorandum 1189 of February 30 re: the purchase of United States Savings Bonds.

Briefly discuss the shortcomings of this example. Ask participants how they would explain the essence of this memo to a new worker in no more than two or three sentences.

D. *How to observe performance.* Most supervisors have considerable experience in observing the performance of workers. Therefore, to this segment of the training program they bring a wealth of information on how to judge whether a man is doing his job well or poorly, quickly or slowly, safely or dangerously. Normally, these more obvious aspects of the supervisorial function can be passed over in sensitivity training. Focus instead on the more subtle problems of observing performance for the purpose of interpreting attitudes, thoughts, and intentions.

Set up four-man teams. Give each man a sheet of paper on which a work situation and the attitude of the worker is described. He is to keep this information to himself. After studying his instructions each man in turn will act out his situation, which is to be interpreted by the three other members of the team.

Some examples:

1. Worker is cleaning up a lathe late in the workday. He has a stomachache and is thinking about going home where two of his children are in bed with the flu.

2. Worker is checking in a shipment. He is angry at being given this assignment which is usually done by someone with less seniority.

3. Worker is soldering wires into an electronic assembly. He thinks his supervisor dislikes him because the supervisor has not spoken to him for several days.

4. Worker is on an assembly line beside another worker whom he detests because he thinks the other worker dislikes people of his racial group.

5. Worker is trucking a casting. He is thinking about his wife, whom he suspects is interested in a man who lives down the block.

6. Worker is studying a blueprint. He does not understand what he sees but is afraid to reveal his lack of understanding because he hopes for a promotion to a better paying job.

7. Worker is shelving stock. He is considering the best way to sneak out several expensive items for his own use.

8. Worker is operating a drill press and thinking about a date he has made for that evening with a woman whose favors he believes he will obtain.

Dozens of possible situations can be developed. Make them as appropriate as possible to your company's operation.

After each sketch has been played through, the three observers are to interpret what thoughts are running through the worker's mind. What is the worker's attitude? What, if any, are his intentions in acting in a certain way? What are the observer's reasons for believing so?

Only after all speculation is exhausted should the actor reveal the actual details of the situation he presented. Then members of the group discuss the reasons for their correct or incorrect interpretations and suggest ways they might have achieved greater accuracy.

If time permits, one or two of the most successful dramatic presentations can be played before the group as a whole, with a general discussion following attempts at interpretation.

E. *Developing positive reinforcement.* This phase involves developing the ability to give praise—an ability often lacking among supervisors at all levels. Here you are seeking to train in ways of finding elements worthy of praise in ordinary work situations, and how to correct or "positively reinforce" behavior by the use of praise.

Briefly describe positive reinforcement as a means to bolster a man's regard for himself and for his job through praise of what he is doing right rather than by criticizing what he is doing wrong. Emphasize the need for this affirmative approach with hardcore workers. Demonstrate by acting out the following, or similar work-related situations, with you as the worker and your assistant as the supervisor.

1. Worker is packing fragile electronic parts. Supervisor says: "I see you're really being careful not to damage any of those parts, John. The way you're going, in another few days your production will be up to all the others."

2. Worker arrives twelve minutes late. Supervisor says: "It's tough to run this operation for even twelve minutes when a good man isn't at his place on the line."

3. Worker drops and breaks a part. Supervisor says: "All the men look up to you as one of the top workers on the shift, Tom. You worked hard to get your good name. Don't lose it by getting careless."

4. Worker has made eleven soldering mistakes which have been caught by inspection. Supervisor says: "Don, I just checked with inspection and they tell me you made eleven errors in soldering today. That's still too many, but I see that you're steadily improving. There were fourteen yesterday, weren't there? I know if you keep trying you can get the mistakes down—you have the ability to do it."

5. Warehouseman with undistinguished, average work record is stacking cartons. Supervisor says: "You know, Jim, guys like you are the backbone of the company. The boss knows he can always count on you to do a good steady job day in and day out. Keep it up."

Point out that the supervisors' statements in these situations are honest, yet each underscored positive elements of the worker's performance, usually as a direct substitute for criticism.

Using four-man teams, have the participants devise work situations where mistakes have been made and where correction is needed, using positive reinforcement as a substitute for criticism. Have these situations presented by two members of the team, while the two observers offer their suggestions for improving technique, comment on the apparent sincerity of the supervisor, and describe their perception of the worker's reaction.

Considerable time can profitably be spent on developing techniques for positive reinforcement. It is a concept some supervisors find difficult to accept and use, particularly those old-timers who have perfected the art of "chewing out" an erring worker.

All members of the group should be asked to relate actual recent experiences in which they corrected worker performance. Have them describe how they handled the situation and how they might have improved their approach. Encourage others to offer suggestions and comments.

PART VI

A. *Experiments in role-playing.* This segment of training calls for the actors to wear black and white masks. Ordinary Halloween masks painted black or white are satisfactory.

Through role-playing you attempt to train at understanding the reaction of the hardcore minority worker on a "gut level." Dramatic situations involving personality clashes, overt racial conflict, and gross misunderstandings should be developed. Rather than supplying the dramatic situations yourself, ask participants to offer examples of conflict or tension from their own experiences, especially examples that can be translated into situations involving Negroes.

In addition to a black-masked worker and a white-masked supervisor, also use "doubles." These two men stand behind each of the actors and offer comments, pointed observations, and criticisms, as if they are the subconscious voice of the actor speaking his real but normally unvoiced feelings, fears, likes, and dislikes.

The following partial example illustrates the technique. Remember in this phase of training, controlled conflict and tension is the essence of the learning experience.

A black worker on the job for about one month is fifteen minutes late. This is the fourth time he has been tardy. He lives a considerable distance from the plant and he has trouble starting his old car on cold mornings. He works at a basic assembling job which he performs a little slower than the norm but at which he has improved in a relatively short time on the job. He was recruited as part of the company's hardcore hiring program and has never had a regular job before although he is twenty-four, married, and the father of a child. The supervisor has never had a black man in his unit before, and is still uncertain what his relationship with the man should be. He is keenly aware that the company management wants the hardcore program to succeed, but he is also resentful because management seems to think "success" means simply getting the man on the job, and fails to realize the production difficulties caused the supervisor.

Supervisor:	I see from your time card that you were late again this morning, Johnson.
Supervisor's double:	*Talking to them is just a waste of breath. I don't think they listen to a word you say.*
Black worker:	Couldn't get my car started.
Black worker's double:	*The way this big shot looks at me, you'd think he smelled something bad.*
Supervisor:	All the other workers manage to get to work on time. This is the fourth time you've been late in less than a month.
Supervisor's double:	*Probably was drunk or high on dope. Or else tom-catting around all night.*

Black worker:	(Mumbles and turns his head.)
Black worker's double:	*Why the hell don't you get off my back, man. I told you the car wouldn't start. What do you want me to do, flap my arms and fly to work?*
Supervisor's double:	*Ornery bastard.*
Supervisor:	This company has gone way out of its way to hire you people. But that doesn't mean you can get away with murder here. We treat all our men the same and we expect . . . (and so on).

During the course of the dramatic situation, or after it has run to its apparent conclusion, have the actors and doubles reverse their roles, or have the white supervisor switch roles with one of the doubles. During this phase you and your assistant must function as dramatic coaches to stimulate lagging situations, and to introduce new possibilities and shift direction where necessary. To keep things rolling, you can whisper specific suggestions to the doubles. Invite members of the audience who feel they have something to offer to serve for a minute or two as doubles. Encourage participants to discuss their feelings frankly, particularly when they assume the black mask. Question them to see if they have gained a deeper understanding of the emotional reaction of black workers.

Besides on-the-job situations, set up dramatic sketches dealing with such matters as marital difficulties, financial problems, garnishments, arrest by police, discriminatory treatment in renting an apartment, buying a used car, and the like. If you know of actual situations involving hardcore workers, use them as well.

Don't shy from situations that turn on overt racist attitudes. At the same time, try to work in situations that have positive overtones, such as those described in the preceding training phase on positive reinforcement. Try to end the session on an affirmative note with a strong and forceful resolution of a difficult situation.

B. *Conclusion of the training period.* Don't strive for a general wrap-up discussion period at the conclusion of training. Save that for a follow-up meeting some time later. Instead use the last several hours as a "decompression period," with refreshments and nothing more serious on the agenda than discussion of the latest ball game. If management treats the gang to a dinner, so much the better. In any case, a period of relaxing is necessary to help smooth ruffled feathers.

C. *Follow-up to the training period.* As follow-up, schedule periodic two-hour Friday afternoon or Saturday morning sessions. Use these sessions to digest and discuss what took place during the general training sessions, as well as for such matters as the following:

1. Discussing and evaluating problems that develop during the on-the-job training of the hardcore worker.

2. Extending and perfecting the training of supervisors.

3. Increasing the sensitivity of supervisors to hardcore problems through additional role-playing exercises.

4. Giving supervisors an opportunity to blow off steam and to engage in a general information exchange on hardcore training.

A final thought about training supervisors: Some companies employ professional trainers to lead sensitivity groups for their employees; others have underwritten the cost of sending supervisors to professionally staffed training centers for sensitivity training. Both good and bad experiences have been reported as a result of these kinds of training. As in most business decisions, a careful study of the pros and cons of various training procedures is advised before choosing one. It is particularly helpful to talk with officers of a company that has undertaken extensive professional sensitivity training before committing your business to such a course.

CHAPTER SEVEN

First Days on the Job: Avoiding Early Disaster

"When I started on this job fourteen years ago," said a Pittsburgh foundry foreman, "for six months I didn't know who the top boss *was*. Nowadays the old man practically leads these new guys in by the hand. Times sure have changed."

They have indeed. Today, in most major companies engaged in hiring the hardcore unemployed, a member of top-level management makes it routine to greet new workers and personally see to it that they get settled on the job. There is good reason to do this. Such display of interest in the new worker forcefully tells supervisors, foremen, and everyone on down the line that management takes more than usual interest in seeing that the man succeeds on the job. Most important, the new worker understands that the company cares whether he succeeds. It makes a difference in how he approaches the job from the very start.

But here, too, good intentions can backfire. In one large Midwestern freezer assembly plant with a good hardcore hiring program, new workers were leaving at a high rate during their first weeks.

"Part of the reason might have been that we weren't giving the new man the right introduction to his job," said the vice president for industrial relations. "He had no feeling that the job meant anything to him or anybody else, and we weren't giving him a sense of how interested we were in his success. We were missing the boat."

The vice president hit on a way to dramatically show each new man the kind of high-powered support he had when he took his new job. When the next hardcore worker reported in, he was startled to find himself escorted along the line by a task force that included the vice president, the plant manager, the personnel officer, the new man's supervisor, and his buddy.

"Well, we realized right away this was laying it on too thick," said the v.p. a bit ruefully. "We'd gone from practically ignoring new men to all this ceremony. The other workers stood around grinning, but some of them were just plain resentful. The new man was embarrassed by all the fuss. We learned our lesson after that one time. Only one man takes a new worker down to the plant now, either me or the plant manager, and we do it without any fanfare—just hand him over to the supervisor and talk a little about the job."

To err on the side of excessive attention to a new man is not where most employers, fresh at hiring the hardcore, go wrong. Many are likely to dismiss entirely the need for a company official to walk a new employee to his job. To many it seems an awkward gesture, difficult to carry out naturally. But it is worth the effort for the positive effect it has in getting a new man started off with an advantage he would not have otherwise.

THE BUDDY'S JOB

Once company brass has publicly shown its interest in the new worker and the job he will do, it is up to the supervisor and the buddy to take over.

A buddy's duties are limited only by his imagination. As suggested in Chapter 5, they can extend beyond the job to helping a new man shop for a used car or to lending him money to tide him over till payday. His first responsibility, of course, is to teach the new man his job, and the time and degree of intensity devoted to that are regulated by the nature of the work and the trained judgment of the supervisor.

But contrary to the wishful dreams of much old-line management, the actual task performed is not always the major part of any job. A new man—any new man—has to find his way through a plant-wide network of curious new personalities, worker-job relationships, recognition of subtle degrees of rank and seniority, pecking-orders, unofficial bosses, plant traditions, taboos and codes—all peculiar to your plant, and all probably having little meaning outside it. But inside, they form a little subculture which, to the new worker from the ghetto who is on a steady job for the first time in his life, is likely to be confusing and frightening. The buddy who can steer a new man through this complex network is worth a little extra reward, and you should show him you recognize his value to the company.

One West Coast furniture factory has a gruff veteran, George, with eighteen years on the job. Since his company started a hardcore employment program, he puts in over half his time as a buddy to new men, working usually with two at the same time. To every new man he has a standard opening: "Let's have a smoke before we get started." His supervisor complains, "It seems like George is always out having a smoke with some new guy. But I'll say one thing for him—he gets through to those guys. I guess he's just got the touch."

Says George, "Hell, all I tell him is who to watch out for and how to keep his nose clean."

If it is really absorbed by the newcomer, the value of that kind of advice runs high, and it may well be more important than some of the practical aspects of being on the job which the buddy must also teach his man—the locations of the locker room, first aid kits, toolroom, stockroom, and the like.

"I give them the tour piecemeal," says George. "No sense in throwing it at them all at once. They'd only forget. Let a man get his bearings first for a couple of days and then take him on a turn around the stockroom, maybe. A little tour like that makes a nice break from the job for a new guy, too. A lot of the stuff they've got to learn just naturally falls into place. The guy gets a splinter or a blister so then show him where the first aid kit is and what's in it."

SAFETY

With other buddies and supervisors George agrees that one of the most difficult lessons to teach a new hardcore worker is to observe safety practices. "Safety's the toughest to get across. Some of these guys seem to *want* to take chances—they like the risk, I guess. But most of them just aren't used to wearing goggles, for instance, so they leave them off and sure as hell something happens. Safety is one thing I really come down hard on a guy for. Most of them, you have to *over*teach them about safety. What I do is wear my own goggles almost all the time with a new man, even when I don't really need them. Shows him how important I think they are. Another thing is safety shoes. Some guy is always complaining that these hightoppers hurt his feet. One guy just wouldn't wear them no way. He always wore those pointy black jobs and if anything would hurt I'd think those would. Anyway, he was ready to quit just because of the shoes. I went to the supervisor and got permission for him to wear just the strap-on steel toes and that worked out okay. He stayed."

In training hardcore recruits in safety, Northern Systems, Inc., a professional training service, uses facilities that are set up like production lines, and training progresses from one station to the next. At various points, trainees are exposed to a safety situation. For example, one side of a training table is colored red for danger. No attempt is made to lecture the trainees about safety. "They are just told to stand at that place," says a Northern Systems vice president. "Curiosity then gets the better of them and they want to know what it all means—a perfect psychological opening for a discussion about safety."

Safety training is approached in another way by one large electronics company. Says an executive of the firm: "Safety has got to be logically explained to this guy before he jumps into the work force. Let him know someone cares about his safety. Get mad if you want, but let him know it is for his own good. With a more negative individual, tell him it's because you don't want him to sue. He'll catch on." And he adds, "One thing, though. If you do care, you can't hide it. If you don't care, you can't hide that either."

Needless to say, a buddy not only must be proficient enough at his own work to easily teach the new worker correct and safe job procedures by example, but he must also have the patience to run through tiresome routines again and again or repeatedly offer explanations without growing annoyed.

"We only use two grades of wood in this end of the shop," says George, "but I don't expect a new man to know the difference between them right off. I just keep explaining the difference until he catches on. Then, when he's got his own job pretty well figured out, I take him around to see what the other men are doing with other kinds of wood and the laminates and plastics. Sometimes I have him help me sort scrap, and he learns something about the material that way too. Mainly, I just keep an eye peeled for chances to explain about new things that pop up, and it doesn't take long—a month or so—before he knows his way around."

LUNCHTIME

Use of materials, safety, operational details of the job—any employer expects to explain these to a new man, whatever his background. But what may come as an unwelcome surprise is the necessity to steer him through rest periods and lunch breaks as well. Yet it is during those times that a hardcore trainee, especially if he is the first or only black man in his end of the plant, may feel most keenly his "difference," his isolation from his fellow workers.

At the lunch buzzer, when the work force splits up into cliques or cribbage teams, the new worker is frequently left to eat his lunch by himself in a corner of the lunchroom. As more Negroes are employed, that corner soon becomes the "colored area," and the integrated program that management is trying to develop is undercut by a segregated lunchroom or cafeteria.

One supervisor approaches the problem directly. "I tell the buddy to include the new guy in on his group during lunch and rest periods, at least for the first week or so. After that the new man can figure out if there's anybody he wants to pal around with. Nobody's going to force him. If he wants to sit in a corner by himself, okay, that's his privilege, once he knows enough about the place to make his own choice."

It happens infrequently that other workers pointedly ostracize a new black worker from their lunch or rest breaks. Where it does come about, usually it is because one or two individuals voice veiled insults or display rudeness, and not because the entire group is hostile. The problem will correct itself if the buddy and a few other members of the group—perhaps at the urging of a supervisor—compensate for their co-workers' bias with an open show of friendliness toward the new man. Bothersome as such a situation may be, it is generally not critical, and should not occur at all if management beforehand forcefully states its equal opportunity policy and makes clear the need for all workers to comply fully as a condition of employment.

HOW LONG THE FIRST DAY?

Just about everything that happens to a hardcore worker on his first day is new to him—machines, behavior, faces, names, tools. New information crowds him on all sides. The fierce noise of a factory may be so unsettling as to disorient him completely. Nervous and uncertain as he was at the beginning of the day, by the end of eight hours on the job he may be desperately bewildered. To a man both mentally and physically unused to the new rhythm and alien pattern of a regular work day, eight hours on the job may in the end seem more like twenty-four. They may simply provide him with more new information than he can absorb. His enthusiasm of the first few hours—at landing a decent job when he thought he would never have the chance, at the visions of a good paycheck forthcoming, at the sense of pride he feels in having at last accomplished something by himself—all may have vanished in depression and weariness. Afraid that he is bound to fail anyway, he may decide it's hopeless to come back the next day.

In order to let the new man savor his early enthusiasm, and to extend it so that it reinforces his first positive feelings about the job until he has gained the confidence that comes with familiarity, some companies have established the practice of shortening the first day. The new man's first shift is cut to four hours, or perhaps even less—enough time to give him the feel of his job, some knowledge of his fellow workers and a sense of the new environment he has entered—but not so much as to overwhelm him with the realization of his own inexperience.

Even when the first day cannot practically be shortened, it can be broken up to good effect. After the new man has been on the shift for several hours, a personnel office representative can bring him to the office for the purpose of signing W2 forms or for some other reason. Or the buddy can follow the lead of George in the furniture factory and break up the day with a visit to the stockroom or shipping room or other parts of the plant important to the new worker.

One Los Angeles chemical plant, which draws increasing numbers of its workers from the black ghetto, has set up a regular four-hour first shift for all its new men. A candidate is interviewed and, if hired, given an immediate medical check. He starts work the following morning, and after lunch break reports to the personnel office where the director provides needed information or answers questions, and then he goes home. His first full shift starts on the second day. The company reports good experience in getting new men through their first few days, usually a critical period of adjustment for the hardcore individual, during which frequent job walk-offs and no-shows occur. The personnel director lays the firm's success to the policy of swift, no-nonsense interview and hiring procedures, getting the man immediately on the job, and letting him warm up to it with a half-shift his first day.

Such a practice may not be possible in some situations, but it can be adapted to most schedules. It's a practice worth trying. An executive of the chemical plant points out, "Frankly, the hardcore new man is a production minus in his early stages anyway. We don't lose a thing by starting him off on half-shifts, even if we carried it out for a couple of weeks. And if it makes things smoother for both him and us, we'd be foolish not to do it."

"THE BIG PICTURE"

One aspect of the enlightenment that has settled over business in the past decades is its realization that a worker who knows the ultimate purpose of his job is a happier man than the one whose information about his work is limited to the size of the nut he tightens and the correct wrench to use. Not many years ago it was popular to describe the effect of the assembly line process on the worker as stultifying and dehumanizing; it was said to shrink the worker's horizons so as to render him less a man. Technological advances were believed to have changed the nature of work so that a factory worker—unlike the artisans of old—was unable to see his job as part of a grand whole. Far from simply being unable to locate himself in the big picture, he was unable even to see the picture. If this is still in any part true, it is no fault of those progressive industrial relations specialists trying systematically to introduce workers to an over-all view of the working world. What they strive for is illustrated in the inspirational favorite story of after-dinner speakers: Two laborers were at work on a construction job. Asked what they were doing, one growled, "I'm laying bricks." But the other said, "I'm building a beautiful cathedral."

Not that you should attempt to infuse your employees with such high-minded sentiment. But what you must do is establish a way for supervisors to introduce hardcore workers easily and naturally to the total function of the plant and the worker's role in that function. You must introduce the new man to the big picture.

There are various ways to carry out that introduction. In a small tire-retreading plant, for example, the new man learning to operate a recapper sees the worn tires arrive by truck, sees them being unloaded, observes for himself the simple steps of their processing beyond his part of the job, and within a few hours sees his own handiwork loaded for delivery to the customer. "What's to explain?" asks the supervisor. "He's got eyes, hasn't he?"

But even in such an operation there is bound to be much that the new hardcore worker won't understand. Bear in mind that the entire world of work is foreign to him, and what seems simple and self-evident to a man who has been on the job long enough to perform it in his sleep may appear arbitrary and pointless to the new man. Even the tire-retread operation has hidden ramifications the new man may never completely comprehend if they are not fully explained. For though he can observe superficially the whole range of work performed, he still may never discover that the shop has a contract to do all recapping for, say, the Speed-Ball Transport Lines. Once he has that information, however, the sight of every Speed-Ball truck on the street will cause him to wonder if it's running on tires that have passed through his hands. On a simple but significant level, worthwhile dimension has been added to his job.

In a large electronic components assembly plant, on the other hand, relating one small specific job to the complex finished assembly may present insurmountable difficulties, further complicated in some cases by security regulations. A black ex-employee from one such plant on the San Francisco peninsula, after being trained in his job through a federal grant, quit after six months. While he didn't claim it was the sole reason for quitting, he did explain that his work seemed unrelated to anything. "I never did really know what I was doing. I mean, I was doing wiring, sure. But what they did with that wiring when I was through, I never did find out. They just came and got the basket when it was full and left me another one to fill up. I suppose I could have asked.

But I figured if they wanted me to know, they'd tell me soon enough."

It's a common attitude among hardcore workers: "If I'm supposed to know, they'll tell me." And if he is not told, he may never find out on his own.

TAKING THE TOUR

The "plant tour" for the new worker should be a routine part of the early training period. It should be carried out as soon as he has shown a grasp of the nature of his job—and this may be well before he develops competence in performing it.

First off, the new man should be shown where and how the results of his work dovetail into subsequent jobs. A foundry core-room worker, for example, would follow his cores from the oven through the dipping operation and on to casting; the man who fastens gaskets on refrigerator doors would walk along the entire line, from the sheet metal shop where the shells are fabricated through the paint booth and on to crating and shipping.

The connection between jobs on an assembly line may seem obvious, but a hardcore black or Mexican-American, uneasy in his job to begin with, may stick closely to his one corner of the plant for months, accumulating only hearsay—and totally incorrect—information on what jobs are done on other floors and behind doors he is not invited to go beyond.

All trips into the plant's far reaches should be led by a buddy or supervisor with whom the worker feels comfortable. Someone who he can ask questions and who will give him straight answers. It is not the best course for the plant manager, or other front office executive, to appear out of nowhere one morning and order the new man to follow him for "a little educational look-see" at the plant. It may prompt a flurry of industry from the men in their path, but the tour will probably be a flop for the new worker.

One supervisor takes his new men down the line at the time they draw their first checks. It's a psychologically apt time, and the supervisor realizes it.

"He's feeling like a big man, ready to celebrate. Maybe in the back of his mind he's even figuring he's got that check, that's enough, and he won't bother to come back the next day. I take him down the line, and he sees the skilled jobs and they look pretty good. I tell him those old-timers once had the same job he's got now. He sees he can move up too, even if I don't put it in so many words. Maybe that's just enough to tip the scales in favor of him staying on the job."

Shrewdly, this supervisor sees possibilities for motivation in a simple plant tour. These are possibilities which, by visiting the right part of the plant at the right time, every employer can tap to the benefit of the hardcore worker. You give him a specific goal to aspire to; it can be something no more complex than a desire to try his hand eventually with a sander or to get into piecework. You enable him to find pride in his work through seeing the uses to which it is put, and he sees where he stands among his fellow workers. It all contributes toward increasing a new worker's motivation to keep his job and do well at it.

BE FLEXIBLE

Important as it is to have a scheduled program of training for your new minority workers, it is equally important for that schedule to be flexible. The new men that come into your shop will be greatly varied in ability, capacity, and the rate at which they learn. If you insist that every one of them fit into a single training mold, the rate of failure will be discouragingly high and the program will very likely fall apart. It's hard to know what training pace will be right for a particular individual until you get to know him, and by then, undue time may already have elapsed. It is unadvisable, too, to let the new man set his own pace; without work experience he simply doesn't know what his pace is, and he may do no more than dawdle or goldbrick unless a certain degree of pressure is exerted upon him.

The trick the supervisor has to master is to recognize what *degree* of pressure to exert, and when to exert it, so as not to press the new hardcore employee beyond his ability to absorb new information—at which point he grows frustrated and dissatisfied with himself and the job. The good supervisor will recognize when that point approaches and push up to it, but not beyond. He determines each man's individual capacity, leads the man close to the limit of it, and keeps him there with steady but not undue pressure. It's not easy, but a hardcore hiring program in general is one that poses a constant series of difficult challenges, and management from the top on down must understand that that will be the case when the program is undertaken.

NO PLACE FOR THEORY

There is, fortunately, no mystery about training the hardcore employee. At bottom, his training is no different than that of any new man: he is put on the job and he learns as he works. Many companies don't even call it "training," referring instead to that early learning period as "probation," or a "breaking-in period." Training, in the sense of an instructor pedantically teaching a student, may never enter the picture. The word itself, along with such terms as "teacher" or "instructor," might well be avoided with the hardcore individual because of its tendency to arouse unpleasant memories of dismal school days. Eliminate or minimize the book-learning aspects in the early days on the job and the chances of a new employee's success are better.

To most jobs the hardcore worker will bring a virtually complete absence of skills. The training period, which no longer is a simple, traditional breaking-in period, starts from scratch. It may be almost literally a matter of showing the new man what foot to put where, and what hand to place on which switch or tool, when to place it there, and exactly how to move it. Take nothing for granted; show how everything must be done, but do it without condescension or impatience.

In its earliest aspects, training should be tied in directly with the tasks the new worker will perform. Whatever he is expected to learn, he must indeed actually perform, with each lesson dovetailing directly into the work he does. This may seem self-evident, but the fact is that some supervisors, having shown a worker the initial aspects of his job, then give verbal instructions on what to do next. Also, it is not enough for the worker to warm up on work which is "just like" his regular task. The concept of the athletic field, that duck-walking or push-ups better fit a man to play football, should not carry over here. Let the man do precisely what he is supposed to do, and walk him through the job from the beginning.

On an assembly line, for example, a new worker may be expected to perform several functions. His job may consist of several components: securing a hinge, fastening a gasket over the hinge, and then turning the part so it reaches the next man in a work-ready position. To the new worker this sequence, simple as it may seem in the telling, can be confusing in practice, especially on a moving line. The supervisor may find it advisable to adjust the worker's task so that he need master only one part of his job before going on to carry out the second and third as well.

Such an adjustment, of course, results in a lessened workload for the new man. But where it definitely facilitates training, it should be seriously considered. If the reduced productivity of the new worker promises to run for a period of several months, supervision should make extended plans accordingly, so that the sudden press of production needs does not push the new man beyond his capabilities.

THE BUDDY TAKES HOLD

At this stage of the game, with the new worker fumbling to get acquainted with his job, it's a toss-up as to who is more important, the supervisor or the buddy.

As George, the old-timer at the furniture factory illustrates, it's the buddy who really indoctrinates the new worker into the everyday mysteries of his job and the shop. The buddy is the modern counterpart of the trusted veteran of a thousand factories of years gone by, to whom each new man used to be turned over by the foreman with no more instruction than, "Show this new guy the ropes."

But today's buddy differs from yesterday's strawboss. He is a good deal more sensitive to what you are trying to accomplish with your hardcore hiring program, and he devotes a lot more time to detailed job instruction. Undoubtedly, his patience is greater than that of the hardbitten old-timer who unofficially ran his corner of the shop with an iron hand.

And patience he needs in good supply. He may have to repeat his instruction of the most simple aspects of the job, and he must do it without irritation or annoyance. It's not always easy. As a foreman in the shipping room of a large Oakland mail-order firm said, "You start to think some of these new guys won't ever catch on, but most do. If they don't it's usually because they don't want to, not because they can't. We give every new man a buddy for the first month. They work together, not just side by side, but with the new man acting as helper. Then after that first month the buddy spends another month working somewhere close to the new man, to answer his questions and keep an eye on him generally. By that time they've run through most of the packing problems they're likely to find—our work isn't all that complicated. Most new men coming in think there's nothing to it—wrapping and packing doesn't look like it takes any skill. But even so, there's a right way and a wrong way to go about it. If we start the new man out right—and that's what the buddy is for—we won't have problems later on."

BLIND SPOTS

Among the problems that can crop up in the early stage of training is the new man's attempt to bluff his way over job difficulties. Most often this arises when he doesn't understand what he's doing and is ashamed to admit his ignorance, since the job has been explained to him several times already, probably with increased impatience each time. If the buddy is not uncommonly alert, the new worker can develop a blind spot that will continue to plague him and in all likelihood lead to later problems.

Such a situation developed in the paint shop of a large appliance manufacturer, where the metal shells for dishwashing machines were cleaned with tack cloths before priming. A new hardcore worker employed as a tacker apparently understood well enough what he was to do—clean the shells just before they entered the paint booth. But a problem developed, in that the primer was not taking evenly on the shells he prepared, causing a variation in color on the finished shells. Upon investigation, it was seen that the tacker, while he appeared to grasp the nature of his work as explained by his buddy, had not in fact recognized that he had been shown a definite, top-to-bottom pattern with which to wipe the shell, a pattern that assured the metal would be completely cleaned. He was attacking the shells haphazardly. Once the need for strict observance to the pattern of wiping was set forth, the new man had no further difficulties.

POSITIVE REINFORCEMENT

In every step of job training it's necessary that the worker be "positively reinforced" in the learning process (see Chapter 6). As explained earlier, about all this means is that the buddy or supervisor find something to praise even as he raises the question of improving some aspect of the worker's performance. It is the opposite from the old strawboss method of profanely chewing-out a new man over a botched job until the offender was cringing in a corner.

Emphasize what he's doing right, praise him for that, and only then move on to whatever needs correction. It's a simple enough matter, but it goes against the grain of many a veteran who is so familiar with his job that he has only disdain for the new man who has trouble learning the ropes.

One way of applying such positive reinforcement is to refer the mistake or oversight to the job, not the man. That is, rather than criticizing the new worker—"Hey, you didn't buff the bottom of this block," you say instead, "Here's a spot the buffer didn't pick up." At the same time point out that all the other surfaces of the block are adequately buffed and stand as a shining example of what the finished job should look like. At the very least this diplomatic procedure allows the new worker, whose self-esteem in regard to the job is at low ebb for the first weeks, to save face. It reduces the necessity for him to stammer out excuses for his ignorance that only further deepen his sense of inadequacy and do nothing to advance the training process.

Indeed, with a little practice, it is an easy matter to find reason to praise or to comment favorably upon whatever it is that a new man is doing right, however little that may be. By traditional shop standards the fact that a man can recognize a crescent from a box wrench is no great shakes, but to a man who first handled either only two days before, it can be a source of pride that will bolster his spirits for hours if his buddy tells him, "You've really caught on to the tools, and that's an important part of the job. Keep up the good work."

TEACHING BY OBSERVATION

On its own, the new man's natural curiosity will likely lead him to observe how others carry out jobs similar to his. But the process can be encouraged and hastened. You can make certain the new man works in proximity to others so as to force his close observation of their techniques. And, like the supervisor who shows the new man around the plant on his first payday, you can make an effort to see that your new worker observes older workers with good jobs that he can reasonably aspire to.

Co-workers can either help or hinder the new man. His progress depends to some degree on informal learning processes— learning absorbed by association with friendly co-workers. Where it does not interfere with their own duties, older workers should be encouraged to give the new man a hand; they can be asked to keep an eye on his work, to answer his questions, to volunteer explanations of what they're doing. At times when a new man's buddy is absent, a trusted older worker should be asked to fill in.

END OF THE FIRST DAY

If he's the "typical" hardcore employee putting in his first day's work, the new man will probably finish his first shift with a great sense of relief at finally being cut loose from the confusion of his unfamiliar work. When he makes his dash for the time clock, the supervisor should make an effort to be at his side to recap in a sentence or two an evaluation of the day's work. "Well, you got through your first day—it'll be clear sailing from now on," or some such reassurance that he can take home with him and use as a rationale for his return to work a second day.

This can be a time, too, when a representative from the personnel office—perhaps the interviewer who hired him, or someone he has met before—can make a point of being on hand to ask him how things are going, inquire if he has any questions, and to pointedly comment, "See you in the morning."

In fact this stress on "seeing him in the morning" is something both supervisor and buddy should also make a point of. Of all the problems encountered with new hardcore employees, the most persistent is the worrisome matter of tardiness (see Chapter 8). If it is handled in the traditional way—a series of warnings leading to the dismissal of the offending employee—a company's hardcore hiring program will run into rough sledding very early. Other methods to prevent the problem from arising must be tried, and some of them may seem rather primitive or unsophisticated—such as having the new man's fellow workers constantly reminding him to come to work on time—but the fact is that such methods do have an effect.

According to the industrial relations officer of a large auto company in Detroit, whose hardcore hiring program was one of the first undertaken by a major employer, the matter of getting a man to come to work on time deserves concentrated attention. His company goes to the lengths of having the buddy call the new man if he isn't in on time. On occasion, if the new man doesn't show up, the buddy is authorized to drive to his house and drag him out of bed.

OTHER WORKERS

During the first day—and throughout the entire early period of the new worker's training—supervisors and buddies must be alert to the attitudes of other workers. If a pocket of resistance to the new man's presence is developing despite earlier explanations of the company's program, it must be dealt with immediately.

Such resistance, or reluctance, to accept the new man can develop not only as a result of outright racial prejudice. It can come about because of the veteran worker's natural reluctance to accept any new man into their social circle until he has proved himself. Or it can result from workers unconsciously viewing employment of new men as a threat to their own jobs.

In either case, fears are not likely to be freely and openly expressed, and a supervisor must evaluate the situation in light of his experience with the men, what he has learned about them, and what he observes in their relationship to the new man. In this way he must decide the nature of the resistance he faces, and must choose appropriate measures to counter it.

His job is not necessarily as difficult as it first may seem—or as it would have been ten or twenty years ago when racial discrimination was more stubbornly entrenched than it is today. In most shops now, outright racial bigotry will no longer be openly encountered. The educational effect of antidiscrimination laws and the impact of civil rights measures have made themselves felt. The feared situation of a worker angrily walking off the job rather than work next to a Negro is seldom found. It is far more likely that discrimination will be subtly veiled, often half-couched as a joke. "Now that we've started hiring *them*, I suppose it won't be long before they'll be running the place."

Here is where the strong stand originally taken by management can again prove its value. The supervisor or foreman or buddy to whom such a remark is addressed or who overhears it can point to the company's policy statement. He should restate that position in his own words, to the effect that "this is what the president has ordered. It doesn't mean anybody will be laid off or lose his job. Everybody is going to get a square deal. It's a policy the company has to follow according to the law if it wants to keep its contracts. And if we lose our contracts, you know what that means to everybody's job. So don't make any trouble."

Supervision on all levels must strongly reflect management's views on the new hiring program. This is one area where the foreman or other supervisory help cannot be one of the boys and side with the griping worker. For example, the foreman who says, "I agree with you, fellows, but let's go along with the company and see if it works," is leaving himself dangerously open to the charge that he is unwittingly abetting the sabotage of the program. Even if in his heart he does agree with the voiced discontent, he must keep his sentiments to himself and never let his mistaken beliefs in any way influence his treatment of the new men. His job is to interpret company policy on the working level, and management should make certain he is committed to carrying out that responsibility without hedging.

CHAPTER EIGHT

Some Common Problems

"A year ago I was bored with my job," a young white plant executive recently told an interviewer. "I was ready to change jobs, get into something else. Now we've got this hardcore program going. It's a hell of a lot of work, and there's always one problem or another. But, you know something? It's exciting. I wouldn't quit now."

This young executive is not alone. The National Association of Manufacturers reports: "Increasingly, company personnel working directly with the hardcore are becoming turned on. Despite their initial feelings of apprehension concerning their involvement in this new venture, they have gotten caught up with its challenge."

At times the scope of the challenge is awesome. "One thing I never thought I'd be doing," said the young executive, "is helping people practically restructure the way they live. But that's what it amounts to when you have to advise them about bus schedules, fighting off finance companies, getting their gas and electricity turned back on, helping them stay out of jail, or how to buy furniture on credit without getting cheated. I never realized the kinds of problems other people have."

INDEPENDENT OPERATORS

The hardcore unemployed individual brings his problems with him when he comes on the job. He is venturing into a foreign environment and the psychological pressures on him are immense. Because he is away from his more comfortable surroundings and usual base of operation, he may be defensive, fearful that he will be subject to ridicule. He doesn't know the "right things" to do.

"From the beginning of their employment," observes the NAM, "many hardcore persons need help in their attempts to overcome long-time patterns of resistance to authority, ignoring clock time and, in general, functioning as independent operators with no sense of how their behavior affects others."

Independent operation may well be an asset in the ghetto where a man often looks out only for his own. Properly channeled, that same independence can be an asset on the job. However, nearly every work environment requires the man to function as part of a team; as such he must observe such elementary requirements as getting to the job on time.

Strict promptness—a sign of moral excellence to most middle-class Americans—generally has little point or purpose in the ghetto, and the new employee may be genuinely bewildered by what seems to him a fanatical concern with time and time clocks. "What difference does a few minutes make" asks the new employee, who has probably never owned an alarm clock, "if the job gets done eventually?"

A company must be prepared with procedures and incentives to modify that attitude, and it is not always easy to arrive at totally effective ones. But in dealing with the never-ending problem of tardiness and absenteeism, there are a number of approaches that some companies have found beneficial, and they can be helpful to others embarking on a hardcore program.

TARDINESS AND ABSENTEEISM

First of all, it is necessary to realize that the new man simply may not "gear in" to the work cycle as easily as people with some knowledge of the working world. This is a problem that may straighten itself out as the man gets accustomed to such new routines as rising earlier than he ever has before, and learns to allow time for getting dressed, having breakfast, and catching the right bus. But it may take time before he gets caught up in the rhythm of that cycle. Then too, the new man may simply be below par physically. If an inadequate diet and irregular hours have taken their toll, the job may be too much for him at first, and it will take a few months for him to get into shape.

Give the new man sufficient time to adjust, but stay on top of the situation right from the beginning. If he is doing anything at all right, he should be praised, so as to reinforce that correct behavior. When the chronically late worker does arrive on time, the supervisor should comment positively: "Glad to see you made it on time. Let's see if you can keep it up for the rest of the week." If it is the morning after payday, when absenteeism triples in some plants, the supervisor should be especially full of praise.

At times the supervisor or buddy may be able to structure the tardiness problem into a situation of self-competition. "You were late only twice last week. Let's see if you can improve on that this week, okay?" In the hands of an understanding supervisor, this simple device may encourage the new man to beat his "record."

Another approach is described by George of the furniture

factory mentioned earlier. "Sure, coming in late or not showing up at all is a real problem with some of these guys. Not all, but some. When that happens, I tell the guy straight out, 'Look, every one of us here has a certain amount of work we've got to put out every day. When you're not here, we've got to put out your work, too. All you do by coming in late is screw up me and the other guys in the section. You ain't putting anything over on the boss—he'll just have to fire you if it happens too often.' Most of them get the idea. I mean, we're not necessarily one big happy family here, but most guys don't want to foul up the men they work with."

This same approach of "don't let us down, we're counting on you," is used to good effect by one of the big automobile plants, which has an extensive and successful hardcore hiring program. One of the plant supervisors says, "If a guy doesn't show up for work, you tell him his friends are going to get after him for letting them down. That's the kind of thing that works." And an executive of Eli Lilly and Company underscores this feeling between workers when he says that many hardcore employees "had a strong desire to establish social relationships at work; if not, absenteeism became high."

At another plant, when one of the new hardcore workers misses the whistle for his shift, a member of a special "buddy committee" is delegated to drive to his home, roll him out of bed, see that he gets his pants on, pour a cup of coffee into him, and drive him back to work. After this has happened once or twice, the message gets through to the new man: His presence is needed on the job, on time and regularly.

Problems of tardiness or absence can stem from ingrained attitudes of the new worker, or they may arise from external causes. Usually these external causes are easier to deal with than, say, fighting a new man's resistance to using an alarm clock.

A long bus ride, with the worker at the mercy of the transit company's ability to hit all transfer points at the correct time, is one difficulty many hardcore workers experience. In fact, companies have found that many problems regarding promptness revolve around buses and bus schedules. One supervisor tells of a new man who was late for the first few days. It developed that he couldn't read well enough to decipher the bus signs. He was ashamed to confess his inability, and it took him several mornings of riding over half the city before he learned the route. After that, he was on time.

Another cause for lateness or absence is the unreliable, secondhand car. One company executive tells of an instance in which the battered car of a new man broke down soon after he was hired. "This man lived many miles from the plant and had no recourse to either public transportation or a car pool. So he proceeded to hitch-hike back and forth to work, adding several hours to the job—portal to portal. But he hung on, determined to keep his job."

Transportation can be such a problem that it overrides all others. Recognizing this, the Urban Coalition in Los Angeles designed a program aimed at easing the transportation crisis of the hardcore unemployed by supplying low-interest financing and insurance for used cars so the new worker could more easily reach his job.

Solutions to purely external problems such as transportation have been well worked over by many companies, since they frequently occur with employees other than hardcore. As described earlier (see Chapter 2), when a company has such procedures available, they should be made clear to the prospect during the first recruitment contact, since he is likely to have unspoken apprehensions about the apparently simple matter of getting to and from the plant. Nearly every company will have well-established car pools; some of these can be tapped. A buddy can be pressed into temporary service for a week or two to pick up the new man. Bus routes and schedules can be explained; and in those cases where needed, bus tickets can be supplied.

On this latter point, one plant manager points out, "For a couple of hundred bucks a company can buy a hell of a lot of bus tickets," and it is a negligible investment if it helps the new hardcore worker form the habit of getting to work regularly and on time.

"DOESN'T QUITE FIT IN"

Time and again a plant representative, when asked how an individual new hardcore employee is working out, will say, "He seems to be doing okay," then pause and add, "but he doesn't quite fit in yet."

The problem of new workers "fitting in" is one which causes unnecessary anxiety to many employers to such an extent in some cases that it forms a barrier to a successful hardcore program. This can happen when the employer has in mind a fixed standard of adaptability and social behavior that he expects all his employees to meet. It need not be a systematized or wholly conscious standard—in fact it seldom is either—but is more a series of middle-class expectations so ingrained in most of us that they are observed without ever being articulated.

In order to fit in, an employee has to get along well with his fellow workers—just how well varies according to the unspoken standard. Generally this means entering easily into the give and take of the group, easily making small talk, exchanging friendly insults, pairing off with lunch companions, quickly finding one's level among co-workers and developing relationships with one's fellows that, although they may never extend beyond the working day, do serve to contribute to over-all work force morale.

These adjustments take place when a man feels that at least a small part of his identity stems from his membership in a particular group. In twentieth-century America, with its rigorous work ethic, a man tends to be identified by the work he does; it puts a convenient tag on him; and most of us, having grown up accepting that tradition, are comfortable with that tag.

Not so for many of the hardcore unemployed who are new to both tradition and job. Unlike other segments of the population, jobs and work are not central to their lives. They don't "plan careers" or talk about work generally. In *Tally's Corner*, Elliot Liebow comments on this phenomenon:

> One reason for the relative absence of talk about one's job is . . . that the sameness of job experiences does not bear reiteration. Another and more important reason is the emptiness of the job experience itself. The man sees middle-class occupations as a primary source of prestige, pride and self-respect; his own job affords him none of these. To think about his job is to see himself as others see him, to remind him of just where he stands in this society. And because society's criteria for placement are generally the same as his own, to talk about his job can trigger a flush of shame and a deep, almost physical ache to change places with someone, almost anyone else. The desire to be a person in his own right, to be noticed by the world he lives in, is shared by each of the men on the street corner.

Under the pressures of this kind of background, the new hardcore employee may make no effort to fit in. He doesn't so much go to the job as let the job come to him. To supervisors and other employees he may appear stand-offish, aloof, even sullen. He may be uncommunicative, failing to answer with more than a grunt when spoken to. He steers clear of other workers at lunch and, fearing that the friendship he desires will be denied him anyway, rudely rebuffs attempts at drawing him into on-the-job relationships.

The upshot of such behavior is that the new man soon manages to isolate himself. If other workers have attempted to be friendly, they soon cease their overtures. The new man retreats further into his cocoon of silence; eventually he leaves the job. A few workers may remember him as "that unfriendly Negro kid who worked here for two or three weeks."

The unfortunate fact of the matter may be that the new man is not unfriendly at all. But he has come to the job with the preconceptions and ingrained mistrust that characterize so many residents of the ghetto, and without massive support he is unable to overcome his fears.

After all, he has been thrust into a totally new environment, one which in its unfamiliarity he may well perceive as alien and hostile, no matter how hard the employer works to provide a friendly atmosphere. Over a period of time his attitude will soften and change, but he may be gone before time can work its alterations.

"A lot of these guys come on the job suspicious, mistrustful," said one plant manager. "They keep watching and waiting to see where the catch is—or, as one of them told me, 'I'm just waiting to see if you're trying to run a game on me.' Well, when they get their feet wet most of them come around. They may still not be the friendliest group in the world, but as long as they do the work, so what? At least they lose some of that defensiveness and stop watching you as if you're planning to turn them over to the cops. What it takes mostly is for the supervisor to show a little understanding. He can't be blowing up at the new men just because they don't answer right when spoken to, or if they don't take orders as well as older guys. Sure, you have to draw the line somewhere, and my foremen do. If the guy is such an oddball misfit that his nastiness gets in the way of doing the job, then he isn't going to last. I mean, a guy can be fairly unpleasant and still keep his job here—but not if the unpleasantness interferes with getting the work out."

TAKING ORDERS

One aspect of the "hardcore attitude" may show itself in the way the new man takes orders or instructions. Given an order, he may curtly nod his head, leaving the supervisor with the impression that his instructions have been understood. Later, when the job remains undone, the exasperated supervisor may lay it to outright insubordination on the part of the new man. He may fail to realize that his instruction simply was not understood in the first place, and the new man refused to reveal his deficiencies by admitting he did not understand or by asking for clarification.

Says George, "I've had new men who wouldn't admit on a bet that they didn't know what the hell I was talking about. They'd nod and then go off and fumble around, pretending they knew what they were supposed to be doing. Then everything would get all balled up if I didn't bail them out in time. I've gotten so I don't take anything for granted, no matter how much they claim they know what they're doing. At least not until I see with my own eyes. I remember one guy, a cocky little fellow, who told me he'd learned all about machines in shop training classes. Well, he couldn't even find the switch on the lathe. But I didn't see any point in rubbing it in. I just told him this was a new model lathe and he'd probably never seen one like it before. I said it had to be operated differently from the ones he was used to. We trained him on it the same way as all the others.

Eventually he worked out okay, although he's still more sure of himself than he has any right to be."

Reluctance to admit ignorance may extend to problems of language, too. A newly hired clerk at a St. Louis company told her supervisor she was quitting because the work "bored" her. Considerably irked, her supervisor was ready to let her go—until he found out that what she really meant was that the work "perplexed" her.

Many a young hardcore man, say supervisors, seem to have the notion that orders, any orders, are given expressly to humiliate him. To accept them without a show of manliness through a little fearless backtalk would be a sign of spineless subservience. If he comes to the job, as so many do, from straight off the ghetto streets, his only previous experience in taking orders from whites in authority will have been from policemen on the street, or in school from teachers, and from that unpalatable experience he dropped out at the first opportunity. In either case, the contact has been unpleasant. Now to establish his imperviousness to that authority he may assume an attitude of nonchalance or scorn. Given sufficient boldness or daring, he may try his hand at manipulation, testing to see how far he can stretch his independence.

In any case, it is uncomfortable for a supervisor. His hard-won authority is always either in question or taken lightly. But fortunately the worker's attitude is generally not permanent, and the supervisor or foreman gains the respect of the hardcore employee in essentially the same way he earns it from other workers: by keeping a cool head in trying circumstances and by consistent fairness in his demands on all workers.

"The greatest asset to motivating the hardcore," says a Honeywell, Inc., employment guide, "is to make him feel he belongs and is getting fair and just treatment." The guide goes on to instruct supervisors "Once he accepts you the battle is half won . . . Be there to help when he needs you, at least until he has adjusted to the world of work. This can take ninety days or six months, but with cooperation from line supervisors, his fellow employees, and the counselor, the chances for success are great."

PERSONAL PROBLEMS

A nineteen-year-old ninth-grade dropout was hired and put to work as an assembler on a household appliances production line. Since the work was fairly simple, involving only the selection and fitting of three parts, supervision was not close. The young man did badly from the very start. This was puzzling to the supervisor, since the worker was obviously dexterous enough for the task, which demanded only that he identify three similar fittings marked by different code numbers, assemble them and pass them on to the next worker. By the end of the first week the worker had fallen so far behind and caused such a slowdown of the line that the leadman asked the supervisor to take him off. Instead, the supervisor assigned a buddy to work closely with the new man. A few hours later when the foreman passed out the payroll checks for that week, the buddy approached the foreman. "I know what's wrong with your new man," he said. "He can't see worth a damn. He tried to read his payroll check upside down and six inches from his face."

It turned out that the young man did indeed have very poor eyesight, but since he scarcely ever read, he had not been forced to use glasses. On the job he was unable to distinguish the code numbers on the fittings and had to sort them out by trial and error. The supervisor had the personnel office call the company physician who made an appointment for the worker with an optometrist.

Physical impairment, such as defective vision, is only one kind of problem the hardcore worker may present. Since he comes to the job with a different social and economic foundation than most other workers, he also brings a different set of personal problems. In a study of its hardcore personnel, Kaiser Steel Corporation's Fontana, California plant set forth some of the needs—beyond the job alone—for the new worker. "He often needs personal help—to keep him out of jail, to get a tow for his broken-down car, to get his kids to a hospital, to get him a ride to work, to get his utilities turned on, to keep the finance company off his back. It may be several months before he gets on his feet."

Whatever the nature of the problem the company will usually have to get involved in it somewhere along the line. For workers with relatively minor problems such help can come from the supervisor or buddy. Frequently, a little sound advice, based on a realistic knowledge of the world of commerce, is all that is required to straighten out a situation.

Discipline—or the threat of it—sometimes may be required to correct a personal problem (see Chapter 10). One large New York manufacturer of steam generators found that the number of garnishments for Negroes consistently ran higher than for whites and developed a strict policy for dealing with the problem. When garnished, the employee is told that "the company expects employees to stay out of debt. An offer is made to help him budget his income, and he is warned that he will receive a three-day suspension for the next garnishment, and be discharged for the third. The number of garnishments has dropped sharply since this policy was inaugurated." It is noteworthy that not only does this company offer counseling to the debt-ridden worker, but it has sought to alleviate the problem that leads to excessive garnishment by directly writing to stores notorious for their easy credit and telling them to make their own collections.

In serious cases management often has knowledge which the employee does not have that enables it to refer the worker to an appropriate source for help. In one plant, for example, a hard-core employee reported to work drunk. He was reprimanded. The following week he again came in drunk. The company gave him an ultimatum: get help or be fired. He chose to get help. The company referred him to a clinic where he received sufficient help so his drinking was no longer a problem on the job.

At Control Data Corporation's Minneapolis plant, one woman was warned about her excessive absences. Then a counselor discovered she was staying home to care for a small son who had an acute bronchial lung ailment. The counselor quickly found a community agency only two blocks from her home which provided twenty-four-hour-a-day assistance for her son.

Many companies now routinely refer a worker with recurring problems to an appropriate social agency. Then, if his problem is sufficiently grave so that his employment must be terminated, at least the agency can continue working with him.

ACCEPTANCE BY OTHER WORKERS

No matter who the new employee may be, there is frequently another older worker ready to give him a hard time. By reason of his experience on the job he feels superior to the new man and has no patience with his ignorance, pointedly ignores him, or in other subtle ways may reveal a fear of the man's threat to his own job security. When the new worker is black, and when he is one of the hardcore to boot, the problem is greatly compounded. No matter how clearly management explains its policies about such harassment, small covert actions on the part of employees who are basically unsympathetic to the new man may yet crop up (see Chapter 9).

Whatever the problem, it must be dealt with forcibly and immediately. In the shipping warehouse of a building materials plant two employees were hunting for a knife to cut the rope binding a crate. An old-timer called to them, "Ask Jimmy (a new black hardcore employee who was standing nearby) if you can use his razor." When Jimmy indignantly replied that he didn't have a razor, the man said, "I thought all you boys carried straight-edged razors." The foreman at once called the older worker aside and told him such behavior wouldn't be tolerated and if anything similar happened again he was duty-bound to report it to the manager. The older worker grumbled a bit, but did call over to the new worker, "No offense meant, kid," and the matter was settled within minutes.

THE FREEZE

What happens if other employees do not overtly discriminate against the new black employee but do not talk to him, offer him help or advice, or associate with him in any way?

Facing such an employee "freeze" or silent treatment, a new worker may soon grow disheartened and leave the job. Even if he continues to work despite the treatment, it is going to be tougher for him to make the grade, since he will have little chance to learn informally, by observation and casual contact with other workers—so necessary an adjunct to the more formal means of job training.

In this situation the buddy is of inestimable value. Frequently, in the new man's early days on the job, the buddy may well be the only employee who will go out of his way to talk to the new man. Much depends on how he handles his assignment. If he is relaxed and easy in his association with the new man, the other workers will soon pick it up and come around in their behavior too (see Chapter 7).

George, the "professional buddy" at the furniture factory, expresses a realistic view of the problem. "You can't force anybody to like every new guy that comes in. Hell, some of them aren't very lovable. But you have to at least treat them like human beings. Me, I treat everybody pretty much like I'd want to be treated. With some of the new guys, I go out of my way to make them feel at home. I try to get them into situations where they have to talk to the other men as part of the job—and the other men have to talk to them. Things just naturally take their course after that. We've had one or two cases where the new guy was getting the silent treatment—maybe it was his own fault for coming on too strong. But the supervisors got me and three or four of the old-timers aside at lunch and said, 'Listen, I want you fellows to give that new guy a hand whenever you can for the rest of this week. Go out of your way to help him get the feel of the place.' So we've never had any problems we weren't able to straighten out. But, hell, yes, it takes a little effort sometimes."

To avoid formation of racial cliques, management can also take such steps as assigning lockers in the worker's dressing room so that solid white and solid black sections do not become accepted as traditional.

SLIPS OF THE TONGUE

Troublesome to many people are the "innocent" slips of the tongue or the use of vaguely racist terms and expressions that are built into the very language. They sometimes require considerable effort to avoid in normal speech. Even when uttered without malice they nonetheless possess the power to wound.

For example, if a white worker says, "I'm free, white and twenty-one" any Negro worker within earshot is instantly on guard.

Many persons who would never use the word "nigger," still find themselves using expressions such as, "That's mighty white of you," or referring to blacks as "colored boys." And invariably the one Indian in a shop is called "Chief," the Mexican-American, "Pancho." However kindly the intentions of the speaker, used in this blanket fashion the terms are about as flattering as if Anglo workers were consistently addressed as "kraut," or "dago."

While many of these terms and phrases may never find their way wholly out of the language, their frequency of use grows less as people are made aware of how loaded they are. In work situations their use may not always constitute the kind of problem that has to be dealt with by the supervisor. A certain degree of this rough word-play is often accepted by many workers. But if the unconscious use of such terms occurs repeatedly and threatens to rupture working relationships, a supervisor is well advised to privately inform the speaker that his language is questionable, and point out the words that are best avoided.

THE PRACTICAL JOKER

Being subjected to mild hazing, or serving as the unwitting butt of a little practical joke, is part of the unofficial initiation rites in many plants. The relative ignorance of the working world shown by hardcore unemployed persons will be a temptation that some plant jokers will find hard to resist.

For most new white workers, being sent on the double to the tool room to fetch a "widget-stretcher" may be harmless enough, and the supervisor generally will turn his head if the prank is not too disruptive. But the hardcore unemployed who has to undergo such jokes will feel very keenly the advantage being taken of his ignorance and inexperience. His self-regard is feeble enough without making him the object of a crew's laughter. It can only serve to undermine his chances of success on the job. With a considerable financial and corporate stake in seeing that the new man does succeed, company management cannot afford to permit him to serve as entertainment for other workers, even when it may all seem to be carried out in the spirit of good clean fun.

Here, too, the buddy, being wise to the underground ways of the shop, can be helpful. At the very start, he should be instructed to help the new man steer clear of the jokers. In some case a word to the joker with the most irrepressible sense of humor, asking—or warning—him to "take it easy on the new guy—he's got enough problems," would be in order.

HEADING OFF PROBLEMS

Some problems of the hardcore worker that are likely to come to attention on the job will "telegraph" their arrival. That is, the supervisor or foreman who is at all attuned to the wavelength of his general work force will see the problems as they approach. Often he can head them off before they become full blown and demand emergency attention. Sometimes it requires almost a sixth sense to pick out danger signs. In one such instance, a new black trainee was assigned to work with a journeyman. It was the first time the older man had anyone in his charge, and he was not happy about it. Privately, he kept telling the new man that he was too slow, that he "would never make it on this job at the rate you're going," and other variations on the same negative theme. The supervisor was not aware of these comments, but he was suspicious of the failing performance of the new man.

On several occasions he talked to him informally, and gradually led him to reveal that the older man was undercutting his work, and that he planned to quit on the following payday. The supervisor at once reassigned the new man to help another worker, and the offending journeyman was kept clear of trainees from then on.

Other aspects of a similar problem may arise. A new worker may be plainly confused about his task, even though his pride refuses to let him admit he needs still further guidance. He should be steered into a different job, or the requirements of the first job reduced so that he can handle it. If this is not done, the new man's capacities will be overtaxed and his resulting unhappiness can manifest itself in various ways disruptive to production. Before the problem reaches that stage, the observant supervisor will make an appropriate shift. Sometimes this can be temporary, with the man returning to his first job after he has gained confidence by mastering the second.

A company has an additional jump on heading off problems of the hardcore unemployed when members of the management team or personnel staff are themselves Negro. As Honeywell, Inc., points out in its guide to the hiring of hardcore persons: The black personnel staffer knows "the problems of the hardcore and can help to erase . . . suspicion . . . [he] can explain puzzling behavior and have a significant value in countering the critics of the company, and can help his own ethnic group understand their often contradictory impulses."

FALSE STARTS IN TRAINING

In the training of the hardcore there are likely to be several false starts. A worker who shows himself dismally incapable of performing the first, or the second, or the third task assigned him may come through brilliantly on the fourth; and having thus caught on, he may find it then possible to learn the once seemingly incomprehensible demands of previous jobs.

As George points out, "I've had men who couldn't seem to get anything through their heads for the first couple of weeks. We'd keep shifting them around, and then all of a sudden they blossom, and there's no more problem teaching them what to do. It takes some guys longer to just absorb things—not the actual learning of a job, but just getting used to the way we operate around here.

It is this "gearing in" to the work process, discussed earlier in this chapter, that often takes time to show itself. It also takes the skill of a good supervisor to lead a new hardcore worker to the point where he is comfortable in the work setting. But thousands of supervisors have done it—and are doing it—and in so doing are guiding their new men to productive careers from which they derive a new sense of dignity and self-worth.

CHAPTER NINE

Keeping Your Program
on the Move

Once the new man has settled down and learned enough about his job so that he does not adversely affect production, many employers would tend to give thanks and let well enough alone. Why ask for trouble by pushing the man along? Yet this push is exactly what's called for if the hardcore program is to result in anything more than putting a few black workers into entry-level jobs and leaving them there, where they will soon show their dissatisfaction with their lack of progress. Stagnation, whether of employee or employer, must not be allowed to set in at any stage of the training process. As the vice president of Eli Lilly has pointed out, there must be "upward movement" of the trainee if he is to remain sufficiently motivated to stick with the job.

Fortunately, the intermediate stages of a new man's training are relatively painless, at least in comparison to his early days. First of all, the worker has survived the crucial transitional period of his first few months in a work environment. He has become acclimatized. He knows his way around. He has learned the details of the job. He has gained at least a modicum of confidence, knowing that he will be treated fairly. Perhaps he has shown all the markings of an excellent worker. Or he may be no more than average, even below average, but still able to do the job.

201

Whatever degree of promise he shows, he has at the very least managed to make some sort of acceptable adjustment to the job—no small achievement in itself—and you may reasonably wish to congratulate yourself. But you must also be aware that the responsibilities of a hardcore hiring program do not end at this point. The mere existence of beginner's jobs isn't enough. Trainees must be able to see some chance to advance. Unless they do advance, the bottom jobs will soon be clogged with unpromotable people. Your program must help the man become promotable.

As in early training, the man must be moved at a pace consistent with his ability to absorb and assimilate new information. Again, it is a matter of gauging an individual's capacity and learning rate, a responsibility that falls to the supervisor, and one that he discharges no differently than he would with any other new employee, whatever his race or background. But it is necessary for the supervisor to constantly remind himself to give the new man the attention he requires to maintain hard-won momentum and motivation.

"After they've been on the job for a couple of months I don't pay much attention to them anymore," says George. "They're tuned in by then. Sure, I keep tabs on them and give a hand now and then, but I don't play the old mother hen anymore. Usually, I've got some other brand-new guy to worry about anyway."

While the buddy slowly bows out of the picture after several months—possibly not for as long as six months—some new workers will still need regular guidance beyond that period. Sometimes this guidance can come from other workers, by observation and other informal means, through asking questions of fellow workers on the use of a tool or the way to best perform some step in a new task or procedure. Such informal teaching situations should be encouraged. But the worker should be systematically introduced as well to situations where he can learn tasks other than his primary one. This may be accomplished by assigning him to assist various skilled workers. Such a procedure can serve to reinforce his motivation, in that he sees the possibility of eventually moving into other slots.

SWITCH SUPERVISORS

From time to time it is also valuable to the worker's progress to switch supervisors. Exposure to new supervisors with different "styles," who will make differing demands, is beneficial in that it broadens the new man's ability to work *for* others, just as shifts in job assignments give him greater experience in working *with* others. At the same time, such variation enriches his view of the working environment. He learns in a practical and personally useful way something about the hierarchy of authority in a shop where, for example, engineers or chemists may not hold the title of supervisor but yet command authority by virtue of their profession. This is knowledge which the worker should have, and which he can best gain first-hand.

OTHER TRAINING MEANS

In many jobs, as the worker progresses and management desires to move him along, there may be other than on-the-job knowledge that he will be required to master. Written material, charts, blueprints, shop manuals and similar material may seem hopelessly difficult to the inadequately educated hardcore employee. Here again, the on-the-job supervisor or training specialist must make certain that adequate steps are taken to assure the assimilation of the material, and that it is concretely related to the job itself.

As much as possible, such theoretical material should be woven into the normal work day. In many cases this will take place naturally: during the course of work, the new man and his buddy or supervisor will have occasion to consult, say, a shop manual or an instruction sheet or a job order. As time goes on the supervisor should delegate that chore to the worker, permitting him to operate on his own in interpreting the directions, so that he becomes more and more accustomed to working from the written word and attains some grasp of its connection with the job at hand.

Many businesses hold classroom sessions, or farm them out to training groups, for new workers as well as old workers being groomed for more responsible jobs. They may deal with such basics as reading and writing, or they may teach the more advanced skills required to move up on the job. Whenever possible these sessions should be unlike formal school settings, without the usual teacher-pupil relationship. The National Association of Manufacturers suggests that such classes "should be small and informal, with seating around a conference table rather than at traditional desks. Some companies use titles such as instructor or advisor rather than teacher or counselor, again departing from traditional patterns."

In this training, as with that done on the job, nothing should be taken for granted. Instruction must be concise, clear and simple, and the entire program put together in such a way that each new step complements the previous one. At the end of each unit of instruction, the worker should be able to discern a concrete goal or some benefit he considers desirable. It may be a change in a portion of his work assignment, or in the way he is permitted to carry out the work, or even in the responsibility he is given—if he is ready for it and if he wants it. It may be no more than, say, a change of shift, or a change in the scheduling of his rest periods. If such goals are held out as desirable within the context of the job, and are attainable only through completing training, they lend a dimension of meaning to classroom sessions that might otherwise seem purposeless to the worker.

LESSENED SUPERVISION

The supervisor has his goal, too, and that is to bring the worker to a point where he will work well without close supervision. Such a point will arrive at widely different times for different individuals. To some workers it may never come at all, but this is something that the supervisor, although he may suspect it, cannot know for sure until he has given the man every chance to prove or disprove it.

The supervisor might feel encouraged to give some workers a free hand after only a month or two. More likely it will take longer than that. To determine just how long, the supervisor can run "tests" in which close supervision for the worker is removed for a half-day period. If the man weathers that first test, the period should be increased to a day, two days, a week.

During this testing process, however, the worker should not feel that he is being told to sink or swim. The supervisor or his delegate should be on hand to make casual spot checks. If the worker is doing well on his own, he should be told so, and appropriately praised early in the process. If he is not doing well, he should quietly be reinstated to the original supervised status, with no implication that he has failed. When it is feasible, the test should be tried again and, if necessary, a third or fourth time.

While the hardcore worker is being tested for his ability to independently carry out a job, the supervisor can use other measures as well to help bolster the man's self-confidence. Let him use his own judgment. This might take the form, for instance, of permitting him to decide the order in which he will take on several jobs of equal priority, or of offering him other opportunities to make simple decisions. In all cases, however, the kinds of decisions he faces should be capable of solution in terms of the actual experience he has been exposed to on the job.

Further, the supervisor should help the worker focus on his own often unrealized capacities and knowledge of the job. This is done by such means as soliciting his suggestions on certain aspects of his work. "How long do you think it will take to finish this part of the job?" Or "What time do you want the shipping department to pick up this job?" Or "Do you think there's an easier or simpler way to do this?"

HOW DOES HE THINK HE'S DOING?

Periodically, the supervisor should ask the new man how he thinks he's doing on the job. He may feel he is performing an absolutely first-rate job, when in fact he is barely meeting minimum standards. On the other hand, with a background of failure and with no confidence in his ability to do anything well, he may feel that he automatically botches everything he touches, even though his work is acceptable. In either case, his perception should be brought into line with reality. If he is not doing as good a job as he thinks he is, he should be corrected so that he does not continue riding for a fall. If his work is satisfactory, he should be told so in such a way as to indicate that his anxiety is groundless.

However, the supervisor who asks a hardcore worker how he thinks he is doing will often get an answer consisting of a shrug and the comment: "I guess I'm doing all right. Otherwise I'd be fired by now." Typically, such a response doesn't simply indicate disinterest in the job. It reveals a lack of experience, or insufficient insight about himself or his work to make the requested evaluation. With many workers an ability to perceive a true relationship to the work will come with time.

Indeed, as the new man gains experience, he may become exceedingly vocal in expressing his feelings about his work, and the lack of appreciation shown for his consummate skills in performing it. He may well insist that he has long been ready to tackle some of the more desirable jobs he sees performed around him. Without dampening the man's enthusiasm, the supervisor must make it clear that certain company policies have to be followed, but that if the man continues his saisfactory work, when the appropriate time comes, he will get full and fair consideration in bidding for any job he desires.

STAYING LOOSE

As in every aspect of a hardcore employment program, maintaining flexibility during the training period is the mark of wise management.

Setting arbitrary training limits on a job—which may be company practice in the normal run of employment—will lead to problems in a program for the hardcore worker. A hard and fast rule such as "six months as a helper and then you're on your own" should be relaxed. Some men will meet such a six-month deadline, but many will not.

Rather than hewing to strict limits, hardcore training programs should be conducted with only general time limits in mind. At the same time, to forestall frustration it is desirable to present the worker with an idea of what those time limits are. "We hope you'll have this job down pat before the end of the year." Or, "Within the next six months you'll probably move on to piecework on the line."

However, even those loose limits should be extended when a worker's lack of progress makes it either desirable or mandatory. But the worker should not take this extension to mean he is being set back. Tell him, "You're doing okay on this job. In another month or two you should have such-and-such mastered and then we'll move you to the line."

The major drawback to an extended training period is the cost of maintaining a worker at less than full productive capability over a longer range than first anticipated. But to effectively train hardcore workers, as a former personnel assistant to General Motors points out, "Companies will have to learn to tolerate short-run productivity losses." In instances of training programs under government subsidy, however, granting such additional time should not be a decisive cost factor. Nor will such extensions be required for all workers. But management should retain enough flexibility to accommodate those workers who can use the extra time to good advantage.

A training subsidy will serve as a cushion, too, when you have to make a decision about discharging a new man (see Chapter 10). That decision should not be made too early. In every business the tendency is to quickly discard deadwood because it costs the employer money. With subsidization, however, you can afford to take a longer, harder, and closer look at a man over a greater period of time than normally. Will an extra month on the job lift him to acceptable levels? Is there something in the training process itself which has blocked his progress? Is too much expected of him? Can he be shifted to a different task?

In the end, of course, some men will give good reason to be terminated. But before that step is taken, you should be sure that you have done all you can to salvage both the man and your investment in his training. In some instances that investment may exceed several thousand dollars—a considerable sum to let go without first making every effort to save it.

MOTIVATION

Over the long haul, a primary difference between the worker who develops satisfactorily and the one who doesn't is the degree of motivation each possesses. The worker who has the right incentives and is properly motivated will tend to identify his best interests with the interests of the company—an ideal situation from management's standpoint.

The seeds of motivation in the black hardcore worker, as in any other worker, lie in several factors: a desire to advance himself; a need to gain the recognition of others; a desire to make a worthwhile contribution; a desire to achieve responsibility or self-reliance; and the need to establish meaningful social relationships.

As the opportunities to achieve these needs through the job become clearer to the worker, he is induced to do his best. He is more likely to report to work on time and have fewer absences, to take greater interest in the quality and quantity of his work, and, generally, to show greater attachment or loyalty to the company.

Reaching the motivational wellsprings in the hardcore worker is not always easy. Because of past failures and betrayals, he may not believe your assertions that he can advance—at least not until he sees that others of his background have moved up the same promotional ladder. He may look with distrust at first upon the praise that seeks to give him recognition, believing it insincere and patronizing and an attempt to "run a game" on him. He may believe that he utterly lacks the ability to contribute anything worthwhile to any pursuit. He may have a deep-seated fear of being thrown back upon his own resources, or of being asked to accept responsibility because this, too, will ask more of him than he can deliver and thus expose his inabilities. And he may shy from trying to establish social relationships for fear of being rejected because of his race or other factors over which he has no control.

Yet such motivational needs and desires do often find fulfillment through a man's work. Many of the hardcore unemployed look toward work experiences to provide them with just such satisfactions. At the San Francisco Adult Opportunity Center, for example, a group of unemployed black men were asked what work really meant to them personally. Their answers varied considerably. "Some felt it was just a 'drag,' a stupid expenditure of energy and time which they would rather use to sleep, go to baseball games, make music, watch TV, go fishing, or spend with their female companions," says a report on the Center. "Most of the men, particularly those over thirty, expressed quite different attitudes. Many recalled a particular job they once had . . . Some spoke of pleasure in mastering a skill, others of feeling good about being part of the mainstream, getting up in the morning and having a place to go to like everyone else. Many of the men revealed their loneliness when they said that the most important value work had for them was the relations developed with other workers. One of the most touching and poignant was . . . a Mr. H who answered slowly: 'You know what work means to me? I'm there in the shop, and at lunch time some fellow says to me, "Want a ride home tonight?" He says it easy like. And I say "yes." And then, after work we both get into the car and we ride home and we talk about things that happened, and then he stops in and has a drink with me.' "

Like any other worker, the hardcore worker harbors basic needs which, when satisfied, influence his performance on the job. If you recognize those needs, and the worker knows they are recognized, his chances of becoming a useful, productive member of the work force are greatly increased.

BACKSLIDING

A new hardcore employee comes through his first few weeks with flying colors. He is always on time, never misses a day; he works with concentration and takes instruction well. His buddy and supervisor think highly of his potential. He gets along well with the other workers.

But then something happens. The quality of his work falls off; his tardiness and absenteeism record begins to grow alarmingly. He disregards instructions. The supervisor can't figure out what has happened.

Behind such backsliding may be a variety of reasons, many of them likely to infiltrate a hardcore program sooner or later. The new man's loss of early enthusiasm is not uncommon. He comes on the job with a certain excitement engendered by the chance to prove himself, to become part of the mainstream. But enthusiasm has a way of running out for everyone, and with fewer resources upon which to feed, it runs out more quickly for the hardcore person.

When he leaves the plant at the end of his shift, the black hardcore worker must still return to the ghetto. He still sees his old streetcorner friends who are on the hustle, and they may show something less than respect for his eight-hours-a-day, five-days-a-week regimen. To help him face their disdain, a new worker needs reasons enabling him to rationalize the worth of his job. He himself may have highly ambivalent feelings about his work—is it worth all the effort or isn't it?

As an observer in a West Coast job development program points out, it is up to the supervisor to help the worker sustain and gradually overcome the ridicule of his peers. This he will do as he develops positive attitudes toward work and the values of the working world. But until—and unless—he develops such attitudes his resolve may waver and he will wish he were back sparring with his poolroom cronies.

Inner conflicts produced by this frame of mind can lead to a number of on-the-job problems. One may be the man's resentment of his lowly status as trainee. The new man sees himself as already proficient in his work and can find no reason why he should not receive the same privileges, prestige, and wages as the experienced worker. The answer to demands of that nature is clear: the man must earn those privileges as others have earned them. The supervisor must make this point firmly—and at the same time show that those privileges are indeed obtainable, and that the worker is in fact well on his way to obtaining them.

Again, the worker's diminishing interest in his work may show itself in an attempt to take advantage of what he perceives as his special status. Feeling himself untouchable as a subsidized trainee, he may do an absolute minimum of work, and even that may be done carelessly and to a chorus of complaint. The supervisor may find him dawdling over easy jobs, returning late from lunch and rest breaks, spending long periods in the toilet, perhaps even sleeping on the job.

Strict and clear limits must be set to curtail such behavior. In such cases a job coach or counselor is valuable in helping to straighten out the worker if the behavior persists beyond the supervisor's warnings. But the supervisor himself must make it understood that no member of the work force—trainee or veteran —is immune from discipline for obvious and disruptive infractions of company regulations.

PROBLEMS FROM OTHER WORKERS

Not all of the difficulties in adjusting to his new work experience arise from the new worker himself. They can be caused by other workers, too (see Chapter 8). Such problems can range from freezing out the new man from all activities to subtle harassment or not-so-subtle ongoing teasing and ridicule that soon makes the job unbearable to the new man.

When a hardcore worker—or the first non-white employee in a plant or department—gets "the treatment" from other workers, it can take a variety of forms. All the dirtiest jobs may be palmed off on him. Other workers will "bad-mouth" him to the supervisor, blaming him for production slowdowns, reduced piecework, and any other untoward happening on the job. His work may be deliberately sabotaged. When he seeks advice, he may be given wrong information and subsequently find himself in trouble with the supervisor. The treatment may extend to scribbles of "to hell with niggers" on toilet walls or the ostracizing of any white worker who offers the new man a friendly word.

Once in motion, this kind of deplorable situation will deteriorate rapidly, and the supervisor is mistaken if he hopes it will correct itself "once the rest of the men get used to having this new fellow around." He has to take a firm lead in laying to rest any notion that such treatment is condoned, to the extent of applying discipline in serious cases.

Fortunately, according to studies of problems experienced by new Negro workers, such extremes of treatment have become less likely as the inevitability of widespread black employment has made itself felt throughout the entire job market.

But what is more likely to happen is that other workers simply go their own way, pointedly ignoring the new man unless it is absolutely necessary to address him or work with him. At such times they may be polite enough, but their acceptance never extends to including the black worker in established carpools, or inviting him to join the bowling team or attend the company picnic.

It is this kind of problem, developing and solidifying over a period of time (as distinguished from the reluctance of the older workers to take any new man into their circle until they get to know him well), that some supervisors find hardest to deal with. A common attitude is the one expressed by a dispatcher for a nationwide moving van company in discussing the first black driver-helper in his district. The new man was doing an adequate but not exceptional job. "Of course," said the dispatcher, "he might look better if he got any real encouragement from the rest of the crew . . . But you can't just push a man on others—he must be voluntarily accepted by them. That is, for the man to be able to do his best. We have three or four white drivers who refuse to work with him—but this is an undercover feeling, not out in the open. I find that he gets better acceptance from our younger and newer drivers."

The driver himself, interviewed separately, has assessed the situation realistically. "I've been well accepted here. If complete acceptance is 100 percent, I've got about 96 percent acceptance. You can't expect everyone to like you . . ."

The points of view in this instance show a standoff between the new man and some of his older co-workers, but it is a relationship without apparent hostility or menace, and not critical from the employer's point of view. However, in situations that are apt to resolve themselves more troublesomely, management will have to step in early in the game. Through reiteration of the company policy behind the reasons for hiring the hardcore unemployed, you must make clear the need for other workers to accept the new man as a fact of on-the-job life. This should be done affirmatively with reference to the positive aspects of the program—new contracts, new markets, new services—so that workers do not feel something unpalatable is being thrown at them on a take-it-or-leave-it basis.

THE SUPERVISOR'S TOUGH JOB

There may be times in a hardcore hiring program when the supervisor will feel he is being asked to walk an impossibly narrow path. He is caught in the squeeze between management and workers, and he has to see that the production system flows as planned with a minimum of mishaps and few disgruntled employees. His job is a tough one, and at times it may seem to him that there is simply no right way to do things.

On the one hand, he has to keep a careful eye on the new man, and praise him for what he does right—which at first may be very little. On the other hand, he must take care that he is not excessively protective of the new black worker, hindering his development by having the buddy do most of his work, or setting work standards so low for the new man that achieving them is meaningless.

He has to be friendly with the new man and attempt to establish the kind of relationship in which good communication is possible. At the same time, he is dealing with a man far less sophisticated about the working world on which he, the supervisor, is an authority. Thus he must take care to avoid being condescending or patronizing—attitudes which the new man will sniff out very quickly and resent.

He must bring each new worker along as fast as that man is capable of moving, so that the new man does not reach a plateau of development and stagnate there. And yet he must also have regard for the slow learner, be willing to offer him additional chances to reveal any late-blooming potential, and not show impatience with a lack of progress so long as the man is genuinely trying.

He must keep a sense of perspective as to what can be expected of the new hardcore worker and still not be unduly permissive with the man. Nor can he afford to be so excessively vigilant that every insignificant detail of the worker's performance is magnified into a serious matter resulting in overcriticism.

The supervisor must see to it also that he does not drag the black trainee into plant politics or "power-plays," as might develop when a supervisor's natural ambition leads him to strive, say, for pushing more hardcore workers through training in less time than any other department, or involving hardcore workers in a drive to set any sort of plant record. Any such activity would obscure the major purpose of the hardcore hiring program.

This is not to imply that an occasional casual competition cannot be set up. For instance, a supervisor or a buddy may be promised a ticket to a ballgame, or similar small reward, if he brings all his hardcore trainees through a given period without a mishap or an absence. Other contests could be conducted upon similar informal lines. But the power play in which a new worker becomes a pawn must be avoided.

SUPERVISORIAL BRUSH-UP

When a new hardcore hiring program begins, supervisors may heartily support it and find it invigorating and challenging. But after a few months of headaches and unhappy experiences with the new men, their enthusiasm may seriously wane. To combat this natural letdown, short brush-up training sessions for supervisors can be helpful (see Chapter 6). Some companies have found these most valuable when they are scheduled as two- or three-hour meetings between supervisors and top-level manage-ment. The participation of company executives in such sessions underscores both the company's continued high interest in the program and the value it places on the supervisors' contribution. Such sessions can be set up as free-form discussions, with the supervisors airing problems they have experienced and soliciting opinions on how to deal with them. In this fashion, innovative techniques that often develop in the shop in a hit-or-miss fash-ion and might otherwise go unrecorded are passed along for the enlightenment of other supervisors and management.

If you have set up a full-scale sensitivity training program as outlined in Chapter 6, the same training officer should conduct the follow-up as part of the over-all supervisor training.

One method of follow-up successfully and dramatically used by some companies calls for selected hardcore trainees in con-trolled bull-session "communication meetings" with supervisors. Regarding the desirability of such exchanges, the National Asso-ciation of Manufacturers says they "stress the importance of getting the majority to understand that minority people have many things to offer middle-class white America. It is a two-way, not a one-way street . . ."

In a meeting or series of meetings where both supervisors and hardcore trainees who have had several months on the job can let down their hair, much surprising information may come to the surface. The bracing quality of such sessions often does much to stimulate supervisorial interest anew, and can put new fire into a training program that has begun to show signs of weariness.

CHAPTER TEN

"For the Good of the Company": Discipline and Dismissal

The most effective worker discipline, personnel men will agree, is *self*-discipline. One of the prime goals of a hardcore program is to instill that quality in the new worker. When—and if—this is achieved the program has succeeded.

Arising out of motivation and incentive, self-discipline stems as well from a worker's sense of identity with his job, his co-workers, and the company generally. Essentially, the self-disciplined worker supervises himself. He does not need the threat of discipline from outside sources. He is motivated from within to carry out his work, even if it means foregoing immediate gratification in favor of future rewards. The ability to defer gratification is not always a part of the hardcore worker's background. He may well be accustomed to living as if tomorrow holds no more promise for him than today. Thus the kind of self-discipline other members of the work force bring to the job must often be developed in the hardcore worker.

Achieving self-discipline is a long-range process, and before it has been realized, there may well be occasions when discipline from other sources is called for. And that source, of course, is the supervisor.

For many supervisors, administrating discipline is one of the most difficult parts of the job. Yet it is also one of the most important. Disciplining a hardcore worker toward whom the supervisor may already be badly disposed, and thus even more determined to treat fairly, may cause even more wear and tear on supervisorial emotions.

In today's enlightened atmosphere, there are relatively few supervisors who watch hawklike for the hardcore worker's slightest error and then pounce upon him in an orgy of overreaction and unjustified criticism. But there do exist many supervisors who are irked by the additional burden of the hardcore training program, the daily problems of which eventually rub raw the nerves of even a good, steady man. Then, when the hardcore worker commits an infraction of the rules, the edgy supervisor hits the ceiling. Everybody understands how it can happen—except the hardcore worker who faces a five-day suspension and loss of pay. He may well feel he is being treated unfairly, or that discipline is being arbitrarily leveled against him. This suspicion is lessened if the company has an established policy regarding discipline.

SOME PRECAUTIONS

If disciplining measures seem to be called for with uncommon frequency for hardcore employees, the warning flag is up that your hardcore training program is in danger. Find out where the trouble lies before serious damage is done. Don't let the program deteriorate into an exchange of hostilities, with the workers' continuing infractions of the rules coming almost as fast as you can slap punishment on the offenders.

This is unlikely to happen if any planning has gone into the program. It is virtually impossible if a strong set of support services—buddy, job coach, counselor—is available, and a sensitivity program for supervisors has been established (see Chapter 6).

But in those cases where it does happen, you may have to dig for the cause. You may find it in excessive vigilance on the part of a supervisor who is not wholly sold on the idea of hardcore training to begin with. The problems he reports regarding hardcore workers may be colored by his prejudices. Especially when a program is in its early stages and inadequate preparatory work has been done with supervisors, problems may be magnified out of proportion, or even manufactured out of whole cloth. Matters that might be overlooked or passed over with a few words if they involved white workers may occasion great concern with a minority worker.

It's been said that by watching any man closely enough for a few weeks and keeping a record of his every questionable action, you can easily justify firing him. Management must be sure that the problems with hardcore workers do not result from overvigilance, from personality clashes, or as the consequence of unhappy older workers feeding erroneous information to the supervisor.

However, all problems won't be imaginary. Many will be extremely real and must be dealt with. Depending upon the gravity of the situation, discipline may or may not be called for. Before resorting to it, consider the feasibility of applying positive reinforcement techniques (see Chapters 6 and 7). By emphasizing whatever the worker is doing right, you may help motivate him to correct the part of his performance which is substandard. For example: "A hard worker who is always on time like you, John, shouldn't have to be reminded so often about a simple thing like wearing safety glasses."

When their services are available, call on the job coach, the counselor, or the buddy to help correct problems before resorting to discipline. At times, simply reminding the erring worker of possible disciplinary measures may be sufficient. Give the worker an opportunity to explain his position and offer his own proposals as to how to amend his behavior. Be flexible. If there is doubt, give the worker the benefit of that doubt. Avoid argument and maintain objectivity. But when, for the good of the company, discipline is unquestionably called for, act swiftly and decisively.

LEVELS OF DISCIPLINE

Not only is a graduated schedule of discipline helpful to the success of a hardcore program but it also improves management's relationship with all workers, old and new. Without such a management reference point, the punishment does not always fit the crime; companies may either be tolerant to the point of chaos, or much too harsh; discipline may seem to be applied discriminatorily, or may be influenced unduly by personal likes and dislikes.

It isn't possible or desirable to have a schedule of set punishments for every conceivable infraction, but most companies do need a general outline of levels of discipline similar to that contained in the collective bargaining agreements of such unions as the United Auto Workers or the International Association of Machinists. Such a set of graduated disciplinary measures lets the new man know where both he and the company stand. It serves to reduce the seemingly arbitrary quality of punishment that bewilders many hardcore trainees. It works as well as a check upon the disgruntled supervisor who, out of misguided principles, might tend to overdiscipline black workers.

1. *Verbal reprimand.* This is the slap-on-the-wrist sort of punishment appropriate only when the offense is relatively minor.

In administering it, tell the trainee *why* and *how* he has transgressed. Explain the specific nature of the offense; explain why it is not permitted; and tell the worker not to repeat it. All this should be done in private. Don't get into an argument; don't threaten—beyond pointing out that company policy makes mandatory more severe discipline if the offense is repeated. What you are seeking is compliance with your order, not an occasion to display strength or authority.

In years past the training process itself often was little more than a string of verbal reprimands. Today even a sympathetic supervisor or buddy may catch himself reprimanding the trainee rather more often than is healthy for the continued success of the program. When offenses occur on the level calling for only verbal reprimand, most often positive reinforcement (see Chapter 7) should be employed. For example, if a man deliberately throws a tool down instead of carefully placing it down, the natural course would be to call him on it. But by avoiding direct criticism, more good, in terms of learning, may be accomplished. "Listen, Bob you've got a perfect record here so far, I'd hate to see you mess it up by breaking any tools. . . ."

2. *Verbal reprimand noted in personnel file.* This must be clearly distinguished from a critical comment made to the worker by the supervisor. The worker should be called away from the worksite and privately reprimanded. Again, he must understand the reason for the reprimand, and be told that his offense is severe enough for a notation of the reprimand to go into his file. Tell the man what the note will say. For instance, the supervisor might say, "This is the third time I've talked to you about this so I have to enter it in your personnel file. It'll say that I spoke to you about throwing tools, and warned you that more severe discipline will be applied if that sort of thing continues."

As with any reprimand, a degree of formality is desirable, so as to impress the worker with the seriousness of the matter. It has been noted that some workers failed to attach much importance to reprimands because in their view the supervisor "didn't take it seriously."

In general, this level of reprimand should be within the province of the supervisor, although he may well want to inform his superior when he takes such action.

3. *Written reprimand.* An example of this discplinary measure:

> Memorandum: To personnel file of Robert Jones
>
> On April 1st, 1970, Supervisor Smith was told by the personnel officer that the time card of production-line worker Alfred Rogers had been rung in at 07:27 a.m. for the above date. Rogers did not in fact report to work on the line until about 08:05 a.m.
>
> Following an investigation by the personnel officer and the supervisor, it was determined that production-line worker Robert Jones had punched the clock for Rogers as a "favor" to him, in order to permit Rogers time to take his car to a service station to be left for servicing.
>
> Punching in for another worker, or causing a worker to punch in for another person, is directly prohibited under all circumstances by company regulations.
>
> This memorandum is to be recorded as a reprimand to Jones, who witnesses by his signature below that he has received and understands the nature of this first warning. He is also aware that subsequent violations will be dealt with more severely.
>
> William Smith   Robert Jones

Before this memo was written, the supervisor and general foreman discussed the matter; their conference can be reconstructed somewhat as follows:

Super.: The last guy who did this got a three-day suspension. He punched the card for a friend who didn't come in all day.

G.F.: But those two were really trying to put something over on us. This guy Jones thought he was only doing his friend a favor.

Super.: Well, rules are rules. They apply the same to everybody.

G.F.: The situations aren't comparable. Look, we both know that this goes on all the time. A driver drops his carpool off and one of them punches in for him while he parks; or some guy stops to pick up coffee for a couple of guys in his crew and they punch him in so he won't be late.

Super.: But in those cases you're only talking about a minute or two, if that. Nobody is trying to get away with anything.

G.F.: Okay, but you're talking as if we only had one set punishment for every infraction. I know it'd make your job a hell of a lot easier if you could say, "Drinking on the job? Give him punishment number 6." Or "Wasting materials? Give him number 42." But every case has to be weighed on its own, no matter who it concerns. We're supposed to be flexible.

Super.: Well, it's true that this is Jones' first mistake. But it's still a serious matter.

G.F.: Right. Too serious for just a verbal warning—but not serious enough for firing. What's left?

Super.: A written warning, or suspension without pay.

G.F.: Okay. Now this is Jones' first offense. Add to that the fact that we're supposed to be running a training program here. Whatever punishment you lay on the man ought to have the greatest potential for constructive learning. What will teach him the most? We can lay a suspension on him that costs him a week's wages and lets all the other workers know he's been slapped down for something when, as far as they can see, he's been a good worker. Morale might be affected. Or we can talk to him and put a warning in his file. Maybe you ought to assign Rogers to another crew, too, so he isn't around to ask any more favors from Jones. But that's my recommendation—give Jones a second chance. That's what this training program is all about. Besides, the reason our disciplinary policy is flexible is to permit some range in punishment. You start at the bottom and work up. If Jones fouls up again, then you slap him with a suspension. But don't trap yourself by handing out so severe a punishment the first time that the next time the only way out is firing. We've got a lot invested in these new guys and we've got to bring them along whenever we can—.

As a result of this discussion, it was decided to issue a written warning to the new man Jones; it took the form of the memo cited. Noteworthy in the discussion between supervisor and general foreman is the understanding shown toward the hardcore training program and the function discipline can serve within it. "It's been laid on us pretty thick that we're supposed to be running a training program," said another supervisor. "All the situations we run up against we're supposed to structure so as to teach the new man something positive. That isn't easy. I mean, if a guy goofs off, my natural inclination is to boot him in the rear and not pussyfoot around."

The kind of discussion between the supervisor and the general foreman is a good example of "constructive pussyfooting," something necessary to help keep a hardcore program moving forward. So as to keep program goals always in sight, it is wise to have two or more supervisorial level people discuss any punitive measures that go beyond the routine verbal warning. In any case, punishment that is recorded in a permanent file should be the result of more than one man's decision.

4. *Suspended for one day.* This disciplinary measure means loss of pay for the worker. It means as well that, unlike most reprimands, his offense will become known to his fellow workers.

Depending on the nature of his misbehavior, they may well see him as a hero for standing up to management. This is especially true if the worker himself sees the day off as a welcome vacation. The loss of only one day's pay may not bother him. Thus, such suspension should always be used judiciously to make sure it has the teaching impact both on the man and his co-workers that management desires. Again, the general foreman should be consulted and the personnel office notified before the suspension is applied.

5. *Additional suspensions: three days to one week.* This disciplinary measure should not be taken before consultation with the general foreman and a representative of the industrial relations or personnel office. A suspension of some duration makes itself felt in the worker's pocketbook, but it also means a temporary vacancy that the supervisor must fill. In the case of a suspension that is ordered while the facts of a matter are being investigated, there is always the possibility that the suspended worker will be found not at fault and will have to be paid for the time he was suspended.

Here, as in all disciplinary matters, make sure the worker understands the rules. Communication problems can be especially thorny with hardcore trainees. In one such situation, a young Puerto Rican worker employed in an East Coast plastic factory was thought to be insubordinate because of his slowness to respond to orders. After repeated warnings, which he took without visible effect, he was handed a three-day suspension. On the first day of the suspension he showed up for work as usual. When it was finally made clear to him what the suspension meant—that he was being punished by not being allowed to work—the man was crushed. He had never understood the fuss about his performance to be of any importance. When he returned to work after the suspension, he proved to be a far more alert worker, since he had been forcibly taught not to take the demands of his job so casually.

6. *Disciplinary transfer and disciplinary demotion.* Transfer or demotion could well take place anywhere along the disciplinary line. For instance Rogers, who persuaded the luckless Jones to punch in for him, received a transfer, not only to remove further temptation from Jones, but as a disciplinary measure as well. On the other hand, transfer should not simply push a trouble-maker into someone else's lap. In some plants, one supervisor may get a reputation for being able to handle the tough cases, and consequently all the problem workers eventually are transferred into his crew. Such a supervisor may not be the right man to supervise a hardcore worker who is having trouble. The individual man and situation must be evaluated before such a transfer is made.

To some workers, demotion may represent a humiliating loss of face which they will bitterly resent. Whether the action will effectively chasten or totally demoralize the worker should be considered before the step is taken. Generally, demotion means some loss of salary. This can be a very real hardship to a hard-core worker and may bring on financial troubles which will soon push him out of the job. It is especially damaging if the worker sees the demotion as slamming shut all doors to further opportunity—even though his own misbehavior brought it about. When such demotion is made, the worker should clearly understand—if that is indeed the case—that he hasn't cut off forever all chances "to earn his stripes back." The supervisor should tell him how long it will be before his performance and behavior is reevaluated, with the possibility of upgrading if no mishaps occur in the interim.

Again, depending on the individual, demotion may represent a very handy solution to a problem. A worker performing badly at one level, because of the pressure of responsibility or other job-connected forces, may be happier in less demanding circumstances. For instance one machine operator who reported to work drunk on several occasions received first reprimands and then suspensions. As a last step before dismissal, he was demoted to helper. With fewer demands from his job, the worker appeared more relaxed, and his drinking was no longer a problem on the job.

7. *Thirty-day suspension.* As the last stop before the end of the line, this punishment should come only after careful consultation between supervisor, general foreman, and a representative of the personnel or industrial relations office. Make certain that the worker clearly understands that the only step left is termination. In some cases, the severity of the discipline can be underscored by offering the man a "choice" between accepting a thirty-day layoff or outright discharge.

After such a suspension, it is desirable to hold a brief counseling session when the worker returns. Remind him of how tenuous is his hold on the job, but also offer support so long as he shows he deserves it.

8. *Dismissal.* While this is always a severe disciplinary action with any worker, for the black hardcore worker it has additional ramifications which should be considered. If the man's performance or behavior is so below standard that he must be fired for the good of the company, then there is no other recourse. At the same time, it means that you are admitting failure in your ability to bring the man through.

The hardcore worker who is discharged will have an unusually hard time finding another job. Knowing this, some companies tend to carry a bad worker rather than take the unpleasant step of dumping him.

Such a course of inaction, although well meant, is always questionable. The business suffers, as does other workers' morale. The worker himself may find in such excessive tolerance confirmation that he can "get away with anything," and thus he becomes virtually untrainable.

At the same time, the responsibility you assume in launching a hardcore program makes certain demands, among them the need to carefully consider the special problems of the unsuitable worker. If you cannot help him, try to find someone who can— a community agency or counseling service. Then, when the man is terminated, he at least has a chance to receive rehabilitative assistance.

In all disciplinary measures, but most especially in cases that result in termination, documentary records should be available of the efforts you have made to save the worker, what discipline he received, and for what infractions. Memoranda, such as the one cited earlier, and similar records, help support your case in the event the discharged worker files charges of discriminatory treatment with federal or state antidiscrimination commissions. Many such agencies will make a preliminary check before formally docketing a complaint. If such company records are immediately available, they can be of assistance in keeping unfounded charges from reaching the more troublesome investigative stage, at which point they would be needed anyhow.

PROBLEMS OFF THE JOB

Should you discipline a worker for behavior *off* the job?

Probably not, unless the problem is of such a nature as to interfere with the worker's productivity or usefulness *on* the job. But in many companies, if a worker somehow runs afoul of the law, is arrested and perhaps briefly incarcerated, he can be pretty sure he no longer has a job. In cases of arrest stemming from crimes of an aggravated nature—armed robbery, rape, or burglary, say—it is understandable why many employers are unwilling to hold the arrested man's job open, or consider re-employing him after his long stay in jail.

But the offenses that are far more likely to remove a worker from a work force for a few days or weeks are of the common, garden-variety nature—gambling, "suspicion" (a frequent cause for arrest in ghetto areas), failure to pay alimony or child support, drunkenness, possession of marijuana, driving after revocation of license, and the like. A man guilty of such offenses will be punished by the proper authority. It is highly questionable whether his employer should discipline him as well—which is what losing his job would amount to. If he is a satisfactory employee so far as performing his assigned job is concerned, any decision to terminate him that is based only on an off-the-job arrest should be carefully weighed by top-level officials in the industrial relations and personnel offices.

Attachment of wages, or other financial problems which start off the job but are forced upon the attention of the employer, are somewhat different matters. The employer has to take some action because he is involved whether or not he wants to be.

But over the past few years employer attitudes toward garnishment have become greatly enlightened from the "debtor's prison" thinking that once prevailed, when a man in debt would be effectively cut off from any chance of repaying that debt. Creditor, debtor, employer, everyone lost. True, the serious annoyance caused by repeated garnishments still require many companies to hold the threat of dismissal over an employee if attachment of his wages recurs. But at the same time most companies with a hardcore program will also offer the man counseling, or make such counseling a provision of continued employment, and actively seek to eliminate the cause of the garnishment.

Again, the kind of spending behavior that traps a man into garnishment is most often not of direct significance to his job. A man who handles his own money badly probably shouldn't be in a position to handle the company's money, but he may still be aptly fitted for work in all other areas of the company operation.

It is noteworthy, too, that harsh local laws permitting garnishment are gradually being tempered, as lawmakers come to realize the arbitrary, frequently unfair and at times even cruel, manner in which garnishment is sometimes carried out.

WHEN HE CAN'T DO THE WORK

In some shops sloppy work or incompetent work traditionally calls for a reprimand or even strong discipline. Under a hardcore program such a policy may still be pursued, but at the same time it must be recognized that the hardcore worker comes to your shop with little competence. If he is now reprimanded for his lack of skills, the entire purpose of the program is undermined.

Still, there will be occasions when discipline is called for; for example, with the man who has in fact developed the capabilities but is now backsliding. Hopefully, discipline will stop short of dismissal, but there will be occasions when there is simply no other way out; the man cannot, or will not, do the work, and termination is all that's left.

Before that final act, however, carefully review the man's case. Have you done everything possible to save him? This should mean that you have exhausted all such means as counseling, additional or new training, transferring to a new job, or different job site, and pointing out his "last chance" status.

But if nothing helps and termination is called for, representatives of supervision, management, and the personnel officer should consult about preparing a written notice of dismissal.

Inform the worker candidly as to why he is being discharged. Wherever it is possible, try to help the man secure another job. Suggest companies that might have entry job levels more suitable to whatever abilities you have noted in the man. Refer the discharged worker to a community or service agency for further help and try to set up a firm contact between him and the agency. Don't accept his vague promise to "look them up sometime." A large California aerospace corporation routinely provides counseling as well as job-seeking assistance to minority workers who are fired because of their inability to carry out the job. In effect, members of the company's industrial relations office run a kind of employment and counseling service for discharged employees. This is usually a one-shot operation, although there have been cases where the dismissed employee repeatedly comes back for help or advice.

LAYOFFS

A general reduction in the work force is a blow to all workers who are idled, but it has a special negative impact upon the hardcore worker who invariably finds himself stuck in the "last-hired, first-fired" category.

When the work force has to be cut, the newer workers normally go first. Almost always the hardcore person will be at the bottom in seniority, and if a collective bargaining agreement is in effect, certain set procedures have to be followed to preserve the rights of older, experienced workers.

Some companies have found that rather than a partial layoff for a long period, complete plant shutdown for a short period is more desirable. This is done frequently in the auto industry. Variations on this method have also been successful, such as a shortened work week, or extended vacations for older workers which keep positions open for newer employees.

Some hardcore training programs with government subsidization can be continued even during a layoff, perhaps by means of a three-day week. Under bargaining agreements, some companies have set up funds to supplement unemployment insurance. With the cooperation of unions, management can sometimes work out a system to temporarily lay off older workers with ample unemployment benefits. With seniority and various benefits riding on their return, these older workers are almost certain to return to work. But this would not be the case with the partially trained newer worker whose lack of benefits or savings makes it essential that he find another job at once. His failure to return can mean that a sizable company investment goes down the drain, particularly if more than just a few men are involved.

When the layoff is unavoidable, make sure the hardcore employee understands that the quality of his work is not the reason he is being laid off. Explain the details of your layoff procedure. Assure him that he will be rehired—if that is in fact the truth. It is most helpful if you can reasonably estimate the duration of the layoff. But if you can't, don't fake it and raise false hopes.

The laid-off hardcore worker is in for a rough time, and anything you can do to ease his plight should be attempted. Explain in detail how he can obtain unemployment insurance. Or, if he is ineligible for that, tell him how to secure welfare or relief assistance. Make sure he understands what he must do to continue his insurance coverage and medical benefits. Here again use your contacts with other employers, employment agencies, or other services to assist the worker in finding temporary work. In some cases, employers have found temporary or part-time jobs for the laid-off worker's wife, thus providing a measure of financial help. In a few cases, the company has made loans to laid-off trainees.

During the period of layoff, keep in touch with the worker through the company paper or by bulletins announcing the progress of callbacks. An occasional telephone call or note from the supervisor or buddy will let the man know that he is still considered as a member of the company family.

Look for ways to get the hardcore back on the job as soon as possible. Sometimes his job can be scheduled for callback earlier than others—for clean-up, painting, make-ready, and the like. Sometimes he can be called in for a day or two in the middle of a layoff.

Other methods of easing the plight of the hardcore worker who finds himself back on the street through no fault of his own will present themselves if company management keeps aware throughout a layoff period that new and special methods are called for to protect their investment in training new workers.

CHAPTER ELEVEN

Painless Transfer and Sound Promotion

One Friday afternoon, a shipping room supervisor told one of his black hardcore trainees who had been on the job about four months: "Bill, the manager wants you to report to the paint shed when you come in on Monday. We're transferring a couple of new men over there."

But on Monday Bill didn't report to the paint shed—nor did he ever show up for work again. The disgruntled supervisor wondered why, never realizing that the proposed transfer had anything to do with it. New men were unceremoniously transferred all the time. Changing production priorities demanded that sudden shifts be made with no time for advance preparation. That was simply the way things were.

Yet when Bill, the ex-worker, turned up later at an adult opportunity center looking for work, the reason he gave for leaving the job was that "they were trying to push me around. Everybody knew I was doing okay in the shipping department, but they tried to transfer me out. So I quit."

What could the company have done? The supervisor had no advance warning of the need for the shift, and the plant manager had little more. How could it have been possible to lay advance groundwork with the worker? The need to maintain production schedules demanded the transfer. But in handling

235

the matter routinely, with no special effort to smooth the way for the transferee, a promising worker was lost, one on whose training the company had invested upwards of a thousand dollars. The expensive lesson that the company learned was that "routine" transfers of the hardcore worker should not be routine at all.

Yet, of necessity, business must constantly make transfers. They may be required for a variety of reasons—changes in production schedules, cutbacks in personnel, production problems, expansion plans. For the good of the company, first-rate workers who are performing their tasks well often have to be transferred. Few if any workers are cheered by the prospect of involuntary transfer from a spot in which they are comfortable, especially when they feel their work is satisfactory, and when the transfer doesn't result in any wage or promotional benefit. But most workers accept transfers required by the company with a minimum of grumbling. Many workers facing transfer show a good face, hoping their cooperation will be favorably recalled the next time management distributes such favors as overtime, promotions, special training opportunities and the like. Most jobwise workers are willing to accept the word of the boss as final, unless there is a collective bargaining agreement to which they can turn. Even under such agreements, as long as seniority is considered, the employer can make transfers to meet the needs of his company. For the worker, the consequent adjustment to a new worksite, to new fellow workers, to a new supervisor and to a new job is looked on as just part of the game.

Yet even the most efficient, well-adjusted worker experiences some physical, emotional, or mental pressure at being transferred out of a familiar job to a new one. And if the experienced, jobwise worker feels the pressure, consider the problems for the hardcore worker. He has no previous work history. He has probably had a hard time adjusting to the job he is already performing. He may have formed tentative friendships with workers on his present job. And after a strained period of suspicion or distrust, he is just beginning to understand the supervisor. To such a worker a transfer from the familiar to the unfamiliar can be too unpleasant to face, and he will simply quit.

LET HIM KNOW THE REASON

Often the hardcore transferee believes in a vague way that his transfer is meant as discipline. This happened in a New York City novelty manufacturing concern that had carefully developed a hardcore training program and had taken on two black and two Puerto Rican women. Because of a change in production needs, the manager was forced to transfer two of the women from a soldering operation to a painting and gilding operation. Both women, who had been welfare recipients for years before coming to the job, seemed well adjusted to their work. They performed well and had satisfactory attendance records. The transfer required only that the two women move from one side of the loft to the other, a shift of no more than 150 feet. But it also involved a change in supervisors. No advance preparation was even considered. The new worksite was in full view of the old; the pay was the same; there was no change in hours; and the new task, if anything, was simpler than the old.

But both women failed to report for work the next day. The day following, both of the other women, who had not been transferred but who had trained and worked with the others, also failed to show up.

This story might have ended here. But the president of the company had taken a personal interest in the success of his hardcore program. Knowing that some misunderstanding must be at the bottom of the matter, he called on the women. He

soon discovered that the two transferred women had understood their transfer to be a form of punishment—for what they
didn't know, but they were too insecure to question the move.
The other two women felt that there was no cause for punishment and quit half in protest and half because they feared that
they, too, would be unjustly "punished" with an unfamiliar job
and a new supervisor.

The president took great pains to explain the real reason for
the transfers, and he soon persuaded the women to return.
Thereafter, no transfers were made at any level in the shop without explanation of why they were necessary.

The experience of this president boils down to some simple
considerations: Be sure that the worker understands that the
transfer is not for disciplinary purposes. Take time to explain
the reasons necessitating the transfer. Use techniques outlined
in earlier chapters to familiarize the worker with his new job,
new supervisors, and fellow workers. If the worker is still relatively new, consider assigning another buddy on the new job.
Be sure the new supervisor is aware that the transfer is not for
disciplinary purposes. Make a point of telling him, *in the presence of the worker,* something to the effect that "you're mighty
lucky to be getting Bill on your side of the shop. He's turning
into one of our best men."

While the company's interests are necessarily foremost, transfer of the hardcore worker should be smooth or its purpose will
be defeated. From the very moment of hire, many companies
begin to prepare the worker for possible transfer. Valuable as
such preparation is, some additional groundwork will be needed
with the hardcore worker. In general, if the man is not secure at
his current job, transfer will probably only create new difficulties
for him. Know your man before you move him.

FOR THE WORKER'S GOOD

A large Philadelphia warehouse began to experience difficulty with a young black worker who had been assigned to assist an older worker in inventory control. The young man, although badly educated, was obviously intelligent. He was quick, responsive, and considered to be a good bet as a trainee. But soon his initial enthusiasm wore off. He began to spend long periods in the toilet. At times he was discovered idling between the stacks of merchandise, and at other times could not be located at all. But instead of summarily firing the man, the supervisor looked over his early record and decided to have him transferred to the loading dock.

It proved to be a smart move. "I don't know what happened to the kid," the loading-dock supervisor later reported. "I heard he was a real goof-off and I was ready to lean on him. Maybe he got religion or something on the dock, but he turned into a helluva worker."

Since the transfer had worked so well—unlike others the company had attempted—a personnel specialist did a little checking. He found that the young man simply had been uneasy inside the cavernous warehouse where dark, narrow isles wound between stacks of merchandise piled fifteen feet high. In the open air of the loading dock, although the work was harder and less interesting, he felt more at ease.

Not all hardcore workers' problems are that simple at the bottom, nor are the problems necessarily solved by transfer. It may be possible to correct difficulties without resorting to transfer—by shifting responsibilities, providing additional intensive training, or by cutting back production expectations for the new man. But where these moves are not feasible or fail to produce the desired result, the possibility of transfer should be investigated before the situation "bottoms out" and you lose the worker.

By waiting too long, an employer can put himself in the position of a small Midwest department store chain that tried to salvage through transfer three young hardcore workers who had failed badly in their stockroom jobs. By himself, each young man promised to be a satisfactory worker. But all three together, with comparatively little supervision, were constantly in trouble. By the time the threesome was broken up and the men individually transferred, it was too late. In spite of some change in attitude and performance when each was on his own, their reputations had already been made. The other workers were suspicious of them; the new supervisors overcritical. All three were eventually dismissed. Yet the problem they presented was known for weeks before anything was done. Had the transfers taken place in time, all three men probably could have been saved.

From a practical dollars and cents point of view, transfer is still a primary way for a company to save its investment in a worker. As a rule of thumb for salvaging the hardcore trainee, consider transfer before termination (see Chapter 10).

WHEN THE WORKER ASKS TO MOVE

A Midwestern telephone company branch launched its hardcore training program by recruiting several young black men for its line maintenance operation. Each man was assigned to a different crew and the crew chiefs were instructed to give them every possible break in learning the job. They were to be taken along on all emergency calls and given maximum exposure to every aspect of the maintenance operation.

Within a week, one of the trainees had developed a reputation for sheer inability to do anything right. The man was apparently awkward beyond belief, and incapable of performing even the simplest tasks. The crew chief claimed it took the full-time attention of an experienced man just to keep him from doing everything wrong. He very quickly became a kind of legendary example of the gross and bumbling, but well-meaning, dolt. As such, the men took him under their collective wing. When he failed to show up for work—usually at least twice a week—his crew would stop by his house and help his mother roust him out of bed and into the truck. When he "somehow misplaced" a five-foot chain saw, they all put in overtime hunting it down. When he tried to sneak away during lunch breaks, they rounded him up for the rest of the day's work. But within eight months, after a "slow start" as was charitably noted in his personnel records, the newcomer developed into a passable worker. At that point, and before his crew could congratulate themselves for having whipped him into shape, he asked for a transfer to equipment installation.

Although this example isn't common, it is by no means unrelated to what can be generally expected after you have successfully trained a hardcore worker at one specific job. Like most members of the work force, he is wholly unaware of the management problems transfer can create, and he will see a denial of his "reasonable" request as pure company stubbornness, if not outright racial discrimination. It is essential that from the very start every worker understands the company system of transfer. He should be made aware of what "the good of the company" as a criterion for transfer really means. He must understand that important as his personal desires may be, and as seriously as they will be considered, in the end they have to jibe with the company's needs or a transfer will not be possible.

WHERE "SPECIAL CONSIDERATION" ENDS

Because of the attention and tolerance shown the hardcore trainee during his training period, he may develop an unrealistic perception of his position and continue to expect special consideration after he has become a regular member of the work force. He may believe he can transfer as he pleases, irrespective of seniority, collective bargaining agreements, the need for his services in a given operation, or production demands.

The worker must be made aware that the company has invested time and money in his training for two purposes: one, as a matter of interest in his welfare and to help him better himself; and two, so that he can become a productive worker and contribute toward the company's profitable operation. From the start he must know that although early demands on him may be limited, in time he will be expected to pull his own weight along with the other workers. Gradually, he will work himself out of his special trainee status and become a full-fledged member of the work force. This should be represented to him as an inevitable and desirable goal.

Once he has moved out of the trainee status, the hardcore worker's request for transfer should be handled much the same as you would any other worker's request. But there are exceptions: some special attention should be given to cases in which the worker requests transfer because of racial problems on his present job; or when you are interested in building a better racial balance among workers in a certain department or crew. In either case, the situation surrounding the need for transfer should be thoroughly explored.

In any transfer, make sure that the worker does not have distorted notions about the desirability of the new job. He may see workers in another section with "easier" jobs and want one for himself. Make sure he is not overreaching his abilities, in which case he will face frustration and failure. Once you have determined these matters, grant or deny the transfer as you would to any deserving worker in your shop, balancing the needs of the company against the needs of the worker.

GENERAL REEVALUATION

In developing hardcore training programs, some companies find an unforeseen benefit: The new program forces reevaluation and modification of general personnel procedures, including those involving transfers. Traditional methods governing transfer may not always be flawless. A Milwaukee appliance factory that shifted workers arbitrarily, with no over-all system of honoring reasonable transfer requests, reevaluated and changed its ways after one black worker quit because he was arbitrarily moved from a job he liked and did well to another job in a different part of the plant. And in a Chicago hotel a Puerto Rican man failed to show up for work for three days after he was summarily denied a transfer to another job which he felt would be more interesting and might lead to a promotion.

The lessons to be learned from the experience of other firms is that when a transfer is made or denied, an employer must provide a sufficient explanation. Don't unwittingly leave the impression that your decision is arbitrary. If no established policy regarding transfers now exists, formulate one and make sure all workers and supervisorial staff know you govern your decision strictly in accordance with it.

PROMOTION

In 1969, an east Texas defense contractor responded to requirements of his government contract by employing some twenty black men and women in a single month. Approximately half of the new workers were from the ranks of the hardcore unemployed. The general foreman, while he cooperated to the letter with management's instructions, nevertheless had strong private feelings that the program was doomed to failure. He quietly ordered the several supervisors under whom the newcomers worked to keep detailed records on them, their work performance, their deportment, their attitudes—everything about them. He planned to have an abundance of documentary evidence to present to management when, as he fully expected it would, the program disastrously failed.

The program did not fail. For various noncritical reasons, two of the workers had to be discharged and two quit, but these were immediately replaced with other black workers. Not only was the general foreman's prediction of failure unrealized but before the year was out he received instructions to select two black employees for promotion to first-line supervisor. Now the same detailed records that had been carefully maintained for the purpose of justifying failure became instead valuable documentation to determine which two workers were most likely to succeed as supervisors. Thankful now for his misguided pessimism, the general foreman named two workers for promotion, and both proved to be good choices.

Even if they were kept for the wrong reason, the records proved useful. Indeed, detailed, up-to-date records are essential if promotions are to be made wisely and well. Such records should include written reports prepared by the supervisor and cover such matters as performance, work habits, and special problems. They should also contain information relating to the worker's expressed job aims, his interest or lack of interest in advancement, how he bears up under responsibility, and his over-all attitude toward the company and its operation. In many companies, such recordkeeping is already a part of company procedure. It has shown its value not only in the selection of promotable black workers but in evaluating all workers, and it also provides an indirect method for evaluating supervisors themselves.

KEEP A MINORITY ROSTER

In addition to keeping such records, consider the possibility of maintaining a separate roster of minority workers who appear qualified for promotion or who seem to be developing in that direction. A separate list of this sort keeps supervisors keenly aware of promotable minority workers. The very fact that it exists constantly suggests the need to groom likely candidates to add to the list. It makes less likely the kind of "color blindness" that crops up at promotion time—the inability to see the nonwhite worker who could move up, not so much because of overt prejudice, but simply because minority workers have not previously been thought of as supervisors and the fact of their availability just does not register in certain minds.

This was the case in a Southern California school district which found itself in need of a supervisor of maintenance. The assistant superintendent in charge of business and the personnel officer put their heads together and tried to come up with the name of a man who could be promoted from the maintenance staff. After reviewing all records without finding the man they wanted, they suggested to the Board of Education that the supervisor be recruited from outside sources. One long-time member of the Board, a physician who was the family doctor of the one Negro in the maintenance crew, asked if this man had been considered. He had not. Neither the superintendent nor personnel officer had thought of him as promotable, although he had worked for the district for many years. Each had known the man for years, and yet "color blindness" set in when a promotion was on the agenda.

TRAINING FOR PROMOTION

Not many firms have programs that systematically train workers for promotions. Yet such a program can be immensely helpful in effectively advancing the Negro workers who are moving out of hardcore status. But the program would not, of course, be limited to minority workers only. Instead, it would be another support service from which all workers would benefit. The fact that such a system will be established as part of the hardcore training program should be made known to all beforehand, since it can help smooth the way to acceptance of the program.

From the moment of hiring on, keep all workers informed of promotional openings. Post notices of those openings with job specifications and invite workers to bid on them. Encourage workers to make their promotable qualities known. Owens-Illinois has a plan to insure that no qualified individual will be overlooked when good jobs are to be filled from the ranks. Called the "Job Preference Program," it provides that any worker at any time may request consideration for a different job by filling out a form on which he lists his training and qualifications. During the annual review of his performance, every employee is reminded that the Job Preference Program is open to him if he seeks promotion or transfer.

Additionally, supervisors should impress on new workers the fact that both job performance and behavior influence the possibility of moving up the promotional ladder. This is frequently a matter that new hardcore workers never totally grasp. Many believe that their mere presence on the job is sufficient to qualify them for any and all privileges.

Among its hardcore workers, a Chicago food-processing plant employed a black woman whose past work history consisted of occasional domestic employment. She was in her late twenties, with children, and had impressed the manager as being of above-average intelligence. She learned her job quickly, with a minimum of instruction. But over the ensuing months, her production rate never rose from the lowest acceptable minimum. In considering how to deal with this, the manager later reported, he called the woman into his office. Without preliminaries, he said, "When I hired you, I made a mental note that you had the stuff to be a lead lady." The woman looked surprised. "Do you want to be a lead lady?" he asked, and the woman nodded. "You have kids, don't you? Do they ever ask for a special treat—money for the movies, a ride to the beach—and you told them it depended on how they acted and if they did what they were supposed to? Well, it's the same way here on the job. Those who do what they are supposed to do—get to work on time, get their production rate up, show a good attitude—those are ones who get promoted to lead lady . . ." In the following months the woman's performance improved, and she was eventually upgraded.

For an effective promotional training program, including on-the-job training sessions or evening skill-improvement classes for potential supervisors, your best training resources are right in your shop. They are your older skilled workers and supervisors who have completed the sensitivity training program as outlined in Chapter 6. Outside training classes may be useful, but the lion's share of the work can in all likelihood be done within your plant. Often skilled workers can be encouraged to participate by means of a bonus arrangement.

Financial help is available too. Through the U.S. Department of Labor, the National Alliance of Businessmen offers a JOBS '70 contract to reimburse costs of providing both training and support services to hardcore persons already employed but who need additional help to move up the promotional ladder (see Chapter 12).

In addition to your in-house resources, use the facilities of local high schools, junior colleges, and trade schools which have courses useful to ambitious workers. Most educational institutions will cooperate, if properly approached. With your help, some will develop a course or two to meet the special needs of your workers. A number of companies have found it to their advantage to defray the cost of such courses to workers, as an added inducement. A California chain store has established the policy of paying both the full tuition and the extra transportation costs for any course—even if not strictly job-related—so long as it in some way potentially increases the usefulness of the employee to the business. All employees are eligible, and working schedules can be adjusted to facilitate an employee's education. "The outlay is not great," said the executive vice president. "We are convinced we get back up to ten dollars in value for every one dollar we invest."

PROBLEMS WITH PROMOTION

Companies with no minority workers in higher positions will have to make extra efforts to catch up to prevailing business standards regarding racial balance in the work force. In so doing, it is easy to step on toes, for this extra effort may be deeply resented by other workers who see it as a threat to their own positions. Even a company with minorities at higher levels will probably hear the common rumor, "Now they're discriminating against whites," as it attempts to further balance its work force. Here, too, as in other situations, a firm, no-nonsense management position, expressed in terms of the company's equal opportunity employment policy, will help calm down rumormongers. You should also be certain that the spearhead of resentment is not a supervisor disgruntled at seeing nonwhites joining supervisorial ranks.

Some companies have attempted to sidestep worker resentment by promoting minority group workers to spots where they supervise only other minority workers. A small Indiana defense subcontractor advanced a black man to foreman and at the same ime "engineered" the work force so that he supervised all the blacks and the one Indian employed. A local civil rights leader pointed out the inequity, and the employer decided to redistribute the black workers.

Give careful advance consideration to the new supervisor's assignment to insure the success of the move. True, all hazards cannot be met beforehand, as one company found when Negro supervisors took over mixed crews: The black workers complained that the new boss was too hard on them and too lenient on the whites, while the whites felt the black supervisor favored members of his own race.

PROMOTIONS AND UNIONS

Extra attention to the promotion of minorities can sometimes run afoul of union prerogatives, too. Companies bound by collective bargaining agreements are often severely limited in their promotional practices. Although promotions from hourly to salaried ranks are usually outside union agreements, most promotions to better paying, more responsible jobs that are steps toward the salaried ranks are controlled by the contract. As pointed out earlier, it is wise to discuss the problem beforehand with various union representatives, the shop stewards in your plant, and the business agents who serve your workers.

If you are stymied on the local level, you may be able to get help from the international union. Most nationwide unions have adopted firm policies of nondiscrimination, and many union officials publicly support job development for minority workers.

Re-examine your labor contract, since this regulates your relations with the union. Sometimes contract changes are necessary or desirable if the hardcore are to obtain decent jobs and promotional channels are to be opened. Such changes cannot be made unilaterally by management or the union, but must be negotiated and then approved by the union members. Contract changes may well involve "trade-offs" between management and union. For example, management may offer an upgrading or promotional training program for union members if the union will relax certain requirements for entry-level jobs, extend probationary periods, or broaden promotional channels. Investigate the possibility of such training-program trade-offs when it comes time to renegotiate your contract.

SOME PROMOTIONAL DO'S AND DON'TS

Don't ask other workers or supervisors if they are willing to work under a Negro supervisor. Promotion is a management function carried out for the good of the company. A routine announcement that the promotion has been made should be all that is necessary. (In this connection it is noteworthy that a survey by the National Advisory Commission on Civil Disorders showed that 87 percent of workers polled said that would "mind not at all" having a Negro supervisor. Another 7 percent said they would mind only "a little.")

Don't promote just because you want a Negro supervisor, no matter who he is. The only available individual may not be ready, or he may simply be unpromotable from the standpoint of good business. A poorly advised first promotion to supervisor is likely to make subsequent advancement of competent minority workers all the more difficult. An "instant Negro supervisor" is sometimes obtained by hiring a black technician or professional worker—engineer, draftsman, designer, chemist—if such jobs hold clear supervisorial rank in your company.

Always consider the desires of the person you seek to promote. He may not desire promotion. The owner of a large Denver restaurant informed a Mexican-American dishwasher who had been employed for four years that he was eligible to fill a vacancy on the kitchen crew which paid slightly more. The man turned down the chance, insisting that he liked his dishwashing job. It was, he said, "a thinking-man's job." He didn't want work that would interfere with his thoughts.

Other employers have at times reported reluctance on the part of upgraded hardcore workers to accept the kind of responsibility that necessarily goes with promotion to certain job levels. They lay this to the worker's fear of "failing in a big way," stemming from his lack of confidence in his abilities. Some men may never develop such confidence, but in others it can be encouraged by bringing the man along in a systematic way, gradually stepping up responsibility. This growing process can be a long-term procedure, but it may result in a thoroughly trained man with the expertise and knowledge to supervise any job in the shop.

When promotion involves moving a Negro employee to a new location, make sure you take into account the difficulty he may have in finding new housing. This may be the factor which leads him to turn down a promotion; he simply may not want to take on the discouraging task of confronting discriminatory landlords. However, it is possible for a company to make its influence felt in a community, and help the new black supervisor obtain housing far more easily than he can by himself. Fair housing groups, which have been organized in most communities, are generally eager to work with business in solving this problem.

FOLLOW-UP

Whether the promotion is from an entry-level job to one requiring just a little more skill, or from hourly to salaried ranks, or from lower to higher management, whatever the nature of the promotion it is important that the man is not simply left to prove himself without your help. Traces of the old "sink-or-swim" attitude are still found in some companies. Men are expected to immediately show their capabilities in higher jobs. At times they may even be subjected to special management pressures to test them.

Where minority workers are concerned, this attitude invites failure. Management should make every effort, including continued training in techniques, communication, problem-solving, and the like, to guard against failure. Open support and frequently expressed interest by top-level management will help serve as positive reinforcement to bolster the new supervisor.

DON'T PROLONG THE AGONY

Despite your total support, there will be times when the promoted man will fail. When the failure is due to limitations he has not revealed until taking on his new position, it is essential that he be transferred or demoted. In either case, adequate explanations should be given and the possibility raised of future repromotion after greater basic experience. To keep a man in a position of authority or in an advanced job when he is clearly failing is not only detrimental to the company welfare and worker morale but it is humiliating to the man himself. Don't put off a decision in the hope that he might still make a go of it. By prolonging the agony, you incur needless expense, reinforce workers' negative attitudes, and subject the individual in question to pressures that reduce his chances of a smooth readjustment once he is reassigned.

For example, a large New York City department store promoted a likely black woman from saleslady to assistant buyer. The woman was a good although not outstanding saleswoman, but the management was anxious to make promotions since there were few blacks among its supervisory personnel. For a variety of reasons, centered mostly on personality difficulties, the woman soon showed she could not supervise other workers. Despite her frequent clashes with both black and white salespeople, management continued to support her until the situation deteriorated so badly that departmental sales fell off, two salesladies resigned, and a rash of customer complaints stacked up. There was no longer a way out. The woman flatly refused a demotion and had to be terminated. She filed a complaint of racial discrimination with the local antidiscrimination commission, and the store was put to considerable trouble to prove through its records that it had acted out of business necessity and not bias.

SOME BENEFITS

A hardcore training program is not worth much if it only results in black workers clogging the entry-level jobs. It would soon defeat itself. There must be upward movement for the new worker. When there is such mobility, the company benefits, not only in having a "home-grown" crop of supervisors who know the company well, but in such intangibles as public relations as well. Any company's image in the community has come increasingly to depend on the way it reveals its concern with major community concerns, and the effective employment of minority workers is paramount among those issues. Then too, as a company's image impresses itself upon the community, recruiting of talented personnel, both black and white, becomes easier.

Developing an effective promotional system for new workers may not be simple. The NAB's JOBS '70 upgrading program is one attempt to make it easier. But tried and true methods of advancing workers into the ranks of management are difficult to set aside, no matter how "horse-and-buggy" oriented everyone admits they are. Yet time and again a company that undertakes strict evaluation, modification, or total scrapping of its promotional procedures develops a new system that benefits all workers, and in the end the company is strengthened.

CHAPTER TWELVE

Sources for Help in Hardcore Hiring

Hacking one's way through the jungle of federal programs for job training—and the thickets of bureaucratic prose describing those programs—is an exhausting chore. Understandably, many businessmen are loathe to tackle it. One of the major difficulties comes when the uninitiated attempt to understand the degrees of overlap between programs. The federal government has made several manful attempts to straighten out that problem by "unifying" and "coordinating" certain programs, but it still has a long way to go. However, all things considered, the amount of red tape and number of restrictions have diminished considerably, making involvement in a government contract less the headache than was once the case.

The programs described here are by no means the only ones that bear upon the problem of the black hardcore unemployed. They are, however, the major programs in the area of job training, and the ones that have proven their usefulness to business.

Other resources, labor union and private, are also briefly described here. The resources listed are not the only ones in a given field. The list is suggestive only of the kinds of services available. Through these resources, the names and addresses of other specific services in your community can be secured.

THE MANPOWER DEVELOPMENT
AND TRAINING ACT

Based on federal legislation passed in 1963 and administered by the U.S. Department of Labor and the U.S. Office of Education, MDTA started with over 75 percent of its funds channeled into *institutional* or classroom training projects that provided basic education. At first only a very small proportion of the funds went to employers to fund *on-the-job* training programs.

Later the classroom-type program was linked with the on-the-job training program in order to more easily reach the unemployed who were past their working prime and for whom a structured classroom education would no longer be useful. The on-the-job part of the training was emphasized and thousands of hard-to-train people moved into productive life. On-the-job training is frequently coupled with supplementary instruction in the general areas of language or theory relating to the skill that the trainee is expected to master. Special support services may be provided—counseling, social adjustment, follow-up, and medical services.

Under MDTA, says Stanley H. Ruttenberg, former Assistant Secretary of Labor for Manpower, "We noted that the employer, with his job-now offer was by far the most successful trainer . . . More than 90 percent of the persons trained on the job were staying on the job. The costs in employer programs were averaging, at the beginning, about $400 per trainee." (By 1969 the cost had grown to about $2,400 per person for ten weeks in the classroom and nineteen weeks on the job.)

As the MDTA program continued to evolve, it began to focus more upon the hardcore unemployed, finally requiring that

65 percent of all persons selected for training come from that manpower category.

In 1967, starting with a pilot program in ten cities, Ruttenberg says, "We handed the whole job of training the hardcore unemployed—from recruitment and testing, to classroom and on-the-job training, with related and supportive services—to selected employers."

The pilot program, which proved industry would employ the hardcore if it was not saddled with the extra costs, was called MA-1. It appeared with variations, progressively numbered, in fifty large cities, and by 1969, it was established in over 130 cities, with a budget of $400 million.

THE CONCENTRATED EMPLOYMENT PROGRAM

CEP, says the Manpower Administration of the Labor Department, "is not really a new program as we normally think of the term. Rather it is a new approach to the problem of the disadvantaged—an attempt to unify and concentrate efforts to provide complete, efficient, and result-getting help where and when it counts."

This new approach, started in 1967, attempts to pull together employment efforts being made for the hardcore unemployed by other federal and state agencies, and tries to involve local businessmen in the job problems of the community. The program also attempts to give full-scale, personalized help to the hardcore, and it seeks to go beyond helping them find a job, sticking with them until they have proved they are able to stay on the job.

CEP projects are planned and carried out locally. All funds and support services are provided by the Department of Labor through one contract with one sponsor, who works with the local state employment agency and may farm out other parts of the contract. There is no one standard method of operation for CEP programs. Each varies according to the needs of the locality. The combination of classroom training and on-the-job training orientation and other services depends upon the needs of the residents. Generally, however, a successful project would depend upon aggressive recruiting efforts in the ghetto to reach the hardcore unemployed who need training.

When the trainee is enrolled in the program, he first receives two weeks of orientation regarding personal appearance, health, job-hunting, budgeting, and the like, along with certain medical care. Job coaches and counselors work with each man on an individual basis. They determine whether to refer him to training or to a job. Once the man has a job, he still receives important follow-up services from his job coach. Helping him find a place to live, counseling, mediating job misunderstandings —such help can be of considerable value to an employer.

Late in 1969, the Department of Labor attempted to correct "serious management deficiencies" in the CEP program resulting from overlapping authority among community action agencies, private employers, and government agencies such as the state employment services. The Department ordered that the "potential for overlap or confusion" must be eliminated before new contracts would be signed with CEP program prime sponsors.

JOB OPPORTUNITIES IN THE BUSINESS SECTOR

The most concentrated, comprehensive hardcore employment program business has undertaken so far is the JOBS program—Job Opportunities in the Business Sector. This is the much discussed "partnership" between the federal government, represented by the Department of Labor, and volunteer businessmen, represented by the National Alliance of Businessmen, formed in 1968.

The NAB "pledges" the jobs and the Labor Department furnishes the workers, using the CEP offices, state employment offices, and other Manpower Administration agencies to carry out recruiting and referral. The pledging employer contracts for federal funds through the Labor Department, which reimburses the employer for costs involved in hiring and training above and beyond what it normally costs to train a new employee. This additional training, since it includes such things as remedial education, correction of minor health problems, personal counseling and testing, transportation, day-care for children, and other services, often costs as much as two or three times normal training expenditures. Such training is sometimes carried out by the employer, depending upon his facilities and inclination, or is farmed out as a package to a professional training firm. A number of such training firms have been formed as subsidiaries of large businesses in order to handle the training needs in all of the corporation's plants or facilities. Their services are usually available to other employers as well; and there are a number of one-man training operations recently sprung up— some of doubtful credentials—which also offer training services. However, it is noteworthy that recent government requirements specify that training be done through "recognized" training centers.

To press employers to work for the highest possible retention rate of JOBS trainees, earlier contracts did not pay off until the man had been on the payroll for nine to twelve months. While this encouraged some employers to develop strong supportive services—such as buddy systems, counseling and the like, since they proved to reduce turnover—it worked a hardship on the smaller employer or small training company, who could not carry the front-end load while waiting for the payoff. However, the consortium concept, in which a number of companies band together around a single training program, served to lessen that problem. In the most recent contract series, JOBS '70, employers are reimbursed monthly, instead of upon completion of training.

The JOBS '70 contracts are available to the private sector, both profit and nonprofit, in 130 cities designated as JOBS areas. All information and documents necessary to admit a proposal for a contract can be obtained through local offices of the Regional Manpower Administration, or the NAB. A contract service representative will provide assistance in preparing the proposal.

Some officials suggest that large employers are the only ones who can afford to participate in JOBS, but former Secretary of Labor George P. Shultz points out that 70 percent of participating firms are small businesses. The remaining 30 percent of large employers, however, may still represent a majority of actual jobs.

At the end of its first 18 months of operation, in which trainees were being placed at the rate of 20,000 per month, a profile of the JOBS trainee emerged:

He comes to the new job averaging a little more than a tenth-grade education.

He has been unemployed approximately half of the previous year.

His previous year's income averaged $2,773.

He has an average family size of 3.9 persons.

73 percent are between ages 20 and 40.

17 percent are under 20.

13 percent are over 40.

78 percent are Negroes; 11 percent white; 6 percent Mexican-American; 2 percent Puerto Rican; 3 percent other.

33 percent earn more than $2 per hour.

65 percent earn $1.75 per hour.

Job turnover averages about 4 percent per month.

THE WORK INCENTIVE PROGRAM

WIN is operated by the Department of Labor's Manpower Administration in cooperation with the U.S. Department of Health, Education and Welfare, and is administered through state employment service offices.

Started in 1968, WIN was designed to move men and women off the welfare rolls into jobs by providing them with the necessary basic training and a broad spectrum of support services—personal and vocational counseling, orientation, skill training in the classroom, job placement, and followup counseling.

Local welfare offices refer appropriate persons to WIN. Most are women. In Maryland, for instance, only 13 percent of the WIN trainees are men.

A five-man team—counselor, manpower specialist, work-training specialist, job coach, and a clerk—work with each WIN participant to decide which combination of services is needed in order to get a job. Only a small percentage of participants are ready to be referred to jobs without first receiving training. While in training, the participant receives welfare payments plus $30 a month incentive allowance from Department of Labor funds. Welfare funds pay for transportation and lunch, and welfare makes day-care arrangements for the children of the participants. Job placement is done by state employment services, often through such channels as JOBS.

JOB CORPS

Perhaps the most publicized and thus best-known training program is the JOB Corps. Established by the Economic Opportunity Act of 1964 and administered by the Office of Economic Opportunity, the program was cut back in 1969 from its earlier dimensions, but it still provides training for considerable numbers of young men and women from sixteen through twenty-one, who are not in school, have had a limited background generally, and are unable to find or hold jobs.

Designed as a "total learning experience," the program is a residential twenty-four-hour program with comprehensive education and job training. Trainees receive room and board, medical and dental care, work clothing, and thirty dollars a month. A "readjustment allowance" ranging from twenty-five to fifty dollars for each completed month is given the trainee at the end of his training. The graduate may move into other federal programs for advanced training. Half to two-thirds of the trainees are Negroes.

The three types of centers—urban centers for men, urban centers for women, and conservation centers, which take 40 percent of all male enrollees—are located on unused government land, such as vacant military bases, or in leased facilities. Operation of the centers is contracted to private business, private agencies, and universities.

NEIGHBORHOOD YOUTH CORPS

Of all the Labor Department-sponsored programs aimed at the disadvantaged poor, the NYC has the greatest enrollment—

nearly 143,000 in mid-1969. Almost half were from minority groups.

Begun in 1964 after passage of the Economic Opportunity Act, the NYC is a program to provide training and work experience for young people between fourteen and twenty-two. A major purpose is to help young people stay in school by offering part-time work coupled with professional counseling. The work that enrollees are given must provide services that would not otherwise be provided, so as to cause no displacement of wage-earners already employed.

Many NYC enrollees move into other Labor Department programs, and in this way enter a labor pool accessible to business and industry.

THE NATIONAL APPRENTICESHIP PROGRAM

NAP grew out of 1937 legislation. In recent years there have been efforts to bring greater numbers of black men into apprenticeship programs. Through *pre*-apprenticeship training, often offered by various other agencies, the hardcore unemployed also have a chance to work up into the skilled crafts or trades.

There are some 350 apprenticeable trades, training for which generally includes two or more years of on-the-job work under the guidance of an experienced craftsman, combined with related classroom instruction. The apprentice is regarded as an employed worker.

Administered by the Manpower Administration through state apprenticeship agencies or the Bureau of Apprenticeship and Training, the system is based on voluntary cooperation among management and labor, industry and government, shop and school. Not all trades require that applicants have a high school diploma. Entrance age limits are generally seventeen to twenty-six.

To encourage Negro participation in apprenticeship programs, the Urban League has taken an interest in assisting applicants to prepare for the entrance test.

U.S. EQUAL EMPLOYMENT OPPORTUNITY COMMISSION

Established by the EEO Act of 1964, the EEOC is primarily a fair employment enforcement agency. But in at least one region—the West—it has received funds to assist employers in finding and hiring minority workers.

STATE AND LOCAL GOVERNMENTAL AGENCIES

The number of resources to which an employer can turn for help in inaugurating or expanding minority hiring programs has grown enormously in the past few years. Today, most state fair employment practice commissions or antidiscrimination agencies, as well as municipal human relations agencies, have "affirmative action" or "positive compliance" programs helpful to the employer. Quite aside from the enforcement functions of FEP laws, these agencies often will provide a review ranging from perfunctory to exhaustive of the methods needed for an employer to pursue a successful minority hiring program. While such agencies usually are not set up to provide the full range of training services an employer needs, their recommendations can well serve as a take-off point, and they function as authoritative guides to obtaining needed assistance in such matters as sensitivity programs for supervisors (see Chapter 6).

Other state and local bodies who can give expert help are special state commissions, or mayor's committees appointed to work on urban problems, unemployment, racial questions, concerns of youth, the problems of schools, and the like.

NATIONAL URBAN COALITION

The Urban Coalition was created in 1967 with a national organization headed by John W. Gardner, former Secretary of the U.S. Department of Health, Education and Welfare, and with local coalitions in major cities. The local groups are made up of representatives of the city's power structure in business, labor, minority groups, religion, and local government. Concern of the coalitions is by no means limited to problems of employment, but encompasses the full range of problems experienced by deteriorating central cities—housing, business, transportation, and health care for the poor.

The key to the success of the alliance appears to lie in the extent to which business actively involves itself. Different coalitions in different cities have had widely varying degrees of success with their programs. In some cities, with little business support, the group has virtually died, while in others it has prospered, enlisting executives on loan from business, interns from government programs, and volunteers to form an effective program.

Many of these undertakings do not directly touch the hardcore unemployed, but others do. In Los Angeles, for example, where the Urban Coalition has had its share of complaints about failing to deal effectively with urban and racial problems, several employment-oriented programs have been offered. One would bring business and industry representatives together with vocational education departments of schools to work with instructors at making teaching more relevant to industry's needs, and also to lend or donate the equipment and material to enable the schools to carry out realistic instruction. Another program would help to relieve the transportation difficulties in ghetto areas by underwriting low-interest financing and insurance for the purchase of cars by trainees or workers who otherwise can't easily get to their jobs.

Each local coalition raises its own funds and plots its own programs. Through ties with community organizations, most coalitions can assist business and industry in recruiting and training the hardcore unemployed.

CONSORTIUMS

A consortium is a group of companies, small, medium, or large, that band together for the common purpose of hiring and training the hardcore unemployed. In the San Francisco area, one such consortium was formed with Lockheed Missiles and Space Company at Sunnyvale as the coordinator. It was formed to provide a simple mechanism for a group of companies to participate in a contract with the U.S. Department of Labor that would reimburse the companies for their cost of training the hardcore unemployed. Any company with "entry level openings in meaningful job categories" and "willingness to waive entry level requirements not absolutely necessary to performance" can join the consortium.

The consortium program consists of a pre-on-the-job training period of four to eight weeks, the range representing the difference in complexity of various entry-level positions.

According to the guidelines set up by the consortium:

During the pre-OJT period, trainees will be members of a class of four to six, all being trained in a single work category. Each trainee will be on the payroll of a particular company, and will receive his paycheck from that company.

The pre-OJT period will also be used for medical examinations, remedial education where required, preliminary vocational training, legal and financial counseling, and will generally address the basic problem of preparing the trainee so that he can perform in an acceptable manner when he appears on the company floor. The pre-OJT period will be handled by Lockheed Missiles and Space Company, who will provide all necessary facilities and staff. Included in this period will be a short training session for the company supervisors to whom each of the employees will report when the OJT period begins.

During the OJT period, each trainee will report to his parent company and enter the OJT portion under the immediate supervisor involved. His counselor at the consortium will be in contact with the trainee and his supervisor during the initial adjustment period to assist in any problems which may develop.

Trainees will be selected to match needs of a job as closely as possible, and to minimize transportation problems. Trainees will be recruited from organizations already established to deal with underprivileged unemployed and underemployed persons, such as the Concentrated Employment Program, the California State Employment Service, the San Francisco Urban League, the City and County Welfare Departments, the Opportunities Industrialization Centers, the Mexican American Opportunities Center, etc. . . .

The jobs for which consortium trainees are prepared are:

tailored to the particular needs of the entry level jobs involved, . . . manufacturing skills, such as electrical assembly, mechanical assembly, sheet metal assembly, etc., to clerical skills such as clerk typists, file clerks, store-room operators;

to operating skills such as key punch operator, telephone operator, reproduction machine operator, etc. No entry level position should be ruled out as a candidate job for the hardcore unemployed—those that require relatively more skills will be handled by using more time for the pre-OJT and OJT periods involved.

Companies participating in the consortium are reimbursed by the U.S. Department of Labor for the cost of the training center, instructors, counselors, medical examinations and corrective measures such as fitting eye glasses, cost of training supervisors, lost time by supervisors, wages of the trainees, and that part of the trainee's wages attributed to training, special transportation, legal counseling, and the like. The operation is set up to involve no additional cost to participating companies.

HUMAN RESOURCES DEVELOPMENT INSTITUTE

The HRDI was established by the AFL-CIO executive council in 1968 to develop greater union participation in programs for hiring the hardcore unemployed. HRDI staff is made up of men and women from twenty-seven different national unions operating in fifty cities with hardcore unemployment problems. In each case the HRDI representative is an integral part of organized labor in his city. He works with local unions and maintains headquarters in the local central labor organization's office. He is charged with the responsibility of analyzing the job and training needs of his community, and to work with unions, industry, and the government programs to meet those needs. Additionally, he encourages unions to sponsor innovative manpower programs on their own.

Working with the NAB in its JOBS program, the Institute has recruited and trained rank-and-file employees to work personally as buddies on a one-to-one basis with new hardcore workers to help them get through their early months on the job. In addition, the HRDI has signed a JOBS program contract to provide sensitivity training for first-line supervisors to help them assimilate new hardcore workers into their crews.

The HRDI also maintains a full-time labor liaison representative at NAB headquarters. The Institute also works with such federal programs as the Concentrated Employment Program, and in establishing programs to recruit more minority young people into apprenticeship programs.

THE OPPORTUNITIES INDUSTRIALIZATION CENTER

OIC grew out of a boycott organized in Philadelphia by Negro churches protesting racial discrimination. It now has branches in some seventy cities where unemployed or underemployed minority people receive vocational training and job placement. Frequently pointed out as an outstanding example of Negro self-help, the OIC program developed along more realistic lines than many such endeavors. For example, it places heavy emphasis on motivating the trainee, and establishes close relationships with business and industry in planning the training, selecting instructors and equipment, and in finding jobs. All instruction from course content to work procedures is determined by its relevance to actual job requirements. Shop standards are maintained. Since enrollment capacity is limited, applicants on the waiting list are put into a "feeder program" to help them maintain their motivation and prepare them for entrance into a working environment.

Financed largely by federal funds, the OIC has received active support from the National Alliance of Businessmen, and such business firms as IBM, Bell Telephone, Philco Corporation, and Western Union, among others.

REMEDIAL EDUCATIONAL TRAINING SYSTEMS

The Board for Fundamental Education, an Indianapolis-based firm, has developed a method for teaching reading, writing, spelling, arithmetic, and English grammar with texts that relate specifically to the job the student will be doing. The BFE system generally is brought in to supplement a company's own on-the-job hardcore training program with, typically, four two-hour sessions a week. The system is designed to aid an employee to reach fourth-grade level in 150 classroom hours or about twenty weeks; to reach eighth-grade level in another 150 hours; and to the equivalent of high school graduation in about another 400 hours. Cost is calculated at about three hundred dollars for 150 hours per person. Among BFE clients have been Eastman Kodak, Olin Chemical, and DuPont.

While BFE uses the basic classroom situation, modified to reduce the inhibitions of that setting, one of its competitors, MIND (Methods of Intellectual Development) has done away with the classroom for teaching the hardcore. MIND lessons are taped and the student works individually, at his own pace, with a tape machine. Monitors check for errors and help the student if he requests it. The student does not feel the usual classroom pressures nor fear revealing his ignorance to fellow students.

According to *Fortune* magazine, MIND's work with "unemployable" applicants at Corn Products Company's Argo plant in Illinois in 1966, got "astounding results." It increased academic skills by the equivalent of 2.2 to 3.2 months in school for every

7.9 hours under MIND instruction. Corn Products now operates MIND as a subsidiary.

Other large companies have established subsidiaries to deal with remedial education needs of hardcore applicants. Northern Natural Gas Company has under its wing the Northern Systems Company. And North American Rockwell established NAR-TRANS, a training, service, and support subsidiary operating in the Los Angeles ghetto. Besides supplying remedial education, NARTRANS places jobless Negroes and Mexican-Americans, after training, in skilled jobs such as keypunching in North American's aerospace plants in southern California.

A major selling point for firms offering remedial education systems is their claim that the cost of such training for the hardcore unemployed is less than the cost an employer experiences in a tight labor market when he advertises for, interviews, and tests dozens of average applicants in order to find the right one.

Many training firms are of small size. As the *Los Angeles Times* points out, "An army of these have sprung up in the warmth and sunshine of federal funds available. Many have nothing but business cards and telephone numbers, hoping for a sub-contract before hiring staff."

The range—and quality—of service offered by these firms varies greatly. The best of them supply competent help in establishing a hiring program right from scratch, on through to providing follow-up service over an extended period and emergency help when needed. The smaller employer especially, without the facilities or staff specialists to set up his own program, finds such services valuable.

The way in which an employer would typically work with a training firm in establishing a remedial education program combined with on-the-job training for the hardcore is documented in the following case study reported by the Urban Affairs Division of the National Association of Manufacturers:

The Laclede Steel Company of Alton, Illinois, in cooperation with the Alton Branch of the National Association for the Advancement of Colored People initiated a program to hire and train hardcore unemployed persons. Laclede contracted with the Training Corporation of America (TCA) of Falls Church, Virginia to counsel and provide basic education to the group to be hired. Recruiting stations were established in areas of high unemployment and members of the NAACP worked with Laclede officials in taking applications.

The recruits spend approximately one week with TCA people who orient them to the program. After a week they are employed on a half-day basis and attend classes the other half day. This lasts for about fifty-five days before the trainees become full-time employees. Following employment, TCA staff is used for follow-up and discussions of such problems as absenteeism that might arise on the job. The TCA counselors provide the recruits with education, group sessions, and discussions about individual problems.

Actual training for the jobs is handled by Laclede supervisory personnel. The trainees are hired into plant jobs, semiskilled and unskilled. These entry-level positions are provided in the labor agreement with the Steelworkers Unions. Once the trainees are on the job full-time, they have the opportunity to compete for better-paying jobs. The jobs pay a minimum of $2.41 an hour.

Laclede defined the hardcore at whom this program is directed as people who have educational deficiencies, unrealistic approaches to the world of work and in some cases, police records. Laclede feels that through TCA a profesisonal training job can be accomplished.

Following the initial seven weeks of the program, Laclede and TCA officials said that the program had "gone beyond our expectations." Of the thirty-one unemployed men enrolled in the training program, twenty-six remained with five dropped for various reasons. Every man in the program had some negative experiences seeking employment prior to enrolling in the program. Two men could not read or write but their initiative enabled them to function well. Many of the trainees were found to have alcoholic problems and nineteen had been arrested. The TCA research indicated that the trainees lacked confidence, lacked realistic attitudes toward work, and had inadequate educations. After participating in the program, the trainees' attitudes were seen to be very positive.

FILMS

While useful films on minority-business relations are not common, there are a few which have particular relevance to an employer's training program for supervisors, or as general information on worker relations.

The Quiet Revolution. A twenty-minute film describing the role of industry and business as they confront the problems of hardcore unemployment. Available from the National Association of Manufacturers, 277 Park Avenue, New York, N.Y. 10017.

The Mythology of Racism. A forty-six-minute film useful for sensitivity training, which deals realistically with the misconceptions about racial differences. Available from Sterling Movies, Inc., 309 West Jackson Blvd., Chicago, Illinois 60606.

There Must Be a Catch. A ten-minute film describing the difficulties a young black dropout has in penetrating personnel office traditions. Available from the Center for Mass Communications, Columbia University Press, 440 West 110th Street, New York, N.Y. 10025.

The Bridge. A twenty-minute description of how business can "build a bridge" to reach the high school dropout. Also available from the National Association of Manufacturers.

An extensive catalog, *Films for Human Relations,* is available from Film Division, The American Jewish Committee, Institute of Human Relations, 165 East 56th Street, New York, N.Y. 10022.

BOOKS

Lists of "must read" books that seek to exhaust their subjects too often only intimidate the reader. He doesn't know where to begin. When he does dig in, he finds many of the books listed don't touch his specific concerns. More often, he ends up reading none and feeling guilty because he hasn't. The books *not* marked with an asterisk below bear especially on the matters business in general encounters in hardcore hiring. Those marked by an asterisk are intended especially for the training officer (see Chapter 6).

Effectively Employing the Hardcore. National Association of Manufacturers, New York, 1968.

Company Experience with Negro Employment. National Industrial Conference Board, New York, 1966.

Ferman, Louis A., et al, editors, *Negroes and Jobs.* Ann Arbor, University of Michigan Press, 1968.

Ginzberg, Eli, editor, *Business Leadership and the Negro Crisis.* New York, McGraw-Hill, 1968.

*Grier, William H., and Cobbs, Price M., *Black Rage.* New York, Basic Books, 1968. (Paperback edition by Bantam Books, 1969.)

*Jacobs, Paul, *Prelude to Riot: A View of Urban America from the Bottom.* New York, Random House, 1967.

Johnson, Lawrence A., *Employing the Hardcore Unemployed.* New York, American Management Association, 1969.

*Katz, William Loren, *Eyewitness: The Negro in American History.* New York, Pitman, 1967.

*The Negro and the City. New York, Time-Life Books, 1968.

*Pettigrew, Thomas F., A Profile of the Negro American. Princeton, N.J., Van Nostrand, 1964.

Ross, Arthur M., and Hill, Herbert, editors, Employment, Race and Poverty. New York, Harcourt, Brace and World, 1967.

*Silberman, Charles E., Crisis in Black and White. New York, Random House, 1964.

*Young, Whitney M., Beyond Racism. New York, McGraw-Hill, 1969.

Some Techniques Used in Employing the Hardcore

Hoffman-Atchley Cabinets of Chatsworth, California, avoided what its president considered the stigmatizing "hardcore" label by calling its new men "manpower trainees." Employing thirty under a JOBS program, the company turned back its government training subsidy to all plant workers based upon their regularity at work, thus assuring both plantwide interest in the training program and reduced absenteeism. To counter lax attendance among new workers, the president met workers as they punched in, saying to those who had missed the previous day, "Where the hell were you? We need you around here. That's the only reason we hired you." That his methods work in motivating workers was shown by reduced turnover as well as a rise in the plant's production and profits. The company president told an interviewer that his trainees made the grade "just as well or better than routine walk-ins who have been hired in the past."

General Electric in Waynesboro, Viriginia used a house trailer equipped as a mobile recruiting office to seek out the hardcore unemployed directly in ghetto neighborhoods. Staffed by one Negro and one white recruiter, the trailer was parked in heavily travelled areas where it readily attracted attention. By establishing a regular schedule of visiting certain neighborhoods, it was able to take advantage of word-of-mouth advertising. The first time out the trailer team recruited eleven hardcore applicants. At its Hotpoint plant in Chicago, GE established a personnel office atmosphere more congenial to blacks by taking down pictures on employment office walls that showed only white workers and replacing them with photographs showing both Negro and white workers.

Union Oil in Los Angeles, in seeking more minority workers, employed a black industrial relations specialist who reported that, as part of his recruiting method, he got three or four haircuts a week—not through vanity, but because "the barbershop is my grapevine. I pick up information on who's back from the service, who's finishing high school, who's looking for serious employment. There might be a new self-help group forming to look for jobs. These things often can be developed into leads for prospective employees."

The Crane Company in Springfield, Massachusetts, dispatched its most skilled interviewers, including one who spoke Spanish, to Job Fairs. At one such fair the team hired twenty-three of fifty-five men interviewed; all of whom were subsequently rated as very good employees.

Hughes Aeropsace in California hired 120 hardcore young people referred from social agencies, ignored their test scores, and trained them for clerical and electronic assembly jobs. However, their supervisors were deliberately not informed that the new workers had no high school diplomas, had done badly on the usual tests, or were to be received differently from the usual new employee. A personnel executive said there was absolutely no difference between the achievement of these new workers and others who met standard requirements.

The Dieboldt Manufacturing Company employed no black or Spanish-speaking workers in 1964. Five years later 18 percent of the work force was minority. This was accomplished by hiring the hardcore at low-skill entry-level jobs and establishing concentrated in-plant training to rapidly upgrade their skills, teach them English, and provide remedial education. Many workers so trained qualified for promotion.

The Texas Division of the Champion Paper Company reviewed its entry-level jobs and found it was able to eliminate educational and test requirements. To fill these jobs it hired hardcore minorities who had been sought out in a house-to-house canvass in ghetto neighborhoods by a job-development project. The company reported these employees to be "exceptionally good."

Illinois Bell offered a series of sensitivity training courses to its first- and second-level supervisors to make them aware of the special needs of hardcore new workers. The company reported an "overwhelming response." Many of the supervisors wanted to do more and undertook volunteer tutoring of ghetto residents.

Western Electric's Kearny Works sought to discover why it had no black supervisors. "We put in a crash program and interviewed every Negro male in the place," said a company executive. "What we learned was fantastic." Negroes with high qualifications were working at jobs far below their abilities. The company began a special training program to prepare some of these men as supervisors, then applied similar techniques with the total work force. Consequently, the company found excellent new supervisors who had been bypassed by former promotion systems.

Pillsbury Company of Minneapolis had 286 minority employees in 1965; four years later it had raised that figure to over 400 by pledging itself to a far-reaching policy of actively recruiting unemployed minorities, training them, deliberately locating new plants so as to aid the hardcore, developing new products to meet the needs of the disadvantaged, and by supporting public policies "that we believe will quickly mobilize our society to effectively achieve the American ideal for all citizens."

Xerox in Rochester, in order to pointedly dramatize the need for greater concentrated effort in recruiting and hiring black workers, issued an edict stating that in new employment the company "should shoot for 50 percent black." A vice president reported, "We have not achieved the 50 percent level in new hiring. But we have pulled our percentage of black employees up to about 11 percent of the total."

Sequential Computer Corporation of Washington, D.C., hired 120 young women from the ranks of the hardcore unemployed to train as data typists. A year later, 80 of them remained. Admittedly, their training included a "little coddling." An executive said, "We gave them extra time off to cash their paychecks at the bank. We loaned them money in emergencies. We arranged legal help, day-care help, and personal counseling." To encourage self-improvement and self-supervision, the data typists were grouped in twelve-women teams. Each team included both experienced and new workers and was headed by an employee promoted because of a good work record. Teammates maintained a close watch on each others' performance which helped keep work standards high.

Emerson Electric in St. Louis used a closed-circuit TV to show hardcore trainees their job operations in detailed slow motion. Such specialized and elaborate training techniques were considered necessary to thorough training. A company executive said that anyone engaged in a hardcore hiring program must ask himself, "Are we ready to spend the extra time to prepare these employees? Unless the answer is a flat yes, the program won't go."

Metropolitan Life Insurance Company in New York hired any dropout who could pass a "native potential" test. Trainees spent four hours on the job and two hours in self-development classes to improve reading and arithmetic skills. Young black and Puerto Rican workers who made good at their jobs were sent to speak in high schools as witnesses to the fact that minority employees could get ahead with the company.

General Motors in Detroit extended a program for hiring marginal workers from the ghetto with an experimental project in which it refrained from firing for tardiness, absence, or lack of ability. Seventy-three percent of the people hired under this special arrangement remained on the job, and the experiment was repeated in another GM plant.

The First National Bank of Passaic County, New Jersey, wanted to keep jobs for minorities foremost among its personnel policies. It set up an "affirmative action file" which contained the names of all minority applicants for whom no jobs were available at the time of application. When a vacancy occurred, the bank consulted the file and considered the persons in it before looking elsewhere.

U.S. Steel Corporation offered consultant services to any group wishing to organize a neighborhood "employment club." A company executive described the club as a way to communicate information about jobs in industry to residents of the ghetto through word of mouth. The club would serve as a central spot in each neighborhood for personnel officers to look for job candidates. It would counsel and prescreen the applicant and save him the time and expense of travelling to individual companies looking for work.

Teamster Union Local 85 in San Francisco offered to train 1,200 hardcore unemployed youths under a U.S. Department of Labor grant. Under its plan, the union will place the trainees on jobs for thirty-day tryouts and guarantee union membership to those who make the grade. The program would "virtually guarantee job placement upon completion of the program," said a union spokesman.

LTV Aerospace Corporation of Dallas was unable to fill assembly-line jobs at its aeronautics plant. In cooperation with the Texas Employment Commission, it recruited 750 industrially unskilled Mexican-Americans from the Rio Grande Valley 500 miles away. The recruits were trained with the help of Department of Labor funds and then moved to their new jobs in Dallas. Through adequate advance planning by both the company and the employment commission, the new workers fit well into both jobs and the community, stayed on the job, and did not experience many of the problems of unskilled newcomers to the city.

A *Detroit Utility Company* approached its hardcore training program with the frank assumption that the trainees were inept and hostile. Coordinated with the usual entry-level job training was a program of sociopsychological training in which, over a twelve-week period, fifty trainees were psychologically prepared for the work environment in training sessions with a clinical psychologist. Supervisors also met to discuss trainee problems. By putting frustrations and hostilities into words and facing them openly, each group developed more realistic attitudes toward each other.

Equitable Life Assurance Society supported its image as an equal opportunity employer through national advertising. A full page advertisement in *Life* magazine showed three small children, one of them black, with text which read, in part, "Who cares if these kids become dropouts? Equitable cares. The future of our country depends on the abilities of the young. That's why Equitable wants to get as many dropouts as it can back on the track to learning. We're taking part in programs where teenagers work part-time at Equitable while they continue in high school. Offering training and counseling to employees who need special help. Supporting stay-in-school programs. . . . Encouraging . . . education projects. . . ."

Lockheed in Georgia found it advantageous not to identify hardcore trainees as such to foremen and supervisors. Company executives felt that the label caused foremen to overreact, either by looking on the new men as "freaks" and rejecting them, or by oversympathetically making excuses for misbehavior, and in either case creating barriers to the trainee's success.

The Campbell Soup Company in Chicago enlisted the aid of the Board of Education in conducting a basic education program for hardcore trainees. The board supplied teachers and materials and the company furnished the space for classes which were held two hours daily on the employee's own time, before or after work. The course was so well received that a program covering grades 1-12 was opened to anyone in the work force who was interested.

Negro Media

Negro newspapers and radio stations beamed to a Negro audience are necessary components in a hardcore or minority hiring program. Whenever help wanted advertisements are placed in general circulation newspapers they should also be routinely placed in Negro papers. An employer's public relations office should be urged to send to black community newspapers any stories involving black workers—man-of-the-month or other achievement awards, significant promotions, new training programs, and the like.

Additionally, the personnel officer would do well to subscribe to at least one such local community newspaper, along with a national Negro magazine such as *Ebony, Sepia,* or *Jet.* Not only will these publications provide your personnel staff with a better idea of Negro concerns and attitudes but by being placed with other reading material in the personnel waiting room, they serve to inform minority applicants of your own attitudes and hiring policies.

	Newspapers	*Radio Stations*
ALABAMA		
Birmingham	*Mirror, World*	WENN, WJLD, WJLN-FM
Montgomery		WAPX, WRMA
Tuscaloosa		WTUG

	Newspapers	*Radio Stations*
Huntsville		WEUP
Mobile	*Beacon*	WGOK, WMOO, WILD

ARKANSAS
| Little Rock | | KOKY |
| Pine Bluff | | KCAT |

CALIFORNIA
San Francisco— Oakland	*Sun Reporter, California Voice*	KDIA, KSOL
Los Angeles	*Sentinel, Herald-Dispatch*	XERB, KGFJ
Sacramento	*Sacramento Observer*	
San Diego	*Lighthouse, Voice*	

COLORADO
| Denver | | KDKO |

DISTRICT OF COLUMBIA
| Washington | *Afro-American* | WOOK, WOL-FM |

FLORIDA
Fort Lauderdale		WRBD
Fort Pierce		WOVY-FM
Orlando		WOKB
Jacksonville	*Florida Star & News*	WRHC, WOBS
Miami	*Times, Star, New Florida Courier*	WMBM, WAME

	Newspapers	*Radio Stations*
Tampa	*News Reporter, Sentinal Bulletin*	WTMP
Pensacola		WBOP

GEORGIA

Atlanta	*Daily World, Voice, Inquirer, Courier*	WRD, WAOK, WIGO, WERD
Augusta	*Weekly Review*	WTHB, WRDW
Columbus		WOKS
Macon		WIBB
Savannah	*Herald, Courier*	WSOK

ILLINOIS

Chicago	*Daily Defender, Weekend Defender, Courier, New Crusader, Gary Crusader, American*	WGRT, WVON, WBEE WMPP

INDIANA

Indianapolis	*Recorder*	WGEE, WTLC-FM

KENTUCKY

Louisville	*Defender*	WLOU

LOUISIANA

Baton Rouge	*News Leader*	WXOK
Lake Charles		KAOK

	Newspapers	*Radio Stations*
New Orleans	*Louisiana Weekly*	WYLD
Shreveport	*Sun*	KOKA
MARYLAND		
Baltimore	*Afro-American*	WEBB, WWIN, WSID, WANN, WXTX-FM
MASSA-		
CHUSETTS		
Boston	*Bay State Banner*	WILD
MICHIGAN		
Detroit	*Chronicle, Tribune, Courier*	WCHB, WJLB, WGPR-FM, WCHD-FM
Flint		WAMM
MISSISSIPPI		
Greenville	*Delta Leader*	WESY
Jackson	*Advocate, Mississippi Enterprise*	WOKJ
Meridian		WQIC
MISSOURI		
Kansas City	*Call*	KPRS
St. Louis	*American, Argus*	KXLW, KATZ, KADI-FM, KWK
NEW JERSEY		
Newark	*Afro-American*	WNJR

	Newspapers	*Radio Stations*
NEW YORK		
New York	*Amsterdam News, Queens Voice, Courier, Manhattan Tribune, Westchester County Press*	WLIB, WWRL
Buffalo	*Challenger, Empire Star*	WUFO
NORTH CAROLINA		
Durham	*Carolina Times*	WSRC
Raleigh	*The Carolinian*	WLLE
Winston-Salem		WAAA
Fayetteville		WIDU
Charlotte	*Post*	WGIV
OHIO		
Cincinnati	*Herald, Call & Post*	WCIN
Cleveland	*Call & Post*	WABQ
Columbus	*Call & Post*	WVKO
Dayton	*Express*	WDAO-FM
Youngstown-Warren	*Buckeye Review*	WNIO
OKLAHOMA		
Oklahoma City	*Black Dispatch*	KBYE
PENNSYLVANIA		
Philadelphia	*Independent, Tribune, Courier*	WHAT, WDAS

	Newspapers	*Radio Stations*
Pittsburgh	*Afro-American* *New Pittsburgh* *Courier*	WAMO, WZUM WAMO-FM

SOUTH
  CAROLINA

Charleston		WPAL
Columbia		WOIC
Greenville		WHYZ
Florence		WYNN

TENNESSEE

Chattanooga	*Observer*	WNOO
Knoxville	*Times*	WJBE
Memphis	*Tri-State* *Defender,* *Memphis World*	WDIA, WLOK
Nashville	*Commentator*	WVOL

TEXAS

Dallas- Fort Worth	*Dallas Post* *Tribune, Fort* *Worth Mind,* *Dallas Express,* *Fort Worth Como* *Weekly*	KNOK
Houston	*Informer,* *Forward Times,* *Texas Freeman*	KYOK
San Antonio	*Register*	KPAE

	Newspapers	*Radio Stations*
Beaumont-		
Port Arthur		KJET
Tyler-Longview		KZEY
VIRGINIA		
Danville		WILA
Norfolk	*Journal & Guide*	WRAP, WHIN
Richmond	*Afro-American*	WANT, WENZ
WASHINGTON		
Seattle		KYAC
WISCONSIN		
Milwaukee		WAWA, WNOV

Training Centers
for Unskilled Workers

Listed here are skills training centers, operating under the direction of the U.S. Department of Health, Education and Welfare, which supply pre-job educational services to the hardcore unemployed. Under a JOBS contract, the employer is reimbursed for all costs he pays the center for appropriate instruction in job-related training.

An employer contemplating a hardcore training program would be well advised to tour a training center in order to gain a first-hand idea of its scope and the applicability of its services to his specific job needs.

This partial list is of those centers "recognized" by the Labor Department.

ALABAMA

> Birmingham MDTA Education Center
> North Birmingham

ARIZONA

> Maricopa County Skills Center
> 246 South First Street
> Phoenix

Tucson Skills Center
(P.O. Box 4040)
55 N. 6th Avenue
Tucson

CALIFORNIA

Community Skill Center
15020 South Figueroa Street
Gardena (Los Angeles)

East Los Angeles Skill Center
1230 S. Monterey Pass Road
Monterey Park (Los Angeles)

Watts Skill Center
840 E. 111th Place
Los Angeles

CONNECTICUT

Hartford MDTA Skill Center
122 Washington Street
Hartford

FLORIDA

Miami Skill Center
3240 NW. 27th Avenue
Miami

INDIANA

Indiana Vocational Technical College
Weir Cook Division
6800 West Raymond Street
Indianapolis

Manpower Training Center
1534 W. Sample Street
South Bend

Lake County Manpower Training Center
Kennedy Building
747 Washington
Gary

IOWA

Des Moines Comprehensive Vocational Facility
2403 Bell Avenue
Des Moines

KANSAS

Central Vocational School
324 North Emporia
Wichita

MASSACHUSETTS

Boston MDTA Skill Center
Lubee Street
East Boston

MICHIGAN

> McNamara Skills Center
> 1501 Beard Street
> Detroit

MISSOURI

> Public School's MDTA Area Training Facility
> 2323 Grand Avenue
> Kansas City

NEW JERSEY

> Jersey City MDT Skills Center
> 760 Montgomery Street
> Jersey City
>
> Newark Manpower Skill Center
> 187 Broadway
> Newark
>
> MDTA Multi Skill Center
> 942 Prospect Street
> Trenton
>
> Camden MDTA Skills Center
> 17th & Admiral Wilson Boulevard
> Camden

NEW YORK

MDTA Center
242 Main Street, West
Rochester

MDTA Center
917 Madison Street
Syracuse

Adult Education Center
Rochambeau School
228 Fisher Avenue
White Plains

MDTA Center
366 Columbus Street
Utica

MDTA Center
55 South Denton Avenue
Nassau County
New Hyde Park

Manpower Division & Training Program
110 Livingston Street
Brooklyn

Williamsburg Adult Training Center
35 Arion Place
Brooklyn

MDTA Center
87 Chinango Street
Binghamton

Jamaica Adult Training Center
150-14 Jamaica Avenue
Jamaica

OHIO

Akron Manpower Development & Training Center
147 Park Street
Akron

Stowe Adult Center
635 West Seventh Street
Cincinnati

Manpower Training Center
2640 East 31st Street
Cleveland

Adult Education & School Services Center
52 Starling Street
Columbus

PENNSYLVANIA

John F. Kennedy Center for Vocational Education
734 Schuylkill Avenue
Philadelphia

SOUTH CAROLINA

Charleston MDT Skill Center
P.O. Box 5272
North Charleston

MDTA Center
Richmond-Lexington
620 Sunset Boulevard
West Columbia

TENNESSEE

MDTA Skill Center
591 Washington Street
Memphis

TEXAS

Fort Worth MDTA Skill Center
1101 West Vickery Boulevard
Fort Worth

Texas Lamar Skill Center
1403 Corinth Street
Dallas

Houston Independent School District
MDTA—CEP Education Building
2704 Leeland Street
Houston

VIRGINIA

Norfolk City Manpower Training Skill Center
Norfolk

WISCONSIN

Milwaukee Technical College Skill Center
1015 North Sixth Street
Milwaukee

Where to Get Information about Government Contacts for Hardcore Training

The Department of Labor has designated certain metropolitan areas as "JOBS cities." Cities are grouped by administrative regions. Information on JOBS contract proposals to be carried out in individual cities may be had from the administrative office designated for each regional grouping.

REGION I

Regional Manpower Administrator, Manpower Administration, U.S. Department of Labor, Room 1907-B, John F. Kennedy Building, Government Center, Boston, Mass. 02203.

Massachusetts: Boston, Brockton, New Bedford, Springfield, Worcester.

Connecticut: Bridgeport, Hartford, New Haven.

Rhode Island: Providence.

REGION II

Regional Manpower Administrator, Manpower Administration, U.S. Department of Labor, Room 712, 341 Ninth Avenue, New York, N. Y. 10001.

New York: Albany, Binghamton, Buffalo, Nassau-Suffolk, New York, Rochester, Syracuse, Utica, Westchester-Rockland.

New Jersey: Jersey City, Newark, Paterson, Trenton.

REGION III

Regional Manpower Administrator, Manpower Administration, U.S. Department of Labor, P.O. Box 8796, Philadelphia, Pa. 19101.

Pennsylvania: Allentown, Erie, Harrisburg, Johnstown, Lancaster, Philadelphia, Pittsburgh, Reading, Wilkes-Barre, York.

Maryland: Baltimore.

West Virginia: Charleston, Huntington.

Virginia: Newport News, Norfolk, Richmond.

Delaware: Wilmington.

REGION IV

Regional Manpower Administrator, Manpower Administration, U.S. Department of Labor, Room 700, 1371 Peachtree Street N.E., Atlanta, Georgia 30309.

Georgia: Atlanta, Columbus.

Alabama: Birmingham, Mobile.

South Carolina: Charleston, Columbia, Greenville.

North Carolina: Charlotte, Greensboro.

Tennessee: Chattanooga, Knoxville, Memphis, Nashville.

Florida: Fort Lauderdale, Jacksonville, Miami, Orlando, St. Petersburg, Tampa, West Palm Beach.

Mississippi: Jackson.

Kentucky: Louisville.

REGION V

Regional Manpower Administrator, Manpower Administration, U.S. Department of Labor, Room 2402, 219 South Dearborn Street, Chicago, Illinois 60604.

Ohio: Akron, Canton, Cincinnati, Cleveland, Columbus, Dayton, Lorain, Toledo, Youngstown.

Illinois: Chicago, Peoria, Rockford.

Michigan: Detroit, Flint, Grand Rapids, Lansing.

Minnesota: Duluth, Minneapolis, St. Paul.

Indiana: Fort Wayne, Indianapolis, South Bend.

Wisconsin: Madison, Milwaukee.

REGION VI

Regional Manpower Administrator, Manpower Administration, U.S. Department of Labor, Room 324, Mayflower Building, 411 North Akard Street, Dallas, Texas 75201.

New Mexico: Albuquerque.

Texas: Austin, Beaumont, Corpus Christi, Dallas, El Paso, Fort Worth, Houston, San Antonio.

Louisiana: Baton Rouge, New Orleans, Shreveport.

Arkansas: Little Rock.

Oklahoma: Oklahoma City, Tulsa.

REGION VII and REGION VIII

Regional Manpower Administrator, Manpower Administration, U.S. Department of Labor, Room 3000, Federal Office Building, 911 Walnut Street, Kansas City, Missouri 64106.

Iowa: Davenport, Des Moines.

Missouri: Kansas City, St. Louis.

Nebraska: Omaha.

Kansas: Wichita.

Colorado: Denver.

Utah: Salt Lake City.

REGION IX

Regional Manpower Administrator, Manpower Administration, U.S. Department of Labor, Room 10064, Federal Building, 450 Golden Gate Avenue, San Francisco, California 94102.

California: Bakersfield, Fresno, Long Beach, Los Angeles, Oakland, Orange, Oxnard, Riverside, Sacramento, San Bernardino, San Diego, San Francisco, San Jose, Santa Barbara, Stockton.

Arizona: Phoenix, Tucson.

Hawaii: Honolulu.

REGION X

Regional Manpower Administrator, Manpower Administration, U.S. Department of Labor, Smith Tower Building, Room 1911, Seattle, Washington 98104.

Washington: Seattle, Spokane, Tacoma.

Oregon: Portland.

DISTRICT OF COLUMBIA

Administrator, Manpower Training and Employment Services Administration for D. C., Manpower Administration, U.S. Department of Labor, District Building, Room 220, 14th and E Streets N.W., Washington, D. C. 20004.

Official State Agencies Concerned with Minority Employment

Many official state antidiscrimination agencies are charged with some measure of "affirmative action" responsibility quite apart from their duty to administer fair employment laws. When such affirmative programs are available they generally mean that a representative of the state agency will furnish expert help to an employer who requests it. Such help can vary from the simple matter of referring an employer to other appropriate sources for assistance or it can involve a complete review of minority manpower resources in the community, working out methods of recruiting, setting up training courses for the new worker, assisting with sensitivity training for supervisors, and providing follow-up troubleshooting as the need arises.

Typically, full-fledged affirmative action programs would be conducted as in the following examples from the California Fair Employment Practice Commission.

When a major utility company became concerned about growing difficulties in hiring and holding minority employees, company management sought the assistance of the FEPC. The company's stated policy had long been one of equal opportunity without discrimination based on race. But in reviewing actual employment practices, the FEPC representative found that a serious lag had developed in the way that policy was being carried out at lower levels. The problem for black applicants, it was discovered, began with the initial job interview: Interviewers were bypassing the company's expressed policy and extending different treatment to white and black applicants. Additionally, there were few minority employees in public contact jobs, and none in management. In discussions with members of the black community, the FEPC also learned that tales of past treatment many Negroes had received in job interviews were widespread, and the community generally considered it futile to apply for work with the company.

For about two years, an FEPC representative maintained regular contact with the firm's employment manager, helping to set up changes in job policy and advising on problems as they arose. He encouraged the company to advertise in minority newspapers, arranged introductions at schools and colleges with high minority enrollments, kept close liaison with the state employment service regarding referrals of minority applicants to the company, aided the company in preparing an attractive recruiting brochure showing minority employees at work in good jobs, and helped seek out public contact positions at which minority workers could be placed. He also assisted the company in a review of its use of aptitude tests, and urged them to adopt a policy of considering some minority applicants who showed a potential to learn regardless of their test scores.

In addition, he helped the firm participate in several local job-training programs for minority youth and assisted in developing an audiovisual program effective in persuading young people to stay in school to gain the kind of training that would lead to good jobs with the company.

As a result of this cooperative work, at the end of three years an excellent pattern of employment had developed. Minority workers were moving into responsible management and public contact positions as employment interviewers, office supervisors, outside salesmen, and field interviewers.

Another affirmative program unfolded when a large rubber company made plans to open a new plant in California's San Joaquin Valley and the industrial relations director met with the FEPC to discuss the best methods of including more minority employees in the work force. The company planned to hire about four hundred production workers for the new factory. About ninety had already been hired although none was Negro. Another one hundred workers were to be employed in the office, and of the sixty-five office people already hired, none was Negro.

The company sought advice on how best to bring in both more Negro and Mexican-American workers. Early recruiting had been done entirely through a state employment office. The FEPC representative met with the manager of that office to discuss ways to include more minority workers in referrals to the new plant. In order to increase the pool of minority applicants, it was suggested that the company also recruit through a second employment office, which was located in an area with a greater population of Mexican-Americans and Negroes. The FEPC representative then informed organizations in the minority community of the new job opportunities and encouraged them to look into them.

In a little over a year, throughout which close contact was maintained between the FEPC staff man and the company personnel office, the new plant hired 466 employees, of whom 26 percent were Mexican-American, 5 percent Filipino, and 4 percent Negro. Of special interest is the fact that these levels of minority representation in the work force very closely matched those of the general population in the new plant's labor market area.

STATE AGENCIES

State Commission for Human Rights, Room 24, Reed Building, Anchorage, Alaska.

Civil Rights Commission of Arizona, 1623 West Washington Street, Phoenix, Arizona.

California Fair Employment Practice Commission, 455 Golden Gate Avenue, San Francisco, California.

Colorado Civil Rights Comission, Room 306, State Services Building, 1525 Sherman Street, Denver, Colorado.

Connecticut Commission on Civil Rights, 92 Farmington Avenue, Hartford, Connecticut.

Division Against Discrimination, Department of Labor and Industrial Relations, 506 West 10th Street, Wilmington, Delaware.

Commissioner's Council on Human Relations, Room 208, District Building, Washington, D. C.

Department of Labor and Industrial Relations, Enforcement Division, Honolulu, Hawaii.

Labor Commissioner, Department of Labor, Industrial Administration Building, Boise, Idaho.

Illinois Fair Employment Practices Commission, 160 North La-Salle Street, Chicago, Illinois.

Indiana Civil Rights Commission, 1004 State Office Building, Indianapolis, Indiana.

Iowa Civil Rights Commission, State Capitol Building, Des Moines, Iowa.

Kansas Commission on Civil Rights, State Office Building, Room 1155W, Topeka, Kansas.

Kentucky Commission on Human Rights, 172 Capitol Annex Building, Frankfort, Kentucky.

Labor Commissioner, Department of Labor and Industry, State Office Building, Augusta, Maine.

Commission on Interracial Problems and Relations, 301 West Preston Street, Baltimore, Maryland.

Commission Against Discrimination, 41 Tremont Street, Boston, Massachusetts.

Civil Rights Commission, 900 Cadillac Square Building, Detroit, Michigan.

State Commission Against Discrimination, 55 State Office Building, St. Paul, Minnesota.

Commission on Human Rights, 312 East Capitol Street, Box 1129, Jefferson City, Missouri.

Department of Labor and Industry, 418 Mitchell Building, Helena, Montana.

Equal Employment Opportunity Commission, State Capitol Building, Lincoln, Nebraska.

Commission on Equal Rights of Citizens, Nevada State Building, Second and Bonanza, Las Vegas, Nevada.

State Commission for Human Rights, 27 Pine Street, Exeter, New Hampshire.

Division on Civil Rights, Department of Law and Public Safety, 152 West State Street, Trenton, New Jersey.

Fair Employment Practice Commission, 137 East DeVargas Street, Santa Fe, New Mexico.

State Commission for Human Rights, 270 Broadway, New York, New York.

Civil Rights Commission, 240 Parsons Avenue, Columbus, Ohio.

Human Rights Commission, P.O. Box 53004, Oklahoma City, Oklahoma.

Civil Rights Division, Oregon Bureau of Labor, 466 State Office Building, Portland, Oregon.

Human Relations Commission, Department of Labor and Industry, 1401 Labor and Industry Building, Harrisburg, Pennsylvania.

Commission Against Discrimination, State House, Providence, Rhode Island.

Commission on Human Relations, 305 Cordell Building, Nashville, Tennessee.

Anti-Discrimination Division, Industrial Commission, Room 418, State Capitol, Salt Lake City, Utah.

Department of Industrial Relations, Montpelier, Vermont.

State Board Against Discrimination, General Administration Building, Olympia, Washington.

Fair Employment Practices Division, Wisconsin Industrial Commission, 819 North Sixth Street, Milwaukee, Wisconsin.

West Virginia Human Rights Commission, West 202 State Capitol Building, Charleston, West Virginia.

Fair Employment Commission, State Department of Labor, Room 304, Capitol Building, Cheyenne, Wyoming.

Most large cities also have human relations commissions, some of whom employ experienced personnel to work with business in developing jobs for minority workers.

Index